Consumer Culture
and
Modernity

Consumer Culture and Modernity

Don Slater

polity

Copyright © Don Slater 1997
The right of Don Slater to be identified as author of this work has been
asserted in accordance with the Copyright, Designs and Patents Act 1988.

First published in 1997 by Polity Press
in association with Blackwell Publishing Ltd.
Reprinted 1998, 2000, 2002, 2003, 2008

Editorial office:
Polity Press
65 Bridge Street
Cambridge CB2 1UR, UK

Marketing and production:
Blackwell Publishing Ltd
108 Cowley Road
Oxford OX4 1JF, UK

Published in the USA by
Blackwell Publishing Inc
350 Main Street
Malden, MA 02148, USA

A CIP catalogue record for this book is available from the British Library.

Library of Congress Cataloging-in-Publication Data
Slater, Don.
Consumer culture and modernity / Don Slater.
Includes bibliographical references and index.
ISBN 978-0-7456-0303-2.— ISBN 978-0-7456-0304-9 (pbk.)
1. Consumption (Economics)—History. 2. Culture—History.
I. Title.
HC79.C6S58 1997
306.3'09—dc21 96–44027
CIP

Typeset in 10½ on 12 pt Ehrhardt by Ace Filmsetting Ltd, Frome, Somerset
Printed in the United States by Odyssey Press Inc., Gonic, New Hampshire
This book is printed on acid-free paper.

Contents

Introduction

This book is an introduction to the field of consumer culture. More specifically, it focuses on *theories* of consumer culture and on the *issues* through which people have organized their thoughts on consumption and culture in the modern world. The fundamental aim of the book is to situate and make sense of these theories and issues as part of the broad development of social thought over the modern period. The book is less concerned with asking, 'What is consumer culture?' and more with how certain modern experiences and dilemmas have been formulated: the rise of commercial society, the relation between needs and social structures, the relation between freedom of choice and the power of commercial systems, the nature of selves and identities in a post-traditional world, the reproduction of social order, prosperity and progress, and of social status and division, the modern fate of individuals and of the intimate, private and everyday world.

The framework of this discussion is indeed *modernity*. The issues and concepts central to thinking about consumer culture are the same ones that have been central to modern intellectual life in general since the Enlightenment. Neither consumer culture as a social experience nor the issues through which that experience has been addressed are new or even recent: consumer culture is a motif threaded through the texture of modernity, a motif that recapitulates the preoccupations and characteristic styles of thought of the modern west.

This way of introducing the field of consumer culture is a response to an endemic problem with this 'field': consumer culture is rediscovered every few decades; or, to be uncharitable, it has been redesigned, repackaged and relaunched as a new academic or political product every generation since the sixteenth century. The latest relaunches – by postmodernism and neo-liberalism in the 1980s – have constituted a particularly profound 'year zero' of the consumer revolution. Postmodernism in particular has produced astonishing insights and productive disruptions. Because of its very nature, however, it has tended to define consumer culture in opposition to modernity, as itself constituting a disruption of modernity. Newcomers to the field, digging their way through the avalanche of new material, might well have difficulty connecting either consumer culture or postmodernism itself to the longer-term context of modern thought which alone can make sense of either of them.

This way of putting things (and of organizing the book) is tendentious. It assumes that postmodern thought and experience can be 'made sense of' in terms of older, modern structures of thought and experience, that neither postmodernism nor postmodernity has blasted these into irrelevance. Hence this book is structured by another feature (which I was not aware of when I started it): a commitment to something very loosely called 'sociology'. Consumer culture is probably less a field (which evokes the steady tilling of a well-marked patch of productive land) and more a spaghetti junction of intersecting disciplines, methodologies, politics. The enduring issue that underlies all of them is the nature of 'the social'. Where productive work has been carried out it has been on the assumption that the study of consumer culture is not simply the study of texts and textuality, of individual choice and consciousness, of wants and desires, but rather the study of such things in the context of social relations, structures, institutions, systems. It is the study of the social conditions under which personal and social wants and the organization of social resources define each other.

How can we relate consumer culture to this nebulous thing called 'the social'? Underlying this book are several central themes through which this connection has been made throughout modern discourses on consumer culture and society. The most central theme is the concept of 'needs', which explores the social relation between private life and public institutions. Ways of thinking about this relation can be further grouped around three central issues: commercialization and the economy; cultural reproduction; 'ethics' and identity.

Commonsensically, being a consumer is about knowing one's needs and getting them satisfied: choosing, buying, using and enjoying – or failing in these. Need is often not seen as a particularly social concept. On the one hand, needs can be seen as natural and self-evident (for example 'basic needs' for food, clothing and shelter); on the other hand, they are often seen as arbitrary and subjective - as 'wants', 'whims', 'preferences' or 'desires' that are entirely bound up with the peculiarities of individuals. Both of these approaches obscure the fundamentally social nature of needs. This must be very clear: needs are not social in the simple sense that there are 'social influences' or 'social pressures' or processes of 'socialisation' through which 'society' 'moulds' 'the individual'. The central point is a different one. When I say that 'I need something', I am making at least two profoundly social statements: firstly, I am saying that I 'need' this thing *in order to* live a certain kind of life, have certain kinds of relations with others (for example have *this* kind of family), be a certain kind of person, carry out certain actions or achieve certain aims. Statements of need are by their very nature profoundly bound up with assumptions about how people would, could or should live in their society: needs are not only social but also political, in that they involve statements about social interests and projects. This connection is partially obscured when needs are treated as natural or 'purely subjective', but it is there none the less. (These formulations are particularly indebted to the work of Kate Soper 1981, 1990; see also Doyal and Gough 1991.)

Secondly, to say that 'I (or we – my social group, my community, my class) need something' is to make a claim on social resources, to claim an entitlement. Needs are both social and political in this respect too: they are statements which question whether material and symbolic resources, labour, power are being allocated by contemporary social processes and institutions in such a way as to sustain the kinds of lives that people want to live. Throughout the modern period the assumption has been that social production should ultimately be accountable to social values. Different ideologies derive these values in different ways: liberalism treats the individual as a sovereign authority; conservatives have deified tradition, historicity and culture; Marxism has an ethical commitment to human creative powers. What they share is a sense that consumer culture stands judged by its ability to sustain desired ways of life – to meet needs. Moreover, and this has probably been *the* central issue in studying consumer culture, there is the question of whether social systems of resource allocation meet the needs defined autonomously by social groups and communities, and do so equitably, or whether these systems (market forces, private corporations, media and cultural institutions, modern 'knowledges', sciences and expertise) have the power to define people's needs for them, or to so reduce some people's access to resources that their ability to define and lead the life they believe to be a good one – i.e., to 'satisfy their needs' – is unjustly restricted.

Thus, there is nothing trivial about consumer culture – though arguments that it reduces social life to a trivial materialism have been common currency for several centuries. Rather, the great issue about consumer culture is the way it connects central questions about how we should or want to live with questions about how society is organized – and does so at the level of everyday life: the material and symbolic structure of the places we live in and how we live in them; the food we eat and clothes we wear; the scarcities and inequities we suffer; the activities open to us in our 'free time'; the unfree nature of much of our time. Even (especially?) the most trivial objects of consumption both make up the fabric of our meaningful life and connect this intimate and mundane world to great fields of social contestation. In the very process of helping to constitute private life, consumer culture has tied the intimate world inextricably to the public, the social, the macro and (as many of the charges against it recount) allowed these to invade the private to a considerable degree. Consumer culture is largely mundane, yet that mundanity is where we live and breathe, and increasingly so as we sense that the public sphere of life has become a consumable spectacle that is ever more remote as a sphere of direct participation. 'Consumer culture' is therefore a story of struggles for the soul of everyday life, of battles to control the texture of the quotidian.

We can talk of at least three great fields of social contestation, which are deeply interwoven. Firstly, the consumption of goods and services requires the mobilization of social resources, and this is always carried out under specific social arrangements of productive organization, technological abilities, relations of labour, property and distribution. The specific arrangements arrived at, the way in which relations of production and relations of consumption mediate each other, place consumption at the heart of questions about what kind of society we are: how is access to objects of consumption regulated: what is the logic that determines the nature of the goods provided to the everyday world; how are our notions of needs, identity, ways of life defined or identified or mediated? In modern society the objects of consumption are largely commodities, if sometimes only potentially or during part of their life cycle (Appadurai 1986): the very ability to carry on everyday life – let alone the scale and quality of that life – is structured by money and market relations. Moreover, the consumption of commodities exposes the everyday to large-scale and rationalized intervention by economic forces and agencies. The great issues which arise from this way of organizing consumption concern the *commercialization* of everyday life, the extent to which its soul is structured in depth by the mediation of economically motivated agents and systems, and the inequities and iniquities of market-based distribution of wealth.

Secondly, the truism that all objects of consumption are meaningful implicates them in a wider field of *cultural reproduction*. The most private act of consumption animates public and social systems of signs, not necessarily in the sense of public display (as in ideas of 'emulation', 'conspicuous consumption' or 'status competition'), but more fundamentally through the process of cultural reproduction: in consuming we do not – *ever* – simply reproduce our physical existence but also reproduce (sustain, evolve, defend, contest, imagine, reject) culturally specific, meaningful ways of life. In mundane consumption we construct social identities and relations out of social resources with which we engage as skilled social agents. As consumption has become an ever more central means of enacting our citizenship of the social world, struggles over the power to dispose of material, financial and symbolic power and resources have become central to the cultural reproduction of the everyday world.

Finally, there is a more nebulous field of contestation in which the character of the quotidian is bound up with questions of identity and ethics: What kind of social actors are we? Many of our questions about the form we take as modern subjects, about how to understand the very relation between the everyday world and the public space, about our moral and social value, about our privacy and power of disposal over our lives, about who we are – many of these questions are taken up in relation to consumption and our social status as a rather new thing called 'a consumer': we see ourselves as people who choose, who are inescapably 'free' and self-managing, who make decisions about who we are or want to be and use purchased goods, services and experiences to carry out these identity projects. In a word, consumer culture is a story of struggle over the everyday partly because it connects up with the social field of 'ethics' (in Foucault's sense), identity and the nature of the self.

In their most general sense, none of these fields of contestation are new. Although commercialization has been a marginal feature outside western modernity, consumption always depends on social arrangements, which we now denote as 'economic', for managing material resources. Objects of consumption are always culturally meaningful and have been used at all times to reproduce social identities culturally. Ethical questions about the scale, nature and social ordering of consumption seem to be universally considered fair game for social, moral or religious regulation of the self. In a word, the profoundly *social* nature of consumption is about as close to a universal presupposition as any responsible social theorist ever gets.

However, this book will not be concerned with the general. The particular struggles around everyday life which we have come to call consumer culture, the particular arrangements through which the material basis, cultural forms and ethical status of everyday life in the modern world are structured and contested – these are a very particular 'achievement' of western modernity, one that arose in recognizable form in the eighteenth century and which came to world historical importance through the globalizing character intrinsic to that modernity. It is the way in which people have thought about this experience that forms the subject of the book. Chapter 1, therefore, sets out a very general characterization of consumer culture as a long-term feature of modernity, including a list of the kinds of attributes by which we can recognize it as a modern, as opposed to recent, phenomenon.

Chapter 2 is about *the consumer* and consumer sovereignty: we will look at how the idea of the consumer has been related to the core modern values of reason, freedom and social progress, from the Enlightenment through liberal political and economic thought to contemporary ideas of 'enterprise culture'. In chapter 3, the focus is on *culture*: for many modern critics of modernity the very phrase 'consumer culture' is a contradiction in terms. This is because it represents the destruction of a stable traditional social order by industrial and capitalist relations that debase real culture, undermine the social values that are necessary for social solidarity and render people's social identities unstable, fluid and a matter for obsessive concern. Chapter 4 takes up the issue of *alienation*: consumer culture is often experienced as an explosive output of *things*, of a wealth and prosperity which promises satisfaction but seems only to deliver poverty, boredom and a sense of estrangement. Chapter 5 is about the *meaning* of all these consumer things and about the place of things and their meanings within social practice. The question of meaning raises numerous questions – largely presented through a discussion of semiotics – about the relations between needs and objects, nature and culture, meaning and social practice. These are pursued in chapter 6 in terms of the long-standing social theoretical attempt to understand how the meaningful character of goods enters into the cultural reproduction of social identity, membership, status and ideology. Finally, chapter 7 is about the most pressing contemporary theme in consumer culture, the claim that there have been epochal changes in economic and cultural relations over the past few decades which have made both consumption and culture more central to social life, which have altered the way in which consumer culture is carried out and the role it plays in social reproduction as a whole, and which have shifted us out of the modern period into 'new times': an era of postmodernity, and of post-Fordist or 'disorganized' capitalism.

Acknowledgement

Like many first children, this book had rather a long gestation, was outrageously overdue, and the labour was long and painful. I would like to thank Catherine Bradley for her support during the earlier years, and two colleagues for seeing me through to term: Helen Thomas, for several years of ante-natal classes; and Chris Jenks, the midwife, for telling me the time was up and inducing the birth. Jo Entwistle has my profound thanks for being there at all stages of the process: she helped in the conception, supported the pregnancy and attended the delivery. As in all reproduction, this child is now on its own and none of those named are responsible for any of its flaws, all of which it inherited from me.

This book is dedicated to my two real children, Daniel and Ben.

1
Consumer Culture and Modernity

Consumption is always and everywhere a cultural process, but 'consumer culture' – a culture *of* consumption – is unique and specific: it is the dominant mode of cultural reproduction developed in the west over the course of modernity. Consumer culture is in important respects *the* culture of the modern west – certainly central to the meaningful practice of everyday life in the modern world; and it is more generally bound up with central values, practices and institutions which define western modernity, such as choice, individualism and market relations. If we were to extract a single defining feature it would run something like this: consumer culture denotes a social arrangement in which the relation between lived culture and social resources, between meaningful ways of life and the symbolic and material resources on which they depend, is mediated through markets. Consumer culture marks out a system in which consumption is dominated by the consumption of commodities, and in which cultural reproduction is largely understood to be carried out through the exercise of free personal choice in the private sphere of everyday life.

Consumer culture was not the only mode of cultural reproduction in operation over the last three hundred years, nor the only one now. One can distinguish residual and emergent, oppositional and eccentric modes of cultural reproduction, just as when we think about modes of production. New Yorkers, for example, raised animals for domestic consumption in uptown Manhattan right to the end of the nineteenth century (Braverman 1974: 274). Today we still like to distinguish gift-giving from commodity-exchange; we also may feel that some cultural goods (for example, friendship, character) cannot be bought; we may even make, rather than buy, some of the things we use. Similarly, the very idea of the welfare state originally represented an alternative mode of meeting needs, one that prioritized collective provision over the private consumption of commodities. Consumer culture is not the only way in which consumption is carried out and everyday life reproduced; but it is certainly the dominant way and possesses a practical scope and ideological depth which allows it to structure and subsume all others to a very great extent.

Nor is consumer culture a purely western affair. It arose in the west, from about the eighteenth century onwards, as part of the west's assertion of its own difference from the rest of the world as modern, progressive, free, rational. But in the idea of consumer culture there was an assumption of dominance and denigration, of the western sense of itself as civilized and righteously affluent, as possessing values that have a universal character. Consumer culture has been a flagship for the advance of western business, western markets and a western way of life. As an aspect of the universalizing project of western modernity, consumer culture has both global pretensions and global extension.

Finally, it may seem odd to define consumer culture in terms of the *modern* west – as a mode of cultural reproduction extending from the eighteenth century to the present. Consumer culture appears to many as fully formed only in the *post*modern era. However, consumer culture is inextricably bound up with modernity as a whole. I mean two things by this. Firstly, core institutions, infrastructures and practices of consumer culture originated in the early modern period, and some of these were well established (at least for some classes and some economic sectors) by this time. Consumer culture is not a late consequence of industrial modernization and cultural modernity, something that followed after the intellectual and industrial labours of modernity were accomplished. It was rather part of the very making of the modern world. Secondly, consumer culture is bound up with the *idea* of modernity, of modern experience and of modern social subjects. In so far as 'the modern' constitutes itself around a sense of the world experienced by a social actor who is deemed individually free and rational, within a world no longer governed by tradition but rather by flux, and a world produced through rational organization and scientific know-how, then the figure of the consumer and the experience of consumerism is both exemplary of the new world and integral to its making.

Looking backwards

This *longue durée* view of consumer culture contradicts some common-sense views of it. Consumer culture, in fact, inhabits an odd time-frame: on the one hand, modern forms of consumption – like modern forms of the market in much economic theory – are often regarded as effectively universal and eternal; on the other hand, in everyday experience consumer culture lives in a perpetual year zero of newness. Consumer culture is about continuous self-creation through the accessibility of things which are themselves presented as new, modish, faddish or fashionable, always improved and improving. In keeping with the fashionable experience it provides, the very idea of consumer culture is constantly heralded as new: in each generation the Columbuses of capitalism rediscover the promised land of affluent freedom; while critics – both left and right – report our arrival in a frozen land of wealth without value.

In what follows, I want to disrupt this sense of eternal newness by telling the history of consumer culture backwards. This will allow us to trace each 'new age' back to a previous one and at the same to get a clearer sense of how consumer culture is bound up with 'the whole of modernity'.

The 1980s saw one of the most powerful rediscoveries of consumerism. The consumer was the hero of the hour, not just as the provider of that buying power which would fuel economic growth (though this was central too, and encouraged through phenomenal credit expansion, deficit financing and income tax reductions) but as the very model of the modern subject and citizen. Exemplified in neo-liberalism – specifically in Reaganomics and Thatcherism – consumer choice became the obligatory pattern for all social relations and the template for civic dynamism and freedom. Collective and social provision gave way to radical individualism (as Thatcher put it, 'There is no such thing as society, only individuals and their families.'). And this individual was enterprising – dynamically and unabashedly self-interested – as exemplified in the yuppie and in the character of Gekko in the film *Wall Street*. The 1980s also heralded the subordination of production to consumption in the form of marketing: design, retailing, advertising and the product concept were ascendant, reflected in postmodern theory as the triumph of the sign and the aestheticization of everyday life. Much-publicized claims about the reorganization of capitalist production and its relation to the state (post-Fordism, disorganized capitalism, flexible accumulation) all argued that Fordist mass consumption – the pioneer of consumer culture – was giving way or giving birth to a newer and truer consumer culture of target or niche marketing, in which the forging of personal identity would be firmly and pleasurably disentangled from the worlds of both work and politics and would be carried out in a world of plural, malleable, playful consumer identities, a process ruled over by the play of image, style, desire and signs. Consumer culture was now all about 'keeping different from the Joneses'.

Both neo-liberalism and postmodernism proclaimed and seemingly endorsed the murder of critical reason by consumer sovereignty: standards of value other than the preferences expressed by individuals in the market-place were derided as elitist, conservative or simply ungrounded. The ideological consumerism of the 1980s then foregrounds radical individualism and privatism on the one hand, and on the other their grounding in a modality of signs and meanings (rather than needs and wants): this consumer culture is proudly superficial, profoundly about appearances. Materialism is neither good nor bad – it's all there is. And when this situation obtains, as Raymond Williams (1980: 185) puts it, we turn out not to be 'sensibly materialistic' at all: unhinged from core social identities and physical want, consumerism becomes a pure play of signs. The ideological miracle carried out by 1980s consumer culture was to tie this image of unhinged superficiality to the most profound, deep structural values and promises of modernity: personal freedom, economic progress, civic dynamism and political democracy. Through the neo-liberal renaissance and the crumbling of Marxism (in the west and the east), consumer culture was seen in terms of the freedoms of the market and therefore as the guarantor of both economic progress and individual freedom.

Ironically, 1980s positions on consumer culture, whether neo-liberal, postmodern or critical, largely presented themselves as reactions against the 1950s and 1960s, as commentaries on the bankruptcy of the post-war consensus (both its establishment version and its opponents). Yet this consensus had presented itself, in its own time, as marking the arrival of the industrial world in the promised land of consumerist plenty. The great theme of the period is the triumph of economic managerialism, through Keynesian economics and welfare statism, over the crisis-tendencies of capitalism exemplified in the Great Depression. The vista of an 'organized capitalism' (Lash and Urry 1987) with smoothly expanding prosperity placed consumer culture near its centre as simultaneously the engine of prosperity, a pre-eminent tool for managing economic and political stability and the reward for embracing the system. The harmonious marriage of managerial collectivism and consumerist individualism – the mixed economy – is precisely what 1980s neo-liberalism loathed, as exemplified in the idea of regulation and in the split between social provision for welfare and infrastructure on the one hand and private sector enterprise on the other. At the time, however, 'You never had it so good.' This is the period of the economic miracle that was so directly experienced in rising consumption standards. It was so good in fact that – within the ideological climate up to the 1970s – critics of consumer culture had to reach for ever more tenuous accounts of how a world both so systemically stable and individually satisfying could be deemed *unsuccessful* by either intellectuals or their erstwhile revolutionary agents.

In fact the image of the post-war consumer and consumer boom is rather schizoid. On the one hand, consumer culture – especially in the 1950s – appears as a new age of conformity, of 'organization man', of the 'other-directed' narcissist, of the mass cultural dope or couch potato keeping up with the Joneses through the slavish mass consumption of standardized mass production goods, the land of Levittown and American cars (Mills 1951; Riesman 1961; Whyte 1957). The consumer is the 'affluent worker' (Goldthorpe and Lockwood 1968–9), steadily building up domestic capital within the framework of long-term job security. The stability of the everyday consuming household was itself anchored within the protective harbour of the Keynesian state, which organized itself around a table with chairs set out for organized government, organized business and organized labour. Fordism, it was argued, provided a prosperous yet empty contentment, involving a colonization of everyday life by corporations and consumption norms which rendered it status-driven and conformist, mass and anti-individualist. Prosperity and the good life meant the *ability* to keep up with the Joneses.

On the other hand, 'the affluent society' (Galbraith 1969) could also involve disturbingly explosive and hedonistic consumption patterns among new social groups which were themselves crucially defined by their consumption: the emergence of the teenager, of the Butlins working class, of the suburban family and so on. The affluent society was a consumer society in which economic prosperity brought insatiable and morally dubious wants, a crisis in values over the work ethic, a bifurcation of desire between respectable consumption (consumption within the framework of the family, the spread of bourgeois propriety through the accumulation of domestic capital) and hedonistic, amoral, non-familial consumption (Bell 1979). On the Marxist side, this period also seemed to confirm a long-worked-out analysis of consumer culture as a form of social and political managerialism, a way to ensure political docility through a mass policy of bread and circuses.

If we date it from the post-war period, consumer culture appears as the culmination of Fordist mass production coupled with Keynesian economic managerialism, both together producing a stable affluence which carries the seeds of its own destruction: moral destruction through conformity or hedonism, socio-economic destruction through the triumph of collectivist regulation, and so on. But post-war consumerism represents the spread of social themes and arrangements which were pioneered in the previous era. The 1920s was probably the first decade to proclaim a generalized ideology of affluence. Above all, it promoted a powerful link between everyday consumption and modernization. From the 1920s, the world was to be modernized partly *through* consumption; consumer culture itself was dominated by the idea that everyday life could and should be *modern*, and that to a great extent it already was. Ewen (1976) and Marchand (1986), for example, demonstrate that the burgeoning advertising and marketing of this era were selling not just consumer goods, but consumerism itself as the shining path to modernity: they incited their publics to modernize themselves, modernize their homes, their means of transport. The exemplary goods of the period are about the mechanization of everyday life, starting with houses themselves, and extending to their electrification; then durables like washing machines, vacuum cleaners, fridges, telephones; then, finally, the automobile for that modern sense of movement into the future and into the jazz age. This is the age of real estate, consumer credit and cars: modern appliances, bought by modern methods, placed in a modern household. The 1920s was probably the first era in which modernity was widely held to be a state that *has already been reached* by the population in general, a state we are in or nearly in, rather than one towards which an avant-garde points: in the consuming activities of the middle-class the ultra-modern future was already readable, already beginning to happen.

The 1920s (and, especially in America, the previous two decades as well) exhibit a similar moral split to the post-war era: Sinclair Lewis's (1922) *Babbitt*, on one side, exemplifies consumerism, 'boosterism', the life of selling and goods, as the route to empty mass conformity (especially within the increasingly privatized, suburbanized and nuclearized family); the flapper, the cinema, the automobile and Prohibition represent the other side: the licentious, youth-oriented, pleasure-oriented orgy of the jazz age, Hollywood and Harlem nights. Again, and quite early on, consumerism shows its double face: it is registered on the one hand as a tool of social order and private contentment, on the other as social licence and cultural disruption.

The 1920s appear as the first consumerist decade, but on closer inspection they seem merely the harvesting of a much longer revolution, commonly periodized as 1880–1930. This era sees the emergence of a mass production system of manufacture increasingly dedicated to producing consumer goods (rather than the heavy capital goods, such as steel, machinery and chemicals, which dominated much of the later nineteenth century). If consumer culture is born here it is because we emphasize several interlocked developments: mass manufacture; the geographical and social spreading of the market; the rationalization of the form and organization of production (see, for example, Aglietta 1979; Boorstin 1973; Fraser 1981; Pope 1983).

Incontrovertibly, it is in this period that all the features which make up consumer culture take on their mature form, but more importantly it is in this period that a modern *norm* emerges concerning how consumer goods are to be produced, sold and assimilated into everyday life. Only now does the following description become normative if not yet universal: goods are designed with standardized, replaceable components which allow them to be produced in very large volumes at low unit cost through an intensive, rationally controlled and increasingly automated technical division of labour.

This is ultimately exemplified in the Fordist model of flow-past assembly lines manned by Taylorized workers. The goods are sold across geographically and socially wider markets – regional, national, global – whose formation is made possible by the interconnection of local markets through new transportation and communications infrastructures (rail, mail, telegraph, telephone); by the concentration of markets in larger cities; by the development of multi-divisional corporations capable of planning and coordinating on this scale; by the integration of markets through *marketing*, using such new techniques as branding and packaging, national sales forces, advertising, point of sale materials and industrial design – all designed to unify product identity across socially and geographically dispersed markets. This is accompanied by the massive development of retail infrastructures (not just shops but also retail multiples, mail order, vertical integration downwards to the point of sale). This massive volume of cheap standardized goods, rationally sold through ever larger markets, is sold to a population which is increasingly *seen* as consumers: they are not seen as classes or genders who consume, but rather as consumers who happen to be organized into classes and genders.

However, if this period marks the true birth of consumer culture it is only because we define consumer culture in terms of mass production and mass participation in consumption. There is no essential reason to do so. We can equally treat the age of mass consumption as the development of a system whose values and aims were inherited from earlier periods, and as the spreading of a culture that had been already well defined in other classes. Moreover, we can consider the fact that critics did not wait for the emergence of Fordist mass production to engage in full-scale attacks and large-scale theorizations of consumer culture (Miller 1981; Williams 1982). Consumer culture existed as a problem for social critics, an ideology for the population and a reality for the bourgeoisie from quite early in the nineteenth century.

Thus we might next look at the prosperous mid-Victorian years from the 1850s to the 1870s. With the industrial and urban pattern of modernization well established as an idea, if not entirely as a reality, and with the economic and political disruptions of the 1840s passed, a new era of confidence is generally held to have been ushered in by the London Exhibition at Crystal Palace in 1851. In a stunning anecdote, Rosalind Williams (1982) points out that whereas this first international celebration of progress focused on exhibiting the triumphs of modern science and technology, by the time of the Paris exhibition of 1889 the objects on display were beginning to carry price tags. The transformation of modernity itself into a commodity, of its experiences and thrills into a ticketed spectacle, of its domination of nature into domestic comfort, of its knowledges into exotic costume, and of the commodity into the goal of modernity: all this was brewing well in advance of mass production oriented towards mass consumption (Richards 1991).

Over this period, consumer culture moves in two contradictory but interrelated directions. On the one hand, consumer culture seems to emerge from the production of public spectacle, from the enervated and overstimulated world of urban experience so powerfully captured in Baudelaire's image of the *flâneur*: in modernity all the world is consumable experience. And all is display: the development of shopping, arcades, department stores, international exhibitions, museums, new forms of entertainment. Cities, department stores and especially international expositions carry powerful collective meanings as symbols of both scientific civilization and national greatness. The world is a cornucopia of consumable experience and goods delivered by modern progress into a modern carnival, and the consumer is the fee-paying audience for the spectacle and experience of modernity (Slater 1995).

On the other hand, and in opposition to the public culture of commodities, consumerism was made respectable during this period by connecting it to the construction of private, bourgeois domesticity. Consumption is to be turned into respectable culture by wresting it from the hands of both the aristocracy (where it signifies luxury, decadence, terminal superficiality) and the working classes (where it signifies public riotousness, the excesses of the drinking, sporting mob). It is crucial that in this period much debate on consumer culture was carried out in terms not of the consumption of goods but of *time*: a debate about leisure (see, especially, Cross 1993; Cunningham 1980) which concerned how to keep public order outside work hours. How, for example, can (male) working-class leisure consumption be diverted from drinking, gaming and prostitution in public places. Yet once excluded from these public places there are fears about what they get up to in their new privacy – fears about health and morals, about subversion and irreligion. What is Victorian philanthropy and reform but the inculcation of new norms of consumption – of healthy domestic, private consumption in the bosom of the family – calibrated by the scales of bourgeois respectability, medical science and moral discourses on sin and criminality (Rose 1992a, 1992b)? In sum, consumer culture of the mid-nineteenth century appears to emerge from a series of struggles to organize and tame, yet at the same time to exploit commercially, the social spaces and times in which modernity is acted out.

One more stop before the terminus: bourgeois respectability, as well as its opponents, drew considerably on romanticism. As we shall see in chapter 3, romanticism and the concept of culture that it produced were in many respects reactions against industrial, commercial, consumer society from Rousseau in the 1750s through revolutionary and nationalist romanticism up to the mid-nineteenth century. It has therefore provided probably the most enduring source of critiques of consumer culture, which it sees as part of a materialistic modernity that lacks authentic collective values and truths.

Yet paradoxically romanticism also bequeathed to consumer culture many of the themes that we consider most modern or even postmodern. Under the impact of a materialistic and monetarized society, romanticism promoted ideas of personal authenticity, an authenticity that derived from what was 'natural', emotional, irrational, sensual and imaginative in the self. Moreover, it associated these sources of authenticity with aestheticism and creativity: everyday life (at least, in the first instance, the everyday life of the artist or genius) should be a process of making the self. The individual's style of goods, activities and experiences was no longer a matter of pure social performance (as Sennett (1977) argues it was for the eighteenth century) but a matter of personal truth and authenticity. The very idea that acts of consuming are seriously consequential for the authenticity of the self (as opposed to mere physical survival or social climbing) is an unintentional consequence of these early developments, as are many of the 'authentic values' in which modern consumer goods come wrapped: naturalness, emotional gratification, ethnic and national cultural values, images of innocent children, natural women and happy domesticity. It is through romanticism that consumer culture becomes both wildly playful and deadly earnest (Berman 1970; Campbell 1989; Sennett 1977; Trilling 1972)

The commercial revolution

Our reverse narrative has now dropped us off in the early modern period. It is here that consumption comes to be understood in recognizably modern ways and in which recognizably modern ways of consuming begin to appear. It is also the period in which we can see most clearly the ways in which consumer culture and modernity are inextricably interwoven.

There has, however, been a considerable historiographical barrier to investigating this connection, a preoccupation, often dubbed a 'productivist bias', with seeing the relation between modernity and capitalism as an *Industrial* Revolution, with production as the engine and essence of modernization. In the most Whiggish versions, modernity unbinds the Prometheus of productive forces from the chains of superstition, authority and tradition: science and technology, the rational technical division of labour and industrial organization, free labour markets, the replacement of status by contract, demographic shifts to the city, all combine in a forcefield of initiative, ingenuity, invention and energy. Industrial machinery – the school pupil's learned litany of steam engines, spinning jennies and Arkwright looms – encapsulates the spectacle of modernization.

The corollary is that consumer culture chronologically *follows* industrialization. Work, after all, comes before play. Moreover, culture in general is often seen to be a matter of economic surplus: until a certain level of material wealth has been achieved, it is often argued, consumption is restricted to basic, effectively non-cultural needs; only above that level can societies sustain that meaning-oriented, 'cultural' choice between desirable goods which characterizes consumer culture. Similarly in economic history, modernization up to the early twentieth century appears as a process of saving, investment and accumulation at a social scale, underpinned by a Puritan, work-oriented ethic. Both the nineteenth century bourgeoisie and the twentieth century Soviet elite saw modernization in these terms – as a period of enforced social saving and investment, of deferred consumer gratification, of a savings plan for the national household. Moreover they *acted* this way quite sufficiently to give the perspective considerable empirical truth. Energies were invested in producing means of production – machinery, metals, infrastructure such as ships and railways – and some primary goods, such as clothing, that involved large markets for staples. Soviet modernization stated this most explicitly: a policy of forced accumulation of productive resources and the dampening of consumer-oriented production and demand in order to catch up in a few five-year plans the accomplishments of a century of western European industrialization.

The 'productivist bias' has been contested by a growing historical revisionism which argues that a Consumer Revolution preceded the Industrial Revolution, or was at least a central and early ingredient of western modernization (basic references and reviews might include Agnew 1986; Appleby 1978; Braudel 1981; Brewer and Porter 1993; Bronner 1989; Campbell 1989; Fine and Leopold 1990; McCracken 1990; McKendrick et al. 1983; Mukerji 1983; Perkin 1968; Porter 1982; Rule 1992; Sekora 1977; Shammas 1990; Thirsk 1978; Weatherill 1988; Xenos 1989). This argument involves looking at developments as early as the sixteenth century, in which we can discern, firstly, a new 'world of goods' (a wide penetration of consumer goods into the everyday lives of more social classes); secondly, the development and spread of 'consumer culture' in the sense of fashion and taste as key elements of consumption; thirdly, the development of infrastructures, organizations and practices that target these new kinds of markets (the rise of shopping, advertising, marketing).

This revisionism started by addressing a contemporary Keynesian question to the eighteenth century. How can industrialization have proceeded on a capitalist basis without the prior existence of adequate effective demand for its produce? To whom could these industrialists sell? Why did they not simply go bankrupt, leaving to the liquidators a pile of rational and scientific inventions and rationally organized but silent factories? The more econometric side of this debate simply assumed that people already wanted more things (assumed that demand was insatiable).

Historians therefore looked for the sources of finance for this demand: the technicalities of the ensuing debate revolved around the relative importance of home versus foreign demand and thus of home markets versus foreign trade and around the importance of demographic shifts, such as rising population and the role of London as a centre of consumption. It also considered shifts in income structure and differential wage rates. (For some of the original discussion, see Coats 1958; Eversley 1967; Gilboy 1967; McKendrick 1974; McKendrick et al. 1983; Rosenberg 1968; Vichert 1971; Wiles 1968; Wrigley 1967.)

However such debates might be resolved, there is a prior (again Keynesian) problem remaining: the propensity to consume. Given more resources, why would people choose to spend them on more things? Simply to assume an insatiable demand for more commodities is to assume, without evidence or explanation, that a central feature of modern consumer culture was already well established. For example, much evidence exists – from many different sectors of the population and many different periods up to the present – that a major struggle for and within capitalism focused on cajoling people not to stop working and enjoy free time independent of commodity consumption once their needs are satisfied, but rather to want more so that they will continue working in order to buy more commodities (see, for example, Campbell 1989: 18; Cross 1993; Sahlins 1974: 1–40; see also Cunningham 1980; Rojek 1985 on struggles over leisure in the nineteenth century). The concept and practice of 'insatiable needs' is not only a historical achievement but a very real social and political battleground (see chapter 3). Making markets and sustaining them requires not only elegant econometric balances but also socio-cultural changes which cannot be assumed. Otherwise, instead of the fallacy of regarding consumer culture as the historically delayed gratification of long industrial labour, we rather assume its basic features to be given and unexplained, not only as preceding capitalism but also as somehow natural and eternal. The central question, then, is: how was the idea and practice of consumption transformed and revalued? And this is a question that must be answered to explain not just consumer culture but the emergence of industrial modernization itself.

Evidence for some kind of consumer revolution around the eighteenth century is certainly plentiful. Firstly, the new historical record offers considerable evidence of a new and expanding 'world of goods' during the early modern period. Contemporaries (for example Defoe) certainly commented on it incessantly. Moreover, we are used to linking the period with a sudden wealth of new commodities derived from discovery and colonial exploitation – coffee, tea, tobacco, imported cloths and dyes, new foods (potatoes, tomatoes), fruits, etc. The west was a master consumer of imperially expropriated commodities before it was a consumer of goods it produced itself (Mukerji 1983; see also Mintz 1985). Analyses of probate documents (for example, Shammas 1990, 1993; Weatherill 1988, 1993), of inventories from shops and chapmen, of commercial manuals and of diaries (for example Mui and Mui 1989; Spufford 1981; Spufford 1984; Willan 1970; and articles in Brewer and Porter 1993) show that entirely new categories of goods appear in homes and shops (e.g. curtains, mirrors); more of traditional categories appear (e.g. chairs and tables); older types of goods are made with newer and more varied materials and are complexly differentiated by prices and qualities (e.g. china plates and cups, clothing); new goods emerge in association with new commodities (for example cups are introduced into homes for drinking the new warm drinks, coffee, chocolate and tea). This 'world of goods' was both wide and deep: while we would hardly look for an 'affluent worker' among Cornish tin miners or Cumberland peasants in the 1690s, we know that an impressive range of relatively cheap goods was being made and bought in Britain. We can add to this the construction of permanent housing (Hoskins 1963); retail and transport infrastructures (Spufford 1984; Willan 1976); clothing markets and other developments from late Tudor times. Finally, amongst the most adventurous pioneers in the new 'world of goods' were the entrepreneurs of leisure: they organized activities such as sport, theatre and entertainment, assemblies, balls and masquerades, leisure and pleasure gardens and so on into commercial events, with fee-paying admission by ticket or subscription. Moreover, the commodification of leisure extends from events to goods: for example toys for children, novels and printed music for the female public – all commodity-based activities (see, for example, Castle 1986; Plumb 1983).

Secondly, the revisionist account of the consumer revolution points to the emergence and social extension of the fashion system throughout this widened consuming public. The system of rapid turnover of styles, the desire for 'the new', creates a new dynamic in consumer demand. This is generally linked to the idea of a transition from traditional to modern society: under the *ancien régime*, social status was relatively fixed and consumption was tied inflexibly to social rank. Fashion, in the sense of the conspicuous and changing display of status through consumption, was largely confined to the aristocracy, not just because of the poverty of other ranks but also largely because of social rigidity. The appearance of fashion marks a moment in which the fixity of ranks and status is breaking down. This kind of analysis tends to equate fashion and therefore the consumer revolution with status competition, emulation and conspicuous consumption: new consumption patterns are tied to a 'trickle-down' process in which aspiring ranks model their consumption on that of higher ranks. This line of thought is widely identified with Neil McKendrick's work (McKendrick 1959/60, 1964, 1974; McKendrick et al. 1983) and is the subject of much debate (see chapter 6) in terms of its adequacy in accounting for either the new scale or new pattern of consumer demand.

Be that as it may, McKendrick's work points us to a third feature of the consumer revolution: the new form and scale of consumption is crucially related to new forms of business and commercial organization, new infrastructures of consumption. McKendrick focuses on the early rise of marketing and consumer-oriented retailing through examples such as Josiah Wedgwood's pottery industry (McKendrick et al. 1983). His interest is in the way Wedgwood exploited an emulation-based fashion system by, for example, tapping into new vogues (producing 'Etruscan' vases in response to enormous public interest in archaeology and classical culture), obtaining and advertising aristocratic and royal endorsements (getting those vases into the homes of noble 'taste leaders'), opening strategically placed shops in order to make a fashionable spectacle of his goods.

The revisionist account has many problems. For example, Fine and Leopold (1990, 1993) raise valid econometric objections concerning its ability to account for industrialization, and reasonable ideological questions about projecting Thatcherism onto Georgian society such that the heroes of capitalist modernization turn out to be eighteenth-century yuppies. The reliance on emulation and trickle-down accounts of fashion are also problematic. However, I want to explore a different objection: the usual revisionist account simply reverses the standard one so that the consumer revolution now precedes the industrial one. An alternative is to see both as part of a *commercial revolution* in which concepts of trade, money, new financial instruments and moveable property, contracts and orientation to commercial exploitation of ever more extensive and impersonal markets generated a vast range of new notions and activities which we deem modern.

The crucial point is that the expansion of the world of goods, the new patterns of consumer dynamism and the new commercial organization all predate anything we might recognize as industrialization by anything up to a couple of centuries. In cloth and clothing production for example – the spearhead of industrialization in most textbooks – the main mechanical inventions start only from the 1780s, while much of the 'industry' was still conducted through cottage-based putting out (i.e. organized on a distributed basis by commercial capitalists rather than through a centralized factory system by industrial capitalists) until well into the 1830s. Yet the production of toys with highly diversified product lines sold on a national market was well established in large-scale enterprises with considerable division of labour and wage-relation from the mid-seventeenth century.

Toy production in fact typified a kind of early modern enterprise studied by Joan Thirsk (1978): the 'projects'. Thirsk uses these 'projects' to demonstrate a revaluation and reorganization of production, commerce and consumption starting from the sixteenth century. The projects and their 'projektors' (early entrepreneurs) originate in a policy of import substitution developed in the context of mercantilism. Worried that demand for foreign 'fripperies' was draining the nation's bullion, government policies and entrepreneurial initiatives strove to increase domestic production through new or reformed businesses. The projects were significantly oriented to consumer goods (for example stockings, buttons, pins and nails, salt, starch, soap, knives and tools, tobacco-pipes, pots and ovens, ribbons and lace, linen and aqua vitae). Moreover, Thirsk argues, their often large work-forces probably also provided the first modern, as opposed to elite, consumers: 'the majority of the population in many local communities did not begin to accumulate much cash in hand until they began to produce commodities other than the staple necessities of life . . . [the projects] gave them cash and something to spend the cash on' (1978: 7). Typically of consumer culture, the workers were simultaneously the makers and the market.

These projects could involve considerable technical and organizational innovation without doubt: for example, the pin-makers that Adam Smith made exemplary of the efficiency gains of the technical division of labour were not, as is often assumed, modern mechanized industrialists but one of the early modern projects as studied by Thirsk. The point is that they innovated (and laid the basis for later industrialization) not primarily as an offshoot of science and engineering or major capital investment (they generally involved little), nor through consumer orientation (in McKendrick's sense of being fashion-led). Rather, they emerged and innovated as part of a policy and practice of commercial opportunism, an orientation towards *trade*. The projects involved large-volume production, to be sold over wide geographically dispersed markets to a 'general public' of consumers rather than locally to known customers.

It is trade and commerce (rather than production or consumption) that looms largest in the early modern mind. They are recognized very early as the catalysts, for good or ill, of the transition from traditional agrarian to modern society. Moreover, it is commerce that provides so many of the new images and concepts through which that society is understood and through which consumption is recognized and revalued in ways that bear the mark of what we now call consumer culture: notions of economy and government, the idea of civil society and of society itself, images of the self, self-interest, reason and desire, new concepts of status and culture.

Firstly, as we will explore in chapter 7, it is in relation to commerce that consumption is redefined in the eighteenth century. In earlier times, consumption meant waste, squandering, using up (without gain), a loss to economic, moral and political flows of value (Williams 1976: 68–70). By the later eighteenth century, the word can be used technically and neutrally within economic and other discourses to signify a natural part of these flows and at the same time their logical terminus or goal: for Smith, 'Consumption is the sole end and purpose of all production and the interest of the producer ought to be attended to, only so far as it may be necessary for promoting that of the consumer.' It is through the idea of commerce that people come to see as necessary and important the social conditions which enable goods to be sold.

Secondly, the revaluation of consumption along the lines of a modern consumer culture is bound up with the experience of a world entirely transformed, not just economically but socially and culturally, by commerce, market exchange and money. Market-based exchange and consumption presupposed that individuals could make unconstrained choices about what goods they wished to buy; and that access to these goods could be regulated solely by the possession of cash, of the money to buy the goods. The idea that people's lifestyles could be determined solely by their money-wealth – rather than by religious prohibitions on luxury and excess, by juridical prohibitions of certain goods to certain status groups, by traditional and communal surveillance, by the cosmological fixity of 'the great chain of being' – indicated a situation of status instability and ultimately status revolution. The spread of markets and market-mediated consumption both required and intensively promoted the breakdown of the old status order, and this is what exercised the early modern mind: the corrosive (or liberating) effect of monetary relations on traditional society. From the late sixteenth century onwards, the hope and dread of a world now more opulently dense with things and more licentiously free to exercise socially unrestricted individual choice was clearly bruited about: the problem or potential of a society in which individuals can make themselves according to their own designs by buying commodities (Sekora 1977). This threat to the old order is not posed by an industrial bourgeoisie alone but rather comprises the erosion of traditional society through all forms of moneyed wealth.

Significantly, 'commerce' meant more than trade in the eighteenth century. From its origins in the sixteenth century, the word has a specific economic sense (it is traffic or intercourse between social beings in the course of buying and selling goods, as well as the whole process and system of exchanging things). But it also carries a general sense of social intercourse, of regular dealings between people, of everyday conversation and interchange of ideas, communication etc. It is a notion of uncompelled encounters between people in the regular and voluntary course of their practical life. For critics of commercial society, the origin of the term in trade (and the idea that modern sociality depends on trade) indicates the disreputability of this new freedom of social interaction. Significantly, 'commerce' also describes sexual and licentious relations (for example, in Fielding, 'Sophia's virtue made his commerce with lady Bellaston appear still more odious' (from *Tom Jones*, 1749; OED) Both commercial and consumer society are often described as a kind of mad orgy (see, for example, Porter 1993a, 1993b).

Commerce was a new metaphor for the social: the free exchange not only of goods and services within a monetary economy but also of ideas, conversation, opinion within a free public sphere (Burchill 1991; Pocock 1975, 1985). This new image is evident in the idea of 'civil society': not just the market, but a whole world of political, economic and private associations in which men (*sic*) could be free, convivial, contentedly opportunistic, self-interested and energetic. Hirschman (1977) captures this relation between commerce and 'civility' in 'political arguments for capitalism before its triumph': commerce, for example in Montesquieu, is a civilizing process because it promotes peaceful intercourse within and between nations; because the passions, unreason, violence and power of both sovereigns and individuals are tamed by the rational pursuit of self-interest; and because private commercial wealth provides the means of resistance to arbitrary authority.

It could be argued that 'consumer culture' (like 'mass society') is one of several terms that comes to replace the idea of 'civil society' and indicates the degeneration of that ideal of voluntary association in which free and equal men enter into commerce and communication with each other. Civil society becomes consumer culture, on the one hand, when the commercial and economic energy on which the former depends is imposed upon it as an external and disciplinary force by, for example, large-scale corporations, the mass media and advertising, and, on the other hand, when civil society is castigated as comprising merely the irrational, arbitrary, frivolous and above all manipulable follies of the mob, the destabilization of status and overturning of hierarchy. Moreover, the use of the term 'consumer culture' can indicate the reduction of the broad social ideal of civil society to the mere pursuit of wealth, the cult of GNP (Habermas 1991).

None the less, ideas of modern consumption arise firstly in the ideal (or dystopia) of a liberal and commercial society comprising free individuals pursuing their interests through free association in the public sphere. The consumer, as we shall see in the next chapter, is one example or one aspect of the private and enterprising individual who stands at the centre of the very notion of modernity. Commercial and civil society required freedom, took liberties and therefore usurped powers. We are familiar with this process in certain areas of historical change: the assertion of reason and science involved a reliance on the individual's resources of knowledge and an independence from received authority, from 'custom and example' (Descartes, quoted in Gellner 1992), tradition, religious revelation. This is a class struggle in thought, a revolution by and for 'self-made men' (Gellner 1992). But Enlightenment man – both as an idealized projection and as a real new form of subjectivity – was not just a rational, freethinking individual in the sphere of science, politics or production: he also learned some of these ways of being by being rational and individual in the experience of going to market and of materially constructing new forms of domesticity, in dressing as a fashionable urbanite and in going to newly commercialized leisure activities.

The outlines of consumer culture

If consumer culture is bound up with 'the whole of modernity' in the ways I have suggested, then a simple definition of it would seem inappropriate. On the other hand, we need some signposts, some way of recognizing just when consumer culture is being talked about. What follows, then, is a limited list of features by which consumer culture has been identified, a list derived from the kinds of material we will be looking at in the following chapters. What kinds of thing have modern thinkers pointed to when they have thought about consumer culture, when they have condemned or applauded modern society as a consumer society? What have they found to be different or dangerous about the way consumption is organized in the modern world? What general modern features and processes seem to have made consumer culture visible and distinctive to modern thinkers as a social phenomenon?

Consumer culture is a culture of consumption

The notion of 'consumer culture' implies that, in the modern world, core social practices and cultural values, ideas, aspirations and identities are defined and oriented in relation to consumption rather than to other social dimensions such as work or citizenship, religious cosmology or military role. To describe a society in terms of its consumption and to assume that its core values derive from it is unprecedented: a militaristic culture, agrarian culture, maritime culture . . . but a consumer culture?

Thus in talking of modern society as a consumer culture, people are not referring simply to a particular pattern of needs and objects – a particular consumption culture – but to a culture *of* consumption. To talk this way is to regard the dominant values of a society not only to be organized through consumption practices but also in some sense to derive from them. Thus we might describe contemporary society as materialistic, as a pecuniary culture based on money, as concerned with 'having' to the exclusion of 'being', as commodified, as hedonistic, narcissistic or, more positively, as a society of choice and consumer sovereignty. The very idea of a culture structured by the consumption of commodities is often regarded as a contradiction in terms (as discussed in chapter 3) because the term 'culture' has been defined as the social preservation of authentic values that cannot be negotiated by money and market exchange. Hence, for example, consumer culture is often equated with 'mass culture', with a society in which the desires and tastes of 'the masses', newly empowered by money and democratic rights, reduce culture to consumption.

Moreover, a central claim is that values from the realm of consumption spill over into other domains of social action, such that modern society is *in toto* a consumer culture, and not just in its specifically consuming activities. The spread of consumption values to the general society occurs firstly because consumption itself becomes a central focus of social life (in the sense that we reproduce more and more areas of social life through the use of commodities, and in the sense that other foci, e.g. work, religion, politics, become less important or meaningful); and secondly because the values of consumer culture acquire a prestige which encourages their metaphorical extension to other social domains, e.g. the extension of the consumer model to public service broadcasting or health provision.

Consumer culture is the culture of a market society

Modern consumption is mediated by market relations and takes the form of the consumption of commodities: that is to say we generally consume goods, services and experiences which have been produced solely in order to be sold on the market to consumers. We do not ourselves make the goods through which we reproduce everyday life. Rather, integral to our consumption is the act of choosing between a range of alternative commodities produced by institutions which are not interested in need or cultural values but in profit and economic values. The consumer's access to consumption is largely structured by the distribution of material and cultural resources (money and taste), which itself is determined in crucial ways by market relations – above all the wage relation and social class.

We can put this most clearly through Marx's terminology (though many of the basic assumptions are very widely shared). The concentration of means of production under private ownership (as capital) means that workers do not, and for the most part cannot, produce the means of their own subsistence, their own consumer goods. These must be obtained indirectly: people sell their labour power for money in the form of wages by producing goods to which they are normally indifferent, in order to be able to buy on another market the goods they actually want (and which have been produced by other equally indifferent workers and capitalists). From this perspective, it is the wage-relation (and not industrial mass production), it is capitalist relations of production (and not its technical forces) that produce the consumer, and do so instantly and automatically. The worker and the consumer are born of the same social relation. The wage relation might produce a very poor consumer indeed, for the most part, and one who cannot go to the market for many of his or her needs, instead either going without, or – up to a late historical period – continuing to produce outside of market relations the means of his or her own subsistence. But it is through the market that consumer culture is defined: consumers are produced when the market emerges as the general means of economic regulation.

To state the obvious, consumer culture is *capitalist* culture. Historically, it develops as part of the capitalist system. Structurally, consumer culture is incompatible with the political regulation of consumption through either suppression of the market or traditionalist sumptuary codes and laws. It does not arise in non-capitalist societies: in the case of both actually existing socialism and religiously fundamentalist states, for example, political control over consumption and the suppression of its 'decadent' culture are crucial. Conversely, when either regime slackens its control or breaks down, in conditions of sufficient technical and material resources, capitalist entrepreneurialism linked to expanded consumer markets does indeed arise.

Consumer culture is, in principle, universal and impersonal

Consumer culture is often identified with the idea of mass consumption because it exemplifies the generalization of commodity consumption to the entire population. However, mass consumption is only one form of a more fundamental principle: the idea of making large volumes of goods for sale to a general public rather than for oneself, for one's household or local community or on the basis of a personal commission. The idea of selling a product that is not tailored to the needs of a known and unique individual or community, but which might be sold to any individual anywhere, presumes impersonal and generalizable relations of exchange as the basis for mediating consumption.

Market relations are anonymous and in principle universal: the consumer is not a known 'customer' but an anonymous subject who can only be imagined and constructed as an *object* – the target of a marketing drive, the profile produced by a market survey, a mass market or market segment. Moreover, if the cultural meaning of the consumer good is not immediately provided by the personalized relations in which it is produced and exchanged, then this too must increasingly be produced and distributed in an impersonal and generalized manner: design, advertising, marketing all start *before* widespread industrialization because of the need to personalize the impersonal, to culturally specify the general and the abstract.

The idea that consumer culture serves a general public also promotes a more positive idea that it embraces 'everyone'. Although we know that access to commodities is restricted by access to money, the consumption of commodities is treated *in principle* as the activity of the entire population. We are all formally free and equal when we go to market, unconstrained in our choices by legally fixed status or cultural prohibitions. Moreover, consumer culture appears universal in so far as it portrays itself as a democracy of comfort and wealth. There seems to be a fundamental human right to consume freely and a technical potential to consume well that is given us by modernity: the right and ability to be a consumer is the ideological birthright of the modern western subject.

Similarly, however, if there is no principle restricting who can consume what, there is also no principled constraint on *what* can be consumed: all social relations, activities and objects can in principle be exchanged as commodities. This is one of the most profound secularizations enacted by the modern world. Everything can become a commodity at least during some part of its life. This potential for any thing, activity or experience to be commodified or to be replaced by commodities perpetually places the intimate world of the everyday into the impersonal world of the market and its values. Moreover, while consumer culture appears universal because it is depicted as a land of freedom in which everyone *can* be a consumer, it is also felt to be universal because everyone *must* be a consumer: this particular freedom is compulsory. It is by and large through commodities that everyday life, and the social relations and identities that we live within it, are sustained and reproduced.

Consumer culture identifies freedom with private choice and private life

To be a consumer is to make choices: to decide what you want, to consider how to spend your money to get it. This exercise of choice is in principle, if never in fact, unconstrained: no one has the *right* to tell you what to buy, what to want. 'Consumer sovereignty' is an extremely compelling image of freedom: apart from the modern right to choose our intimate partners, it provides one of the few tangible and mundane experiences of freedom which feels personally significant to modern subjects. How emotionally charged within everyday life is the right to vote?

The 'freedom' of consumer culture is defined in a particular way which is crucial to modernity, especially its liberal version: consumer choice is a private act. Firstly it is private in the positive sense that it occurs within a domain of the private – of the individual, the household, the group of friends – which is ideologically declared out of bounds to public intervention. The relation between freedom and privacy is crucial to the idea of the modern individual: reason, for example, was conceptualized by much of the Enlightenment as a private resource, found within the individual, with which *he* (as we shall see, the hero of this story is specifically male) could resist the irrational social authority of tradition, religion, political elites, superstition. Private, individual resources were also defined in terms of the *interests* of the individual, which only he could know and which he had every right to pursue. Consumer choice is merely the mundane version of this broader notion of private, individual freedom.

Secondly, however, consumer choice is private in the more negative sense that it is restricted to the household, mundane domesticity, the world of private relationships. Any particular act of consumption is private in the sense of having no public significance. We do not consume in order to build a better society, to be a good person and live the true life, but to increase private pleasures and comforts.

Consumer culture is marked by this double sense of privacy and its relation to choice and freedom: individual empowerment, meaning, investment in the future, identity etc. are bound up with a restricted area of life. The constant complaint of critical traditions is that in becoming 'free' as consumers we barter away power and freedom in the workplace or in the political arena in exchange for mere private contentment.

Finally, and perhaps most importantly, the privacy of individual choice seems to contradict social order, solidarity and authority. If individuals define their own interests, how can society hold together? If choice is governed by private individual preferences, what happens to enduring cultural values? In many respects, this is the main preoccupation of critics of consumer culture, both conservative and radical: if we cannot judge or regulate the desires of individuals, how can they work to constitute a good or progressive or authentic collective life?

Consumer needs are in principle unlimited and insatiable

In most cultures, the possibility that needs may be insatiable indicates a social or moral pathology (sin, corruption, decadence) or a very particular status marker for social elites (the excesses of competitive display). In consumer culture, uniquely, unlimited need – the constant desire for more and the constant production of more desires – is widely taken to be not only normal for its denizens but essential for socio-economic order and progress.

The idea of insatiable need is bound up with notions of cultural modernization: the increased productivity of modern industry is widely understood as both a response and a spur to the capacity of people's desires to become increasingly sophisticated, refined, imaginative and personal, as well as people's desire to advance themselves socially and economically. As we shall see in several chapters, these capacities can be heralded as either a quantum leap in human civilization or a descent into decadence. On the other hand, it is generally accepted by most parties that a commercial society is systemically dependent on the insatiability of needs: put crudely, commodity production requires the sale of ever-increasing quantities of ever-changing goods; market society is therefore perpetually haunted by the possibility that needs might be either satisfied or underfinanced.

This fear emerges in many forms and through a variety of historical experiences. There is the perpetual fear that workers will choose more time rather than more goods as the reward for industrial progress (see, for example, Campbell 1989; Cross 1993; Sahlins 1974). The redefinition of leisure time as consumption time, the commodification of leisure, has been crucial in sustaining capitalist growth. Experiences of global economic depression in the inter-war years give rise to an elaborate structure of demand management strategies (Keynesianism, welfare state). It has also been argued that advertising and marketing have not only addressed demand deficits for particular brands and products but also participated in changing values from a puritan orientation to savings, the future, the preservation of goods and sobriety to a hedonistic ethos of spending and credit, orientation to the present, rapid technical and aesthetic obsolescence, the turnover of styles and goods and a playful culture.

For many authors, it is precisely in this domain that the fundamental and ultimately self-rending cultural contradictions of modernity (and its crumbling into postmodernity) arise: economic modernization is characterized, on the one hand, by rational planning, discipline and labour underpinned by a work ethic; yet, on the other hand, it structurally depends upon fostering irrational desires and passions, a hedonistic orientation to gratification in the present which must surely undermine it.

Consumer culture is the privileged medium for negotiating identity and status within a post-traditional society

In Europe, the *ancien régime* inherited the feudal idea, if no longer quite the actuality, of a social structure comprising fixed and stable status: a world in which social position is ascribed by birth and is fixed as part of a cosmological order (for example 'the great chain of being') in which each entity has an ordained place and has attached to it exclusive rights, privileges and obligations. The latter include rights and obligations to a particular lifestyle. Hence sumptuary laws are important forms of symbolic regulation: that certain animals can be eaten only by nobles (poaching laws), that guild members must wear uniforms, that retainers must wear livery, that the right to move house should be conditional. In a word, crucial areas of consumption were fixed both in order to mark out positions within the status order, and also in order to regulate and police it. Revivals of sumptuary laws were rife in England as 'the great chain of being' began to rust away over the seventeenth and eighteenth centuries with the birth of commercial society.

Modern concepts of individualism, founded on modern practices of market exchange, sweep away the possibility as well as the desirability of a fixed status order. The move 'from status to contract' makes social mobility a matter of principle: mobility either upward or downward, for status is now an achievement of the moment (there is always new and more dynamic money threatening you from below) and not an attribute ascribed to one as part of an inheritance from the cosmic order. In a post-traditional society, social identity must be constructed by individuals, because it is no longer given or ascribed, but in the most bewildering of circumstances: not only is one's position in the status order no longer fixed, but the order itself is unstable and changing and is represented through ever changing goods and images. Access to goods is regulated purely by money, yet these goods still signify social position, and in increasingly complex and creative ways.

Goods can always signify social identity, but in the fluid processes of a post-traditional society, identity seems to be more a function of consumption than the other, traditional, way round. The extreme version of this is found in the idea of postmodernity: society appears as a kind of fancy-dress party in which identities are designed, tried on, worn for the evening and then traded in for the next. Appearances – the images we construct on the surfaces of our bodies, our living spaces, our manners and our voices – become a crucial way of knowing and identifying ourselves and each other, but again, precisely at the moment when these signs have become detached from any fixed meaning or reference. In the new, modern world, we rely on appearances; but only in the old world did those appearances have reliable meanings, were they fixed items in a fixed code.

Consumer culture is crucially about the negotiation of status and identity – the practice and communication of social position – under these conditions. Regulation of these issues by tradition is replaced by negotiation and construction, and consumer goods are crucial to the way in which we make up our social appearance, our social networks (lifestyle, status group etc.), our structures of social value.

*Consumer culture represents the increasing importance of culture
in the modern exercise of power*

Consumer culture is notoriously awash with signs, images, publicity. Most obviously, it involves an aestheticization of commodities and their environment: advertising, packaging, shop display, point of sale material, product design etc. have a long history within commercial capitalism. There is an explosion of visual and verbal discourse on, about and through objects (Leiss et al. 1986). Although these features have again come to the forefront of thought over the 1980s, they have been both evident and much discussed from the very dawn of commerce as the ordering principle of everyday modernity.

Firstly, problems of status and identity, as outlined under the previous point, promote a new flexibility in the relations between consumption, communication and meaning. It is not so much that goods and acts of consumption become more important in signalling status (they always were crucial) but that both the structure of status and the structure of meaning become unstable, flexible, highly *negotiable*. Appearance becomes a privileged site of strategic action in unprecedented ways.

Secondly, the nature of market exchange seems intrinsically bound up with aestheticization. As indicated above, commodities circulate through impersonal and anonymous networks: the split between producer and consumer extends beyond simple commissioning (where a personal relationship still exists) to production for an anonymous general public. To reconnect consumer and product within this mediated space both must be personified again, given meaning, and a meaning which connects them. For example, Haug (1986) theorizes this in the notion of 'commodity aesthetics': the producer must create an image of use value in which potential buyers can recognize themselves. All aspects of the product's meaning and all channels through which its meaning can be constructed and represented become subject to intense and rationalized calculation.

This gives rise to some of the central issues of sociological debate on consumer culture. On the one hand, the eminently modern notion of the social subject as a self-creating, self-defining individual is bound up with self-creation through consumption: it is partly through the use of goods and services that we formulate ourselves as social identities and display these identities. This renders consumption as the privileged site of autonomy, meaning, subjectivity, privacy and freedom. On the other hand, all these meanings around social identity and consumption become crucial to economic competition and rational organization, become the objects of strategic action by dominating institutions. The sense of autonomy and identity in consumption is placed constantly under threat. Hence the constant and constitutive controversy over whether consumption is a sphere of manipulation or freedom, whether the consumer is sovereign or subject, active or passive, creative or determined, and so on.

Moreover, there has been a considerable shift in how theorists perceive the role of culture in social organization. For earlier critics of consumer culture, what passes for culture in capitalist societies appeared to be at the service of economic and political power: advertising, for example, fostered in individuals those needs which were most useful to the system, both in the sense of increasing demand for commodities and in the sense of identifying individuals with the commodity system in general. Much post-Fordist and postmodern theory, on the other hand, argues that culture is now organizing the economy in crucial respects: the value of goods depends more on their cultural value ('sign-value') than on their functional or economic value; advertising and marketing are no longer functions subordinate to production but are actually commanding discourses within firms; more and more commodities take the form not of material goods at all but of signs and representations (for example information, software), of services and 'experiences' (for example tourism, leisure). The logical development of consumer culture (as of advanced capitalism as a whole) seems to be in the direction of the 'de-materialization' of the economy.

Conclusion

The fact that we can trace consumer culture a rather long way back, and that we can list a number of features through which it has been identified throughout modernity, is not a matter of pedantic historical interest. As we shall see in the following chapters, the fact that consumer culture is bound up with 'the whole of modernity' means that the concepts, issues, and critiques through which we try to understand it also have long histories. If the choice of 'theories of consumer culture' now on offer in today's university bookshop is not to be reduced to a matter of pure consumer preference, then they too must be understood as part of a history of modern times. In the next chapter we will start by looking at what 'the consumer' and 'consumer choice' mean.

2
The Freedoms of the Market

Hero or fool?

The consumer is a schizoid character in modern thought. On the one hand a ridiculous figure: an irrational slave to trivial, materialistic desires who can be manipulated into childish mass conformity by calculating mass producers. This consumer is a cultural dupe or dope, the mug seduced by advertising, the fashion victim, the striving *nouveau riche*, the Babbit keeping up with the Joneses, yuppies who would sell their birthright for a mess of designer labels. Ostensibly exercising free choice, this consumer actually offends against all the aspirations of modern western citizens to be free, rational, autonomous and self-defining.

On the other hand, the consumer is a hero of modernity. This may appear strange, since heroism is traditionally associated with noble distance from the base pursuit of material gain. But the consumer became a hero precisely when bourgeois culture broke this association and dignified itself in a historically new dramatic form: its liberal tradition connected material gain, technical progress and individual freedom through the motivation of the *pursuit of self-interest*. This laid the basis for a 'democratic' heroism: in the individual's most banal and previously undignified desires (for comforts and for wealth, for trade and for industry) could be discerned the heroic will and intelligence that could transform nature and society and bend them both to mastery by the freely and privately chosen desires of the individual. The consumer is heroic because he (*sic*) is rational and autonomous and because only his self-defined needs can give legitimacy to economic and social institutions. The 'masculinity' of this bourgeois hero is part of the picture, as is the supposedly feminine character of the irrational, manipulated and domestic consumer.

Rational or irrational, sovereign or manipulated, autonomous or other-determined, active or passive, creative or conformist, individual or mass, subject or object – these are the dichotomies through which the consumer has been viewed since early modernity. The first term in each of these pairs is usually associated with a form of liberalism or utilitarianism; the second term with the opposition, such as critiques of modern (mass) culture (chapter 3) and critiques of commodity relations (chapter 4). In this chapter I want to explore these terms from the perspective of liberal-utilitarianism, the tradition which both sets up the consumer as hero but also, unwittingly, defines its other face.

We will start with recent imagery of a heroic 'enterprise culture' which clearly links the consumer to core Enlightenment themes of freedom, reason and progress through concepts of choice and the market. We can trace this heroic consumer back to early liberalism and then see how – in utilitarianism and neo-classical economics – rationality, autonomy and social dynamism were narrowed to attributes of 'economic man'. One consequence of this narrowing has been decisive for modern understandings of consumption: 'rationality' comes to describe *how* individuals may pursue their desires, but says nothing about *what* desires they pursue, about where their needs come from, about whether they are good or bad. This has produced, firstly, a seemingly unbridgeable division in our knowledge of consumer culture between the economic study of 'rational action' and the study of 'needs', which is carried out as a cultural or psychological study by other disciplines. There is a second, normative, consequence however: the consumer is heroic in so far as *he* is depicted as one aspect of rational economic man; in so far as *she* is regarded in terms of specific needs (which cannot be defined through reason), the consumer appears as irrational dupe. Finally, Foucault's work has recently been used to cut through the terms and polarities set up by liberalism: he moves on from asking whether or not we are 'free to choose' in consumer culture to ask how the concept and strategy of freedom have been used to construct the modern self, how we have learned to see ourselves in terms of freedom and choice.

Consumer sovereignty and enterprise culture

'Consumer sovereignty' is the most powerful image of the consumer as social hero and has been a major ideological rallying cry for liberal assaults against 'collectivism' – socialist, communist and Keynesian – from the 1920s to the Cold War. Within the tradition of liberalism, consumer sovereignty means two things: firstly, that consumers have sovereignty over their own needs, desires, wants, identities. Individuals have both the right and the ability to formulate their own plans and projects. In other words, needs and desires are private: individuals (or households) constitute a private sphere which must be free from interference by external social authorities who might wish to define and impose overarching social aims and projects. For liberalism, the state is the most threatening public authority over needs; but the monopolistic firm, exemplified in the manipulative advertiser, can also threaten consumer sovereignty. It is in these senses that consumer sovereignty is about 'freedom of choice'. Secondly, however, liberalism holds that the consumer is sovereign in a market society – and only in a market society – because competition, enforced through the price mechanism, ensures that producers must respond to the expressed preferences of consumers. By allocating their scarce means (money) amongst available goods in terms of the amount of satisfaction they might obtain from them at a given price, consumers hold a very effective axe over the heads of producers. Consumers are sovereign, then, in that firms only survive by accurately and efficiently satisfying their desires. This works, of course, only if consumers are already sovereign in the first sense (that they, and not firms or states, have the freedom to define their own needs) and if the prerequisites of competition obtain.

Consumer sovereignty, then, is about freedom in the form of personal liberty and about the accountability of social institutions to private interests. But it is also about social dynamism and progress: by making institutions directly and competitively accountable to individuals' desires, liberal society, it is held, fosters initiative, enterprise, efficient use of resources, imagination and that exuberant, even mischievous go-getting opportunism, that shameless and total egoism, by which western capitalism has loved to depict itself. Consumer sovereignty is inextricably bound up with images of the west as a cornucopia of goodies, the great bonanza. Moreover, given that, for liberalism, consumer sovereignty connects individual desires and social institutions through the *rational* calculation of self-interest (as we shall detail below), consumer sovereignty brings together the three defining obsessions of modernity: freedom, reason and progress. Hence the heroism of consumption: the most trivial purchase of a Chicken McNugget is an enactment of individual self-determination, of the rational calculation of ends and means, and of the energetic social advancement produced by these forces.

Consumer sovereignty was the most popular Cold War wedge between east and west, one that – unlike the apocalyptic balance of nuclear terror – struck into the heart of everyday life. The contrast between the bounteous (American) west and the grey, sclerotic Soviet east turned on the notion that stifling the individuals' capacity to define and pursue even the most trivial of their desires resulted both in an entire loss of freedom and in an inefficient, corrupt and above all materially *unsuccessful* social system. In aspiring to plan production and distribution, the Soviet system, it was argued, inevitably subordinated the needs of the population to bureaucratic planning, instituting what Feher et al. (1984) cogently label a 'dictatorship over needs'. In the absence of a market system disciplined by consumer sovereignty, it did this in increasingly undemocratic ways, taking on the economic, political and ideological power to enforce on its people only those needs it found convenient to satisfy. The norms and character of consumption were therefore established technocratically and as part of an attempt to balance problems of political stability with technical economic requirements, rather than in response to the dynamic of cultural reproduction. The latter was to be managed through political or politicized institutions (the party, youth and cultural organizations, public spectacles) that colonized everyday life in ways unimaginable within a market society. Thus political unfreedom was closely linked to the stifling of consumer freedom. At the same time, such a system was incapable of carrying out its own project: without the price mechanism of the market, planners firstly had insufficient (or invalid) knowledge of who needed what, when and where and therefore could not coordinate social resources; and secondly they were not disciplined into efficiency by competition (see, for example, Altvater 1993; Breitenbach et al. 1990; Feher et al. 1984; Hodgson 1984; Nove 1983). Rational social planning appeared to produce unfreedom, irrationality and lack of progress and dynamism. On the other hand, while officially denigrated (and linked to the decadence of the west) the heroic consumer who connects freedom and social dynamism through the market pursuit of self-interest seemed to persist. Consumer culture survived in the seeming desperation for western consumer goods, for a culture of Coke and jeans: culturally, western consumption represented material success and private pleasures, but also the outcome and evidence of personal freedom. The same ideals and activities survived in the informal, unofficial black economy of market-like relations in which people got what they wanted through intricate patterns of private exchange (and which was economically crucial in sustaining the eastern economies by making up for the deficiencies of central planning). Moreover, this informal economy exemplified precisely those values through which we identify consumer culture with western modernity in its heroic phase (enterprising individualism, rejection of authority in private life, autonomy defined as self-creation, private domesticity as the locus of meaningful social life). If civil society disappeared as a reality from Soviet life, its values seemed to persist more in consumer dreams than anywhere else: capitalism, consumerism and a free civil society were felt to be entirely of a piece.

What emerged so harrowingly for western socialists in 1989 was the extent to which eastern citizens had indeed come to see consumer freedom exercised through the market as both the epitome and the linchpin of all other freedoms, and the extent to which *all* collective provision for need (e.g. rights to employment, childcare, health, education, a measure of economic equality) were neither valued nor connected to the idea of freedom. To the eyes of the western left, the scenes of millions of ordinary citizens turning to the street throughout the cities of the east to refuse a corrupt system in the name of civic freedom was a truly heroic return to enlightened modernity. The speed with which this was swept aside in favour of an identification of all freedom with the right to go shopping over the Berlin Wall was terrifying. The reunification election in East Germany was the real meaning of the 1989 revolutions: civil society meant consumer society, civic freedom the freedom to shop freely. The collapse of actually existing socialism was seen by most eastern European citizens as a return to the mainline of western modernity (freedom, democracy, civil rights etc.) but in an image of the west which seemed a magnification of the west's own worst fears. Could Enlightenment have seriously come down to Coca-Cola culture?

In the west, the neo-liberal revival exemplified by Thatcherism and Reaganomics had already radically promoted consumer sovereignty as the link between freedom and dynamism. The model of consumer choice came to be seen as the most adequate model for *all* forms of modern citizenship and social action, the market as the only means of social coordination that secured both freedom and progress. Thus the 'rolling back of the state' was to be accomplished either by outright return to the market through privatization or through internal markets and a model of consumer sovereignty even in public services which remained in state control. Thatcherism in particular waged its war against a kind of grey sovietism at home: the run-down council estate, the demeaning social security office, the long hospital queue – these represented both a lack of freedom to choose and a bureaucratic inefficiency that resulted from not needing to respond to consumer needs individually voiced through market demand. The language of freedom and the language of consumer choice became virtually identical. Freedom meant the individualistic freedoms of the market and being 'free to choose'.

As in eastern Europe, consumer choice was itself one part of a broader notion of 'enterprise culture'. To release the modern citizen from the 'nanny state', a cultural revolution was in order, one that replaced traits of dependency, indiscipline, passivity inculcated by 'welfare socialism' with the values of 'enterprise' associated with market behaviour and with the stimulus to individual energy aroused by competition. As Heelas and Morris (1992: 5–6; cf. du Gay 1996: 75–95) note, enterprising producers and consumers are mutual conditions for neo-liberalism: producers, private or public, are enterprising only if they are competing for consumers' custom; while consumers must themselves be enterprising, and indeed demonstrate in their actions all the properties of enterprise by which producers are usually defined: 'initiative, energy, independence, boldness, self-reliance, a willingness to take risks and to accept responsibility for one's actions . . . ' (Keat and Abercrombie 1991: 3). Hence Thatcherism saw consumerism as a form of active citizenship involving home-ownership, the buying of shares, private insurance and so on. The enterprising consumer looks at their goods more as capital than consumables, as investments – rational, risk-taking and calculable – in an enterprise of the self or the family: 'the sphere of consumption itself takes on some of the characteristics of commercial life: working out how to maximise retirement income, treating one's home as a business investment and so on.' (Keat and Abercrombie 1991: 9; similarly, in Friedman's (1957) 'theory of permanent income' rational consumers plan consumption, and saving, in terms of their expected income over their entire life-time). Whether as producer or consumer, then, the enterprise culture heroizes the same 'active self-motivated individual, accepting responsibility for its own fate, keen to identify clearly its aims and desires, to remove barriers to its fulfilment, to monitor its success in realising them . . . ' (Keat and Abercrombie 1991: 11).

Enlightenment, liberalism, markets

The consumer is a hero, we could say, not when he or she is simply buying or enjoying things (for this can be depicted as impulsive, irrational, manipulated) but when these activities are viewed as one aspect of a broader concept of 'modern man' – man as self-defining, one who pursues his self-defined interests rationally, freely and energetically. Liberalism derived its image of the consumer from the broader ideal of 'Enlightenment man' and then came increasingly to find the ideal relation between this individual and society in market institutions and economic relations.

Reason and autonomy

Barbara Kruger's incisive summation of the 1980s cultural revolution, 'I shop therefore I am', crystallizes the link between the enterprising consumer and Enlightenment man. At first glance, the phrase simply suggests that people have been reduced to a superficiality in which they have an identity *only* by buying and consuming things: it evokes the postmodern consumer who exists only through commodity-signs. Yet the reference to Descartes' *cogito* brings out the depth and superficiality of this figure: 'I think therefore I am' is the most powerful western statement of the relation between individualism, reason and freedom. Descartes believes that he has arrived, solely by the use of his individual capacity for reason, at the one secure knowledge claim that he can make about the world. This claim, unsurprisingly, is itself a statement that defines the individual in terms of its rational capacity.

Descartes' vision makes individual freedom and individual reason interdependent: individuals are free and autonomous in so far as they are not defined by others (especially not by social custom or authority) but through their own reason. Reason is the inner resource by which modern individuals contest and liberate themselves from the irrationality of traditional society. (Kant later defines 'maturity' in terms of autonomous self-definition, the individual who reaches, through his or her own reason, a universally valid, yet entirely self-constituted self: Immaturity is the inability to use one's understanding without guidance from another' (Kant 1983: 41).) In the self-assessment of the *philosophes* it is reason that frees man from *ancien régime* superstition and irrationality; for liberals, it is rather reason in its more social form of the individual's free pursuit of self-interest through rational economic and political action. In either case, the individual comes to be seen as essentially self-defining, as achieving identity through choice rather than ascription by a traditional social order: he must use his reason to decide who he is, what he wants, what his interests are and how they may best be pursued.

Enlightenment made the individual the philosophical centre of the world; liberalism made the individual its moral and political centre: social institutions must be subordinated to the free and self-defining individual. Especially over the past two decades, we have tended to see (neo-)liberalism as an argument about specifically economic liberties: deregulation, *laissez-faire*, privatization. But liberalism is a broad *political* project. Its fundamental value and goal is personal liberty – defined as the individual's freedom from social interference – and its concern is to secure the social conditions necessary to allow individuals to define and pursue their own interests. This is freedom in Berlin's 'negative' sense: freedom from interference, a right to privacy; a freedom whose only limit is that individuals are not free to do that which will compromise other individuals' freedoms (i.e. which might harm them). Various social means might promote this freedom, above all democracy and capitalist markets. But they are indeed means, not ends in themselves: the fundamental commitment is to private personal liberty. Thus, neo-liberals such as Hayek (1976) and Brittan (1988) both carefully distinguish liberalism proper from *laissez-faire*. Where markets (or democracy) compromise individual liberty, liberals will regulate the market.

By making personal liberty the central and overriding social value, liberalism argues that personal interests – desires, choices, beliefs – can be the only sources of social legitimacy. Liberalism begins, for example in Hobbes and Locke, by questioning the legitimacy of social authority from the standpoint of the individual. It argues that social institutions can claim legitimacy only in so far as they arise from, express, represent the desires of individuals (and their families, i.e. the private realm). This is grounded in social contract and natural rights theories which argue that social institutions indeed arose from the voluntary association of individuals on the basis of their needs and interests. These associations can be dissolved when they no longer reflect or respond to the sovereign desires of individuals.

This theme can be stated rather more radically, as in Thatcher's claim, 'There is no such thing as society, only individuals and their families.' This statement is meant literally within the liberal tradition: social authorities and institutions have no real existence in their own right. They can be analytically reduced (and must be politically and economically reduced) to the actions and wills of the individuals who make them up. This theme has a very broad currency in social thought. In the form of 'methodological individualism' it is used to theorize society as a mosaic of individual actions; in economic thought it reduces economy to the market behaviour of a multitude of individuals pursuing their self-interests. Conversely, the pursuit of self-interest by individuals is deemed a sufficient condition for 'society' (though it does not exist) to be orderly and progressive, as with Smith's 'hidden hand' of the market.

Thus liberalism places individual choice at the centre of social theory: social institutions must derive from or respond to the way in which individuals formulate their private, self-defined interests as social demands, as choices of these goods, those policies, these laws; choices that are made by individuals purely as part and parcel of their pursuit of their own agenda. This is the only secure foundation for liberty.

Markets

On this basis we can go back to the notion of 'consumer sovereignty': it exemplifies the concern of the liberal tradition to ground social processes in the privately formed desires of individuals, to ensure that that privacy is safeguarded and to make of it a resource for contesting or disciplining the power of social institutions. The liberal tradition develops these themes philosophically, politically and juridically, but it is the market and the rational economic behaviour of individuals which constitutes it that is at the heart of things. Over quite a long period, the holy trinity of reason, freedom and social progress comes to be seen as manifesting itself pre-eminently in the *economic* pursuit of self-interest by economic man. We will characterize this firstly in its most clear form, neo-classical economics, which develops from the 1870s to become over the course of the twentieth century not merely the mainstream of economic thought but the general model of social order through which the consumer is defined.

The neo-classical market is a mechanism for translating individual preferences, privately formulated, into a socially coordinated allocation of resources among different spheres of production and between individuals with different kinds and degrees of desire. Its crucial aspect is that all events in the market-place, all outcomes (different prices, levels of production, kinds of goods etc.) can be explained as the result of individuals pursuing their privately defined interests. Just as 'there is no such thing as society' for good liberals, the market itself is not a social authority, nor is it even, properly speaking, a 'social institution' (which would imply that it has aims, organization, management, roles allocated by a plan or organization chart). Rather, the market is seen as an impersonal mechanism or means of coordination which allows social order to emerge from the anarchy of diverse individual desires (see Thompson et al. 1991). Smith's 'hidden hand' produces order as well as welfare as the unintended outcome of intentional individual acts. Moreover, as he and the tradition constantly stress, the attempt to *will* particular outcomes is self-defeating: no authority can either know or control the infinitely complex simultaneous equation of individual self-interests.

Rather, social coordination through the market is achieved when all individuals, with their disparate desires, rationally orient themselves to the common denominator of *price*. This notion involves a very complex idea of what 'social action' means, and how it relates to 'private interests'. Essentially, desire is a private matter in that consumers appear in the market already knowing what they want: their desires are formed outside the market and before they engage in economic (public) action. The nature of their specific desires (whether they are shopping for apples, oranges or F-111 Stealth bombers) is irrelevant to both the economist and to the consumer. This is because *in the market* consumers do not relate to producers, other consumers or products in terms of their particular needs, but only through the calculation of price. As a consumer, I enter the market already knowing what things I want, how much I want them and how much money I have at my disposal to purchase them. With this knowledge, I arrive on the market and find that apples, oranges and Stealth bombers are available at particular prices. If the price of oranges, for example, is too high (as determined through the rational calculations described by marginal utility theory), I will buy fewer oranges. If others feel the same, producers cannot sell all their oranges at the current price and, given competitive conditions, will reduce their price to a level at which the sum of consumer decisions about the worth of oranges to them individually (as opposed to the other things they want) will result in all oranges being bought. Conversely, if the price is low in relation to people's demand for oranges, more will be demanded and producers can raise their prices and still sell them all. The same logic applies to the supply side: producers will seek efficiency gains (through organization, technology, lower wages) allowing them to produce more goods at lower prices.

Price is not, for liberal economic thought, a reflection of the 'value' of goods: this is regarded as a metaphysical concept. Price is simply a social compromise between the agendas of wants followed by each private individual. It is an aggregation or averaging of individual decisions rather than a social entity in its own right. Price is also the common denominator in relation to which individuals (producers and consumers) can orient themselves. One could identify two orienting functions for price. Firstly, it is a common denominator or unit of calculation by which economic actors can compare a potentially infinite range of possible courses of action. All questions can be reduced to the rationally calculable question, 'How much will it cost?' We will look at this below in terms of utility. Secondly, price provides an information system: providing it is able to fluctuate freely (through competition), and providing that all economic actors have a complete knowledge of prices in order to orient their actions rationally to it, price automatically aggregates the multitude of individual decisions about utility and communicates this information to producers, who in turn not only can but must respond, lowering price when demand falls, raising it to take advantage of rising perceptions of the product's relative utility.

Price is therefore considered an efficient mechanism for allocating social resources in terms of the only standard liberalism recognizes: the preferences of individuals. These preferences discipline the behaviour of firms automatically: they need not desire to satisfy individuals' needs but must march in close step with the marginal utility calculations of those individuals in order to stay in business.

Reason and choice

The consumer is the hero of the ideal liberal relation between individual and society: consumers are private individuals rationally pursuing their self-defined interests through a mechanism (the market) that socially coordinates individuals' actions without compromising the autonomy of their choices.

However this idealized view of how things could be depends on some fairly peculiar assumptions about how individuals relate to their needs and desires. These are assumptions about what it means to pursue self-interest *rationally*, and they are clearly embodied in the dreaded figure of *homo oeconomicus*. As we noted above, in neo-classical economics consumers already privately know what they want before they arrive on the relevant social scene – the market. Neo-classical thought is concerned solely with what happens next: with theorizing *how* they pursue what they want, not *what* it is that they want. We are dealing here with *formal rationality*, because we are dealing with the logic and procedures through which individuals calculate the best means to maximize the satisfaction of desires that are themselves assumed (they are already determined, defined and known by the individual). Orientation to price is a formally rational process: given limited means (money) and unlimited desires for goods, what pattern of spending will maximize my satisfaction? The reasons I might give for a particular choice of goods do not refer to the particular nature of these satisfactions but only to the logical structure of my calculations.

This approach has been defined as a 'praxeology': a formal model of the structure of rational action rather than an account of 'consumer behaviour' in any social or cultural sense. When we think about consumers in everyday life, we tend to think about *what* people want, about their particular needs and desires, about particular objects, activities and experiences that might satisfy them: 'I want *this*.' We think about consumers *substantively*, as having concrete, actual, specific wants. We might even make statements about the good or bad reasons an individual could have for wanting something. We constantly assess statements like, 'He needs that in order to . . .', 'She bought that on a whim', 'I like the new styles but they are impractical'. This kind of thinking can be described as *substantive rationality*: we relate particular desires and acts to particular values and reasons. Substantive rationality is very much cultural thinking: in the case of consumer culture we think about needs and goods in terms of their meanings within a specific way of life, values and social relations.

The most crucial point about liberalism and neo-classical economic theory is that this kind of thinking is ruled out of bounds in a wide variety of ways (for related critiques of the consumer in conventional economics, see Campbell 1989; Clarke 1982; Douglas and Isherwood 1979; Etzioni 1988; Fine and Leopold 1993; Godelier 1972, 1986; Hodgson and Screpanti 1991; Lane 1991; Plant 1989; Robinson 1983). One could say that although liberalism and economics place individual choice at the centre of their moral and social world, it is something they can say very little about: we do not get to see individuals coming to formulate their desires and interests, only the way in which they calculatedly pursue them. The decisive issue for this approach is how consumers move from substantive desires (for that dress, this holiday) to formally rational action. In liberalism and neo-classical economics, the move is one of abstraction: individuals abstract from the diverse particular qualities of needs and objects one single quality, a common denominator, which all are said to possess – *utility*. Utility is defined simply as the capacity of an object' to satisfy a desire. The nature of the desire is irrelevant: utility simply represents the abstract, empty desire-satisfying attribute of a good. I go to market knowing I want particular things, such as books and cinema tickets. At current prices, the £10 at my disposal will buy one book or two tickets. At this point, a culturally inclined observer might examine the ins and outs of my tastes for different types of culture, for sociable as opposed to private activities, my dedication to study, or whatever. The conventional economist, on the other hand, will look at how I might rationally compare these two expenditures and make a choice on the basis of the amount of utility (the total sum of satisfaction) that each outlay of cash might secure for me.

Utility, in a word, is what makes us able to compare apples and oranges. Bentham, who originated this line of thought with utilitarianism, defined utility as 'that property in any object whereby it tends to produce benefit, advantage, pleasure, good, or happiness, or reduce pain' (Ryan 1987: 66). What might constitute a utility is purely a matter of an individual's definition of '. . . benefit, advantage . . .' at any given time. Goods, according to this way of thinking, do not have utility in themselves, but only in the eyes of a beholder. However, if utility is entirely a matter of private individual judgement, it makes it difficult for an observer (such as an economist) to identify a utility in the real world (let alone 'utility' as such), as it would require accessing the subjective experience of the consumer. Neo-classicism (and utilitarianism) solve this 'by definition': we (as social observers or economists) know that a good 'has utility' if someone is willing to buy it; we know this because we have already assumed, by definition, that if someone wants to buy a good it can only be because that good 'has utility' for them. This is often described as 'expressed' or 'revealed preferences': the act of buying indicates, by definition, a preference. This is not – as many have pointed out – a theory of need or consumer culture by any stretch of the imagination: it is a tautology which says nothing about particular needs but simply infers their presence or absence from the act of buying. To say that someone bought something because it represented a utility to them adds nothing to our knowledge of why they bought it, what their motives or needs were. Utility, to reiterate, is the core of a formal concern with how we calculate in pursuing our interests rather than a substantive concern with what those interests are or how they came to be.

Utility is a highly formal and abstract concept because it replaces the multiplicity of human desires with a single desire, the desire for utility; it replaces the variety of social motives with the single, and individual, self-interested motive of 'maximizing utility'. In a sense, it replaces 'society' and 'culture' (the substantive character of human wants in particular ways of life) with 'reason', with abstract calculation and with quantification. It is important to add that the same formal logic is applied to 'supply' as to 'demand', to goods themselves as to needs and preferences. As explored, for example, by Lancaster (1966, 1971) and Ironmonger (1972), neo-classical economics treats the goods which consumers find on the market as 'given' and unchanging. This is a particularly unrealistic assumption in a consumer-oriented economy in which the nature of markets – their boundaries, content, structure – are being constantly redefined, fragmented and segmented by introducing new goods or redefining ('repositioning') older ones. Indeed, one can define the entire function of advertising and marketing as the redefinition of market structures and relations (above all, competitive relations) through the substantive, cultural redefinition of goods (Slater 1985, 1987, 1989).

Finally, all these assumptions are stated in the form of claims about how real individuals do, can or should act. Certainly Bentham took it to be an unshakeable, foundational truth that all individuals were motivated not by particular needs but by a general desire to increase pleasure and minimize pain and that therefore all individual actions and social policies should be analysed and judged rational and proper, in terms of their consequences for producing a total sum of pleasure or pain, utility or 'disutility'. All action and judgement derive from calculating quantities of this one substance, utility. Bentham propounds what he terms, unfelicitously, the 'felicific calculus', or 'hedonics' (Lane 1991), a schema of factors which enter into the individual's and the theorist's (or legislator's) assessment of possible courses of action with regard to utility. For example, chapter IV of *An Introduction to the Principles of Morals and Legislation* is devoted to schematizing the factors that must enter into understanding or estimating the 'value' of pleasures and pains: their intensity, duration, certainty or uncertainty, propinquity or remoteness, fecundity, purity and extent. Chapter V itemizes the kinds of pleasures and pains (simple or complex) which are to be assessed by these criteria (Ryan 1987: 86–97). It is uncertain whether Bentham seriously intended people to put actual numbers to these factors, but the principle he follows is essentially quantitative: reduce a diversity of things to a common denominator so that they can be quantitatively compared. What is certain is that when, as Lane puts it, 'hedonics' finally merged with economics in the neo-classical theory of the later nineteenth century, the very idea of prices as a mechanism of social coordination depended upon the capacity of individuals to reduce their desires to the single currency of utility so as to be able to compare and make choices between courses of action. In this formal capacity lay their rationality.

Economic amoralism

The split between formal and substantive rationality, then, produces a rather strange silence about consumer *culture* as opposed to rational calculation. This is not an accidental oversight on the part of the liberal tradition but entirely in keeping with its fundamental concern: personal liberty in the sense of the privacy and self-determination of the individual. By restricting itself to analysing formal, calculating rationality, liberal economics refrains from making any judgements about the substantive needs and desires of individuals. For if liberal thought were to accord to itself the right to speak about 'what people want' as opposed to 'how they calculate', it would constitute itself as a social authority over individual needs. It would therefore offend, firstly, against its own most cherished principle (the privacy of individual interests) and, secondly, against its own aim and function (to state the social conditions under which that privacy can be safeguarded while at the same time those interests can be successfully pursued). Liberalism, as we have just seen, *cannot* say much about actual consumption; but it also *will* not.

We could describe liberal economics as 'economic amoralism'. It does not matter whether individuals are expressing a preference for heroin, nail varnish or opera tickets, for more hospitals or more nuclear warheads: the analysis will have the same logical structure. The form that should be taken by the material wealth of modern society is dictated not by overriding social goals and judgements as to what makes for a good life (for example, more hospitals, less heroin) but by the privately formed preferences of individuals, which cannot and should not themselves be judged. The consumer must be sovereign because the individual is sovereign. The beauty of the market is that it refrains from moral judgement: every thing has its price if individuals express a demand for it.

Rigorous liberalism makes individuals the sole authorities over their desires and their ability to pay the sole mechanism determining whether those desires should be satisfied. It is this economic amoralism that gives contemporary neo-liberalism such a populist, anti-elitist character (similar to postmodernism). To say that market forces should decide everything is to say that desires cannot be judged morally, only pragmatically (can they be met at a profit?). However, this theoretical commitment to liberty and non-interference has never stopped liberal regimes from making substantial and moralistic interventions; it just makes them self-contradictory. To take one example: in the run-up to the British Broadcasting Act in 1988, Margaret Thatcher held two seminars at Downing Street. In the morning, she met with neo-liberals and came out advocating complete deregulation of public service broadcasting, seeing the ideal as viewers (consumers) paying for each programme individually in order to maximize producers' response to consumer choice. In the afternoon, she met with neo-conservatives, including Mary Whitehouse, and emerged with a call for regulation (i.e. censorship) of sex and violence on TV in order to defend traditional family values: i.e. a substantive agenda of what is deemed good for people to view. The ability of figures like Thatcher and Reagan to bind together neo-liberals concerned with formal freedoms and neo-conservatives defending traditionalist substantive values was based more on political skill than on intellectual consistency (as their successors learned to their cost).

This tension between the amoralism of a system based on individual preferences and the presumed need for collective cultural values or cultural authority as a basis for social order has been central to critiques of consumer culture, as we shall see in the next two chapters. For the moment we might cite Marx's sardonic comments on the game that liberal-utilitarianism and conservatism often play:

> You [political economists] must make everything which is yours *venal*, i.e. useful. I might ask the political economist: am I obeying economic laws if I make money by prostituting my body to the lust of another . . . ? His answer will be: your acts do not contravene my laws, but you should find out what Cousin Morality and Cousin Religion have to say about it; the morality and religion of my *political economy* have no objection to make, but . . . (Marx 1975: 362).

Economic amoralism is logically tied to a founding premise of modern thought, the separation of facts from values. In the optimism of early Enlightenment thought it was assumed that once the clouds of social superstition and authority (i.e. the irrationality of traditional society) had been chased from men's minds, they would come to know, through reason and observation, who they really were and what they really needed. Moreover, individual reason would reveal a universal and natural humanity. Reason would uncover both true facts and true values (Gellner 1992). David Hume's 'scepticism' and the positivist premises which descend from it epitomize the dashing of such hopes and do so in a way that is directly applied to consumer culture. For Hume, following in the Lockean tradition, reason arises solely from sensation and is therefore limited to observation of that which exists; it is therefore incapable of moving from 'is' to 'ought', of moving from what it knows to be the case to stating what should be, of deriving values from factual knowledge (crudely, unlike the physical properties and movements of an object, its 'value' or 'rightness' cannot be observed). Reason therefore cannot prescribe the ultimate ends or meaning of life. It cannot legitimately give particular values or goals scientific, moral or political authority over the preferences individuals define for themselves and choose to pursue. Science, for example, can produce knowledge of how to regulate our bodies (diets, exercise, good environment) in the interest of the pursuit of beauty, health, preservation of youth or whatever. However, by Hume's rules – which liberalism has generally followed – these goals and their order of importance cannot be decided by reason. If individuals devote most of their energies to looking young, fit and attractive it is simply their choice and therefore ultimately irrational (neither proved nor disproved by reason), however rationally they pursue it.

The real centre of Hume's world, like the consumer's, is the mundane pleasures and appetites. Hume came, as Ignatieff puts it, to 'trust in the certainties of secular passion' (1984: 88): that which reason could not prove was 'artlessly and effortlessly delivered by the everyday happiness of life' (89) – the enjoyment of eating, conviviality, beauty and so on. In a word, the reality of the individual is constituted by his desires and his will or, in the contemporary eighteenth century term, by his *passions*. Hume declares that 'reason is the slave of passion' because reason, unable plausibly to define the substantive ends of life, should properly serve those defined by the passions and the 'certainties of pleasure' (91). Thus, Hume recognizes that the desires of the individual are not to be regulated by others not merely because they *should not* be (in the name of liberty, privacy, natural justice) but more because they *cannot* be: reason has no legitimate purchase here. Reason, mirroring the general course of modernity, can dethrone the absolutism of traditional values but by the same token cannot provide socially authoritative values to replace them (see also Xenos 1989).

The separation of facts from values is inscribed in the very ideas of utility and preferences and therefore in the basic image of the consumer. Utility is specifically *not* defined in terms of need but in terms of pleasure or satisfaction. In most of its common-sense definitions need implies an objective standard defined in terms of goods that are in some sense essential: what we need to do or to have in order to survive, be moral agents, achieve desired social ends etc. Hence we often talk about basic needs, real needs and authentic needs (see chapters 4 and 5). Needs are often distinguished from wants, desires, whims. The latter are seen firstly as non-essential (one can live or be a proper social member without a BMW, a cappuccino-maker, a four-slice rather than a two-slice toaster), and secondly as subjective: they are arrived at through the imagination, status competition or cultural sophistication of individuals. The ability to distinguish between needs and wants, however, presumes the ability to make certain empirical and moral distinctions. Firstly, one requires a knowledge of the 'real needs' of humans in comparison to which 'mere desires' can be deemed inessential (however urgently felt by the person); secondly, one needs a moral conception of how humans *should* be or what they *should* do, in relation to which certain desires can be judged wrong or inessential. Indeed, the two generally go together: notions of what humans naturally are are derived from moral-political conceptions of what they should be, and vice versa.

The idea of 'preferences for utilities' evades all these issues. The concept allows no distinctions between good and bad, essential and inessential, needs and wants. There is simply an agenda, private to the individual, of satisfactions to be pursued. There is no moral or cognitive authority by which those preferences can be judged. Consumers are first of all 'sovereign' over their own desires, and then, through market forces, over the institutions whose profits depend on satisfying those desires with commodities.

Thus, 'economic amoralism' as a way of thinking the consumer has, firstly, an ethical basis (personal liberty) and, secondly, a cognitive one (the limits of reason when it comes to values). However, there is also a third, *technical*, basis for economic amoralism. Substantive needs, 'passions', values, culture – all the stuff of life – come from outside the market. In economic jargon, needs are 'exogenous' with respect to markets. They and the substantive social world in which they are formed are treated as a background, a context or an environment against which formal economic reason operates. Needs only appear within the economic sphere in the form of 'facts': so many people will buy this commodity at that price. The empirical knowledge of consumption that liberal economics produces takes the form of market research rather than cultural analysis: market research presents statistical information, the counting up of facts about who wants what.

Again, this limitation arises from principle, not oversight. Liberal economics tries to argue that markets can be efficient allocators of resources, that they produce 'welfare', that they will do so under certain conditions (perfect competition). But how are efficiency and welfare to be judged? Neo-classical economics does not have a theory of value (such as the labour theory of value in political economy and Marxism) that can argue, for example, that market prices are reasonable or not depending on whether they reflect some objective standard of worth. Rather, as we have noted, prices are related solely to the social averaging of individual preferences, of the subjective evaluations of the consumers. The problem here is that preferences cannot constitute a standard for judging efficiency or welfare (a kind of theory of value) unless they are independent of the thing they are judging. As Galbraith famously put it:

> If the individual's wants are to be urgent, they must be original with himself. They cannot be urgent if they are contrived for him. Above all they must not be

contrived by the process of production by which they are satisfied. . . . One cannot define production as satisfying wants if that production creates the wants . . . (1969: 146–7).

Mainstream economics therefore *assumes* that needs are exogenous, that they are an independent variable, one that should be explained (if any explanation is deemed necessary) by anything other than economic relations: otherwise neither particular market situations (prices) nor the market as such could be technically assessed as to efficiency or welfare. The market had better be amoral – non-interfering and indifferent to what people want – if it is to have any meaning.

In fact, Galbraith argues that contemporary capitalism constantly attempts to create or determine needs (and thereby control prices) through technologies of planning, including advertising.and marketing. Capitalism, he argues, is now characterized by a 'revised sequence' in which firms are sovereign over consumers rather than vice versa precisely because they can determine what people want. For Galbraith, this is tantamount to arguing that markets no longer exist in advanced capitalism. Advertising and marketing, for example, by intervening substantively and culturally through images, styles, psychology and so on, result in a kind of artificial urgency of desire: consumers will want a particular good at any price. Thus, if needs are not exogenous then markets cannot even be said to exist; and prices cannot, by definition, represent optimal allocations of resources. The very idea becomes meaningless. In fact, because advertising is seen as an attempt to alter the substantive needs of consumers, many commentators treat it not so much as a form of economic behaviour at all, but as a kind of unwarranted intrusion of psychological or semiotic technologies into the economic sphere. A classic example of this is Vance Packard's *The Hidden Persuaders* (1977).

Thus, morally, cognitively and technically, neo-classical economics fortifies the privacy of the liberal individual against all judgements and dictats. The consumer is sovereign by right, by default of reason and by technical definition. Yet the price paid for the perfection of formal reason is an inability to say very much, morally, cognitively *or* technically, about consumption.

Economics and its 'others'

The importance of liberal-utilitarian thought is not limited to its having provided one (albeit hugely prestigious) theory of consumer behaviour. It has also been party to developing a whole structure and division of labour in thinking about consumer culture, above all an epistemological division of labour between various social science disciplines. Economics is defined as the study of formal rationality, of the consumer as decision-maker, and, as we have seen, cannot and will not say very much about what the consumer is deciding about. Specific needs and objects constitute a background or environment within which rational action takes place, as implied by the concept of exogeny. So who is to paint in this background? Or, in other words, where do needs come from and who is to study them?

Many answers have been provided; all start from the split between formal and substantive rationality. Firstly, needs can simply be taken for granted in various ways, usually by behaving as if they were self-evident (everyone knows what they need). Analysts simply draw on their background knowledge of their own culture. Or needs can be treated simply as inexplicable *facts*: things that you count through market research rather than explain through social theory. Secondly, needs can be assumed in more rigorous ways. For example, needs can be seen as 'natural', as intrinsic to the nature of human bodies or minds. They can then be provided to economic thought by various other disciplines: by biological and physical sciences, which would, for example, relate needs for food, clothing and shelter to the bodily requirements of physical reproduction and health by anthropology as a study of universal needs that transcend cultural diversity, by a psychology that grounds need in individual emotional or cognitive structures or, from the Enlightenment onwards, by 'philosophical anthropologies' which attempt to provide rational accounts of the essential character of the human. These approaches are generally characterized as 'essentialist'. Thirdly, needs can be treated as socially constructed, variable, diverse, or as mediated by specific social contexts, social influences or processes of socialization. Sociology, cultural studies, history and anthropology all provide 'theories of needs' in this sense. Finally, there have been various brands of consumer behaviour theory which attempt to throw all of this together; the general aim is to construct models depicting how all this 'environment' and 'social influence' affect the rational decision-making process.

Thus, the split between formal and substantive rationality has in important ways produced the intellectual structure through which consumer culture has been studied: a division between the study of formally rational behaviour (economics) and the study of its irrational, cultural content (the rest). Of the many problems with this division of labour not least is the disappearance of consumer culture itself. It is actually very difficult to find disciplines in which one can study, within one framework, both the economic and cultural forces which structure consumption, and yet it is precisely the *relation* between economy and culture that defines consumer culture.

Rationality and embeddedness

Another way of defining formal rationality is through the concept of 'disembeddedness': economic action is separated from cultural and social relations and is carried out in a separate sphere, the economic. We may ask, firstly, whether this is an adequate description of modern market societies and, secondly, whether such a modern notion of 'the economic' can validly be applied to other societies.

Mainstream economics is the most peculiar social discipline in that it is the only one that defines itself not by a subject matter ('society', 'non-modern cultures', the 'human mind', 'social policy') but by a particular characterization of that subject matter. For example, economics is 'the science which studies human behavior as a relationship between ends and scarce means which have alternative uses' (Robbins, quoted in Nelson 1993: 25). This is commonly interpreted to mean that economics studies the logic of rational choice and consequently presumes that its object domain consists of formal means–ends rationality. This is quite a presumption, tantamount to defining a discipline in terms of a particular theory. Moreover, it sets up a normative standard of behaviour: it looks, in all societies and in all sectors of its own society, for that form of behaviour, formal rationality, which supposedly defines western modernity.

The most authoritative alternative definition of economics is that of Karl Polanyi (1957a, 1957b) for whom it is the study of 'how human societies provision themselves'. This definition makes no assumptions about the existence of a domain of specifically economic institutions, forms of behaviour or rationality. Quite the reverse: Polanyi argues that human provisioning is normally embedded in a wider range of social institutions. Functions that modern citizens and economists might classify as 'economic' (e.g. the distribution of income, the allocation of consumption goods, the regulation of the division of labour and so on) have in previous times been performed by social relations, structures and institutions which we, as moderns, classify as non-economic. For example, in clan societies, familial relationships (kinship ties, patriarchal authority etc.) rather than impersonal market mechanisms may regulate who consumes what, when and by how much. The 'economy' is thus *embedded* in other social relations, and may be governed not by formal rationality but by such things as social reciprocity or politically mediated redistribution. The nineteenth-century heyday of free market capitalism, the 'Great Transformation', represents for Polanyi a very brief moment of extreme disembeddedness (and even this must be qualified by the fostering and regulation of emergent markets by the state) in which human provisioning was detached from other social relations and regulated by formally rational calculation. In most social systems, however, substantive social relations do not represent (as they do for neo-classicism) merely an external or exogenous environment. They are rather internal to, the very stuff of, 'economy'.

If economists and others are to go looking for disembedded formal rationality in non-modern (and much of modern) societies, they will find them to be *ir*rational, because provisioning there proceeds through substantive relations and reasons (the debate sparked by Polanyi was actually called, in anthropology at least, the debate between the formalists and substantialists). In the next section, we will see the consequences of this for women, whose consumer choices are considered substantive and embedded rather than formal and disembedded.

There are problems with Polanyi's approach too. Of most consequence is a tendency to assume that non-modern societies do not involve formally rational calculation. This ignores the widespread existence of markets and monetarization (even when they are marginal or 'enclaved'), but it also ignores the broader issue of the part played by rational calculation even in highly embedded relations. For example, Bourdieu (1989: 3–10) offers a riveting account of gift exchange, related in interesting ways to Mauss's (1990) seminal discussion. Gifts are generally seen as the very opposite of commodities in that they have meaning and value purely through the social relationship in which they are embedded (Polanyi, for example, describes this in terms of reciprocity, Baudrillard in terms of 'symbolic exchange'). Yet in order to constitute an act as gift-giving as opposed to, say, payment, much rational calculation is required. If I reciprocate immediately, I might be taken to be paying rather than giving a gift; if I reciprocate with too big a gift I might offend. Thus I have to make calculations about value and equivalence.

The safest conclusion is probably that there is more formal rationality in non-market economies than Polanyi will allow and more substantive rationality in market economics than liberalism will allow (Granovetter 1985). In terms of the consumer (who ironically has received very little attention from the new economic sociology which has sprung up from these arguments), the conclusion would have to be that both formal and substantive rationality, in close relation, are always involved, and that an approach which places them in different realms and disciplines is not going to be very useful. A very clear example of this is the practice of shopping (Slater 1993). 'Going shopping' means going to a 'market-place' (a mall, a supermarket, a shopping precinct and so on): a social place and time involving many kinds of social activities and social relations. As we have seen, mainstream economics looks at the market rather than at market-places, and the market is a highly abstract set of forces (supply and demand curves brought into relation by price through individual rational calculations) which can be mathematically modelled as an enclosed system, and which comprises only one 'motivation', the abstract one of 'maximizing utility' in the form of either profit or satisfaction. On the other hand, the market-place where we go shopping is a socially organized event filled with an astonishing range of activities and relations. Both traditional and modern market-places, for example, involve the spectacular display of goods, all kinds of entertainments and amenities (restaurants, performers, theatricals, cinema, toilets, protection from the weather), spontaneous social attractions that arise from the congregation of crowds of people, security and regulation and so on.

It can also be argued that market-places and shops serve a range of functions: not just the circulation of commodities, but being a focus for social gathering and collective identities, where people meet and hang out, a focus for civic political and cultural symbolism and identity, a focus for tourism, a place to steal or to sell, to busk or to beg, to make speeches or to hold marches, and so on. Markets, in this sense, are not purely economic but complex social events and institutions. The same goes for what consumers do in markets. They day-dream and window-shop, they meet friends, they see a film or eat a meal, they go with their family, on their own, with friends (in each case constituting a quite different kind of occasion), they shop for groceries or for a wedding dress or for a gift (each of which involves not only different 'external' motives but different kinds of market action), they may consider shopping a major leisure activity or a horrible chore. They may also engage in rational price calculations. (There is now a vast literature on shopping, much of which connects with these issues, though usually by way of postmodernism: Adburgham 1981; Agnew 1986; Benson 1986; Bowlby 1987; Bronner 1989; Chaney 1983, 1991, 1993; Fiske 1989; Gardner and Sheppard 1989; Jameson 1984; Lunt and Livingstone 1992; Miller 1981; Mui and Mui 1989; Reekie 1993; Richards 1991; Shields 1990, 1992; Slater 1993; Walkowitz 1992; Williams 1982; Wilson 1991; Wolff 1985.)

Enlightenment man and the female consumer

I started this chapter by asking whether the consumer was a hero or a dupe. The answer, for the liberal-utilitarian tradition, was that the consumer was a hero to the extent that he (*sic*) was autonomous and self-determined, and that this autonomy depended on his rational capacities, on his ability firstly to know and define his own needs (to be sovereign over them) and secondly to pursue them rationally (for his needs to be sovereign over social resources, largely through the market). This consumer's needs could be as lunatic or perverse as desire might make them so long as they were calculated by a rational ego.

Yet we also have an image prevalent in both everyday life and social theory of the consumer as a dupe or dope. This consumer – the mass, conformist consumer – is defined precisely by its failure to live up to this standard of 'maturity', of reason and autonomy. Firstly, the consumer as dupe is a slave to desires rather than a rational calculator of them, is defined not by its formal rationality but by its substantive desires, whims, impulses. Its desires are not autonomous but determined by others, by the needs of family, by social pressure, by fashion and trends, by advertising, marketing and the media. Indeed, the everyday consumer is not seen as the rational calculator of self-defined desires but rather as the *object* of rational calculation by other forces, the target of a marketing drive or advertising campaign. Finally, as we have seen, this consumer is not even part of the subject matter of economics – the study of rational man – but rather falls into those disciplines (psychology, sociology, cultural studies) that study *substantive* needs: needs when they are regarded as both irrational and *caused* or determined, as things to be explained not by autonomous self-creation but by the nature of the body or the pressures of society.

But is this other consumer the product of a failure to live up to enlightenment ideals or the product of the exclusionary nature of those ideals? Enlightenment spoke a language of universal rights which covertly excluded much of the population. It all depended on who was referred to by the term 'man'. Thus Lockean liberalism restricted the social contract to property-owning adult white males, an exclusion only gradually surrendered over several centuries' fight for a universal franchise. Women's access to public life and private autonomy was similarly restricted through their legal rights to ownership. In this sense, Enlightenment merely legitimated older patriarchal forms of control over women and subordinate males through claims about the capacity of (certain) men to be rational, autonomous, cultured and social, as opposed to the identification of women and subordinate men with nature, unreason, childishness and other-determination. This legitimation, which excludes significant groups from adult public activity, then uses their exclusion as further evidence that they *ought* to be excluded (see, for example, Bauman 1993; Bordo 1987; Gilroy 1993; Sydie 1987).

For example, feminist critiques of mainstream economics argue that women are deemed irrational, and therefore not to be proper economic actors at all, on the basis of an exclusionary definition of rationality, and one based on men's experience (Ferber and Nelson 1993). Paula England argues that the rationality model is male-defined in that it assumes a self which is foreign to women's experience and devalues it: the model is of a 'separative self', one in which humans are 'autonomous, impervious to social influences, and lack sufficient emotional connection to each other to make empathy possible'

(1993: 37). This model is reflected in three central assumptions about economic theory: that interpersonal utility comparisons are impossible (each individual has his or her own utility function which cannot be judged from the perspective of anyone else's); that tastes are exogenous to economic models and are unchanging (they come from the separate and private interior world of the individual ego); and that actors are selfish in market behaviour (that their utilities are independent of other people's utilities). Moreover, as we have seen, the idea that needs are exogenous assumes a complete separation between emotion and reason, between substantive needs and values on the one hand and their formal calculation on the other (50). 'Maturity' – the emergence of an ethically approved self – is defined purely in terms of individuation rather than of connection with others, a capacity for intimacy, nurturance and so on. The latter are identified with loss of liberty and autonomy, as a compromise of sovereignty.

As a whole, this model of the 'separative self' relates to men as public actors and denigrates women's work in reproduction, their social skills, their emotional life and so on. Secondly, it ignores the extent to which male autonomy in production and the public sphere depends on women's reproductive labour. Men's rational pursuit of their own utilities depends on women doing precisely what economic theory deems impossible: merging their 'utilities' with those of their families, comparing and often subordinating their utilities to those of others in the household, perceiving their own utilities as dependent on those of others (for example achieving pleasure or ethical dignity through promoting the 'utilities' of their partners and children). Changing or abandoning the liberal economic view of rationality and autonomy would obviously produce not only a different picture of consumption and consumers but also a different *judgement* of them. It would mean ethically acknowledging forms of social action which are currently devalued or taken for granted.

The sheer outrageousness of basing theories of consumers and consumer culture on notions of rationality that exclude and denigrate women's experience has to be measured against the fact that so much consumption – most consumption decisions, purchases and labour in consumption – is carried out by women. This arises from a gender division of labour which divides public and private, production and reproduction, and assigns women, ever more intensively over the course of modernity, to domestic reproduction. More specifically, as consumer culture and commodification gather pace and structures in the twentieth century, the woman's responsibility for domestic reproduction is increasingly defined, through advertising, home economics and other educational discourses, state policy and media portrayals, as a responsibility to manage consumption. As domestic reproduction increasingly comes to mean building a home by buying commodities, women are increasingly defined as 'experts in consumption'. The man brings home the pay packet that the woman spends (either in good domestic management or, in a popular image, impulsively and irrationally).

Unfortunately it is not only liberalism that leaves out of its theories of consumer culture precisely the people who are 'responsible' for consumption. In fact, in writing a book that surveys such theories, I have symptomatically found it difficult to raise these issues consistently: they get structured out of the field. For example, the 'hero' of 'culture' as a response to 'post-traditional society' (next chapter) is the generally male 'romantic self', the poet, the artist, the genius in search of authenticity. Critiques of alienation and reification (chapter 4) deify *homo faber*, man as producer, transformer and master of the object world, a world constituted by 'labour' rather than 'reproduction'. Theories of signification (chapters 5 and 6) are more promising, but tend to dissolve gender difference into semiotic difference or, in the case of cultural studies, overvalue and overemphasize expressive and rebellious forms of consumption such as subcultures that are identified with men as public actors as opposed to the mundane, private and conformist consumption which structures so many women's everyday lives. Finally (in chapter 7), post-Fordism subsumes women's reproductive work within a functionalist account of systemic reproduction (public labour takes priority again), while postmodernism, constantly claiming to speak about 'difference' and 'others', rather tends to generalize about the fate of a generic and thus ungendered 'subject'.

Moreover, given the terms set up by the liberal Enlightenment, it is unsurprising not only that women are considered irrational in being identified with substantive and domestic consumption, but that the 'consumer as dupe', the consumer split off from the Enlightenment ideal, is generally seen as 'feminine'. Mass consumption and the mass cultural audience, for example, attract gendered imagery. They are described as whimsical and inconstant, flighty, narcissistic; they can be seduced, or their resistance overcome, by stimuli or persuasion in order to achieve market penetration (Huyssen 1986: chapter 3; cf Thornton 1995: 104). Hebdige (1988c) similarly recounts that the post-war consumer boom, particularly when seen as a process of Americanization, was described as a 'feminization' of British culture. Hoggart, for example, sees consumer culture as a feminization of the virile authentic working class. A clearly related imagery is provided in Bourdieu's account of taste hierarchies, the experience of carnival as opposed to symphony hall. Bourgeois cultural consumption is defined in terms of a Kantian aesthetic in which the audience calmly and knowledgeably *contemplates* the art-work; popular consumption is characterized by emotional and bodily immersion in an event.

These images point up another way in which the consumer is 'other' to enlightenment man. It is not just that the consumer is neither rational nor autonomous: the consumer is also an object of calculation, a means to the ends pursued by rational economic men. When viewed from the boardroom or advertising agency, they can be seen as manipulable, child-like in the irrationality of their desires. Their needs – their substantive culture – are not seen as ends or values in themselves but as technical problems which must be dealt with. Seeing consumers as the object rather than the subject of rational calculation renders them 'other' to the one doing the calculating. Moreover, there is something like a vicious spiral involved: the more that consumers are perceived as targets for intervention by advertising, marketing, retailing, etc., the further they fall from the ideal of rationality and autonomy, the more contemptuous the characterization of them becomes, and the more they are identified with subordinate social groups. And, of course, the more they are identified with social subordination, the more they can be perceived as irrational, manipulable targets or as 'vulnerable' consumers, such as children or the elderly, who are the objects of social concern. Marchand vividly describes the 'othering' of the consumer in 1920s American advertising, in which the advertisers could view the consumer from behind the safety of desks they rarely left (described as a condition of 'deskitis') and contemptuously talk of advertising to 'Mr and Mrs Moron and the Little Morons' (Marchand 1986: 67). As one 1920s advertising agent cited by Marchand (67) sums up the view from the market: 'After all, men and women in the mass are apt to have incredibly shallow brain-pans. In infancy they are attracted by bright colors, glitter, and noise. And in adulthood they retain a surprisingly similar set of basic reactions.' Raymond Williams's classic statement (1985) that there are no masses, only ways of organizing people as masses, describes the same situation: denying the rationality of consumers and seeing them as a manipulable mass are profoundly interrelated, and both start from the position of someone who considers himself rational treating 'them' as 'other'.

To summarize, Joyce Appleby asked the important question (1993: 162): 'Why, in the floodtide of Enlightenment enthusiasms for freedom . . . was free consumption never articulated as a social goal . . . Why is it . . . that consumption, which is the linchpin of our modern social system, has never been the linchpin of our theories explaining modernity?' The answer may well be that 'free consumption' was not articulated *separately* from the broader liberal ideal of the rational pursuit of self-interest. Bentham's 'felicific' calculator is never called 'a consumer'; instead, like the 'enterprising individual' of the 1980s, producer and consumer are one man embodying the same rationality and freedom whatever interests he pursues and in whichever social sphere. Free consumption, in this view, is never a separate social goal or aspect of modernity. Indeed, when consumption and consumers are seen as separate, as 'other', they are no longer a social ideal but social subordinates. The irony is that liberalism itself can make the consumer separate and 'other' through its exclusionary, formal notion of rationality and through the use of that rationality to make people the objects rather than the subjects of self-interested action.

The strategy of freedom

The opposition between hero and dupe has probably constituted the central debate about consumer culture. Are consumers free or determined? Can they actively and creatively use social resources to construct meaningful and satisfying lives? Or are they passively constrained and determined by a system which is able to define their needs for them? Does advertising create or control needs or do consumers pursue interests they have defined for themselves? In Galbraith's terms, what or who is behind the 'urgency' of the consumer's needs?

Yet, as we have seen, both hero and dupe seem to be produced by liberalism itself. By identifying modern heroism with rationality and autonomy, some consumers can fail to measure up to the standard or to be the objects of others' 'heroic' efforts. Moreover, one of the ironies of this debate has been that most parties to it seem to share the same basic liberal assumption: that freedom and determination are opposites, and that an increase in freedom means a decrease in social regulation and power, and vice versa. The debate is then in principle, if rarely in practice, an empirical one. Are consumers *really* free and autonomous or *really* manipulated?

More recently, Foucault's later work has been used to try to break through this problematic by arguing that freedom and power are not opposites, but rather that freedom can operate as a very effective strategy *of* power, a tool of power, a creation of power. The issue then becomes not the truth or falsity of liberalism's claims that the consumer is sovereign but rather the question of how the concept of choice, or the choosing self, has been used to construct modern social order; the issue is not whether liberal institutions have 'liberated' individuals from power, but the historical role played by the liberal discourses and practices of freedom in producing modern forms of power.

What Foucault effectively provides is a reinterpretation of liberalism as a historical phenomenon or, in his word, as a form of 'governmentality'. 'Government' is a concern with the 'conduct of conduct', with 'managing and administering social and personal existence in the attempt to introduce economy, order and virtue' (Rose 1992a: 143). 'Governmentality' signifies a structure or logic for regulating conduct which is articulated through knowledge and practice. Governmentality is not located in the state alone but (much as in Althusser's ISA's or Gramscian hegemony) spreads through a vast network of institutions and practices: indeed, the devolution of power, its 'capillary' character, is crucial both to Foucault's general concept of power and his specific analysis of liberalism. Liberalism neither rules through direct or coercive control over its populations, nor – as in its self-image – refrains from rule through the restraint of state powers. Rather, liberal government relies on the self-managing capacities of individuals and therefore compels and requires them to manage themselves, to act freely, responsibly and with rational foresight. These capacities of individuals are 'a central target and resource for authorities' (Rose 1992a: 143). Similarly, the free market as an institution is not a sphere of freedom from the state but a mechanism encouraged by the state to allow it to manage 'at a distance' a complex social process it cannot directly govern (Burchill 1991: 127).

Liberalism relies on self-managing subjects but believes that their innate capacities are automatically liberated once traditional, irrational social authorities are defeated. Foucault, as a post-structuralist, believes that forms of subjectivity are produced, not liberated or repressed: liberal society must produce individuals, the famous 'enterprising self' with which this chapter started, who

> will make a venture of its life, project itself a future and seek to shape itself in order to become that which it wishes to be. The enterprising self is thus a calculating self, a self that calculates *about* itself and that works *upon* itself in order to better itself . . . good government is to be grounded in the ways in which persons govern themselves (Rose 1992a: 146).

Liberalism's fundamental interest in the individual is not really its freedom and autonomy but its capacity for self-government or self-management. 'Citizenship is to be active and individualistic rather than passive and dependent. The political subject is henceforth to be an individual whose citizenship is manifested through the free exercise of personal choice among a variety of options' (Rose 1992a: 159).

Foucault's analysis of liberal governmentality maps out the production of freedom at the political level or policy level. This level of analysis seems, at least in retrospect, to complement the institutional analyses of 'human technologies' which constituted the bulk of his published work: the books on madness, medicine, prisons and sexuality. A central theme running through this work, especially through the 'bio-politics' of the *Discipline and Punish* period, was that 'liberal' reform of these institutions purported to 'liberate' the mad and the bad by shifting attention from the punishment of the body to the care of the soul. In fact, as the image of the panopticon was employed to show, this 'liberation' did not release an authentic humanity but rather produced a self that was 'normalized', self-surveilling and colonized by relations of power at a far more profound level. As in the analysis of liberal governmentality, the modern citizen is both an object and resource for the management of population.

His very late work took up the same themes at yet another level, that of the self. Power operates not only through policy and discourse/practice at the institutional level, but also through 'ethical techniques of the self' (Foucault 1988: 146) 'which permit individuals to effect by their own means . . . a certain number of operations on their own bodies and souls, thoughts, conduct, and way of being, so as to transform themselves in order to attain a certain state of happiness, purity, wisdom, perfection, or immortality' (Foucault 1988: 18). For Foucault, it is 'the kind of relationship you ought to have with yourself, *rapport à soi*, which I call ethics, and which determines how the individual is supposed to constitute himself as a moral subject of his own action' (Hacking 1986: 235). At all these levels of analysis, liberal society is geared to the inculcation of a self-managing and choosing self. The modern self is 'institutionally required to construct a life through the exercise of choice from among alternatives', and to be the kind of person who is capable of doing so, to conform to the 'norm of the autonomous, responsible subject, obliged to make its life meaningful through acts of choice' (Rose 1992b: 153; see also du Gay 1996). In this light, the consumer is the epitome of the liberal individual, and consumerism can be seen as a pre-eminent social training ground in its ethical production. It is where we apply to ourselves, at the most intimate and detailed levels, the operations by which we understand ourselves in terms of choice. Yet for Foucault, unlike for liberalism, becoming a choosing self is not a liberation but a strategy of modern governance.

Conclusion

For the liberal tradition, as we have seen, the individual secures freedom at the expense of social authority. The consumer is connected to this kind of freedom by the exercise of choice on the basis of reason, a form of reason (formal rationality) thath brooks no social authority and judgement but which rather disciplines society through its economic action in the market. For liberalism, this represents and secures a state of individual freedom – the sovereign consumer and enterprising self with which we began the chapter. For the critics of modernity and consumer culture whom we will explore in the next two chapters, it is precisely through this rationality, and particularly its economic form, that modernity has caused cultural devastation and social alienation, has made the very idea of community and true society a nostalgic memory or utopian dream. And it is in this light that consumer culture comes to be seen not as individual liberation but as anomie, not as social progress but rather as pathology.

3
Consumption versus Culture

Introduction: post-traditional society

For the liberal wing of modernity, enlightened men and heroic consumers emerge from the dismantling of traditional society. On the other hand, for the critic of modernity – whether reactionary or radical, and generally a confused amalgam of both – this process of social deregulation produces anarchy, alienation and the debasement of all values. Modern commerce, democracy and enlightenment dissolve the social bonds and values that previously held society together and gave the individual a place within it. In their place, the forces of liberal modernization leave mere material self-interest and economic calculation, neither of which is able to provide new values which could secure either social stability or individual identity.

'Culture' was one of the crucial terms through which anti-liberal forces counted the cost of modernity. '*Consumer* culture', in this perspective, is merely an ersatz, artificial, mass-manufactured and pretty poor substitute for the world we have lost in post-traditional society. In fact, it is the antithesis and enemy of culture. In it individual choice and desire triumph over abiding social values and obligations; the whims of the present take precedence over the truth embodied in history, tradition and continuity; needs, values and goods are manufactured and calculated in relation to profit rather than arising organically from authentic individual or communal life. Above all, consumerism represents the triumph of economic value over all other kinds and sources of social worth. Everything can be bought and sold. Everything has its price.

'Consumer culture', therefore, is a contradiction in terms for much of modern western thought. The phrase comes to us dripping with irony, for the very term 'culture' was designed to signify all that has been destroyed by the world which produced the consumer. The aim of this chapter, then, is to explore 'consumer culture' as an oxymoron: two incompatible terms locked together by modernity. We need first to explore the opposition between the ideal of culture and the utilitarian, post-traditional, commercial world. At the heart of this opposition are arguments about the nature of need: whereas liberalism linked the deregulation of desire to individual freedom and economic growth, proponents of culture as an ideal argued that material prosperity without a binding framework of social values produces unrelenting dissatisfaction (or false satisfactions), as well as a tyranny of 'false' society (in the form of fashion, envy, conformism, mass culture) over depthless and disoriented 'free' individuals. Finally, the sense that consumer culture is part of a crisis of social deregulation emerges most clearly as a crisis over identity: in the deregulated pluralism of modernity, identity is neither ascribed nor fixed by a stable social order but must be chosen or constructed by individuals. Consumer culture exemplifies this situation of choice and simultaneously exploits and intensifies the cultural deficits of modernity.

Culture, ideal and debased

Culture as a social ideal

Culture can be thought of as either ordinary or ideal: it can be, on the one hand, a way of describing the meaningful character of the life of a collectivity or, on the other hand, a more rarefied sphere of valued cultural objects (art and literature, thought and philosophy), as well as of the values embodied both in those objects and in the elites that produce or appreciate them (aristocracies of blood and status, of the mind, of the spirit). The continuing power of Raymond Williams's *Culture and Society* (1985) comes from showing how these two notions of culture are profoundly and historically bound up with each other as ways of thinking about and responding to modern society. He demonstrates that even in the most rarefied aesthetic concepts of culture (high culture, art), we are dealing with a form of *social* thought.

The idea of culture as part of the 'culture and society tradition', Williams argues, is a social ideal, a model of social values and processes which constitutes a 'court of appeal', a tribunal before which everyday life in the modern world must bow for judgement. Firstly, proponents of culture in the 'higher' sense believe that the higher values they find there *should* be the values that govern everyday life, should be embodied in the material order of society: the concept of culture is a critique and evaluation of everyday life in the modern world. Secondly, there is an argument that in the pre-modern world these *were* the social values that governed everyday life, or that they will be in a post-bourgeois world: it is only in the modern world that these values are chased out of everyday life and can subsist only in rarefied social spaces, in culture as a preserved heritage. The very existence of (high) culture as a separate sphere is a standing indictment of the diremptions of modern life and of its spiritual and human bankruptcy. Finally, culture as a social ideal *must* fulfil a social function; it must provide or at least preserve those ideals of community, self-hood, 'the good' and so on by which social order may be maintained or critiqued in the name of a better order.

The concept of culture is after values that arise within the way of life of a people, which give that people solidarity and identity and which authoritatively judge what is good or bad, real or false, not only in art but in everyday life. To use the terms of the previous chapter, it is culture that should provide *substantive* values. These values, it is generally argued, were once given by the traditional social order but, in the transition to modernity, were destroyed by reason, by the money economy and by political democracy. Culture in this respect is a profoundly anti-modern concept and specifically an attack on the formal rationality of Enlightenment, liberalism and utilitarianism. As we have seen, liberal society is in principle and more importantly in practice indifferent to the substantive nature of individual desires and cultural values. Both are left to the preferences of individuals in the present, and these preferences are beyond social control or judgement: modernity releases individuals from communal surveillance by the local community and status order into the anonymity and 'licence' of the city, the free labour market, the destabilized status order. Liberal modernity deifies reason, which may govern how people pursue their interests but is unable to say anything socially or morally authoritative about what interests they *should* pursue. But if values are matters of mere individual preferences mediated solely by money, how can society hold together, and how can we distinguish between good and bad social values? Indeed, as we have seen, liberalism to a certain extent denies the very idea of society as such, of a collectivity possessing a moral authority over its members.

Liberal-utilitarianism may believe that contractual relationships, entered into voluntarily by people rationally pursuing their own interests, provide an adequate technical basis for coordinating social action. The idea of 'culture' articulates the belief that they are not a sufficient basis for social solidarity. Solidarity requires a framework of meaning and morals which stands above the individual. The absence of such a framework in modern life obsesses social thought throughout the modern period and may even be – as Turner (1987) argues – the central problem which constitutes it. Besides the terms 'culture' and 'commerce', a wide variety of contrasting terms have been used to define the same crisis: culture versus civilization, status versus contract, mechanical versus organic solidarity, community versus association, praxis versus labour, use value versus exchange value. In each case the first term marks a form of moral–cultural regulation, which is replaced by the co-ordination of individual actions through impersonal mechanisms such as the market, law and the technical division of labour. These oppositions all arise from 'a nostalgic science of society, since implicitly it is forced to identify with the past as a source of values for the critique of the present' (Turner 1987: 237). What Turner says of social thought, many authors (for example, Marcuse 1964, 1972; Bell 1979) extend to the entire project of modern art and philosophy:

> the higher culture of the West . . . was a pre-technological culture . . . derived from the experience of a world which no longer exists. . . . It was feudal not only because of its confinement to privileged minorities, not only because of its inherent romantic element . . . , but also because its authentic works expressed a conscious, methodical alienation from the entire sphere of business and industry, and from its calculable and profitable order (Marcuse 1964: 58).

The culture and society tradition arises in opposition to modern commercial society, attacking its formal rationality, materialism and egoism and the cultural banality and emptiness of its great gods 'self-interest' and 'utility'. These can generate wealth, but not value. The sources to which the concept of culture has traditionally looked for real value mark it out as deeply connected to romanticism. As we shall explore further in the next chapter, the liberal enlightenment appears to treat the entire world as comprising mere objects that are to be owned, used, calculated, amassed in the pursuit of self-interest. Romanticism and the concept of culture argue that there are things larger than the individual – community, nation, race, nature, spirit, the ideal of art – which alone can produce those values that will render the individual authentic, real. These are the true 'sources of the self' (Taylor 1989), and they can be neither produced nor sustained through self-interested reason: their proper medium is (variably) history, feeling, sensibility, emotion, the unconscious.

To take a crucial example, one of the dominant metaphors of culture as a social ideal is *organicism*. Williams (1976) notes that the word 'culture' itself derives from metaphors of organic processes (cultivating, growing, nurturing). It only becomes a reified concept and an abstract noun at the historical point at which critics believe that this process is no longer present in the everyday life of industrial civilization. At this point, culture only exists as a thing, as artefacts (art) that are preserved and nurtured (cultivated) by intellectual, moral and social elites outside and uncontaminated by everyday life.

Organicism implies wholeness, naturalness and integration. Modernity is about alienation, mechanism, analytical and social separation. If we take the traditionalist route, F. R. Leavis provides a good example in his notion of 'organic community'. Firstly, this is a pre-industrial culture, the culture of village and craft civilization, in which social and natural relations produced 'an art of life, a way of living, ordered and patterned, involving the social arts, codes of intercourse and a responsive adjustment, growing out of immemorial experience, to the natural environment and the rhythm of the year' (Leavis and Thompson 1933: 3). Organic community presumes, firstly, the natural relation of man to nature embodied in craft rather than mechanized manufacture, agriculture rather than industry. The pastoral, the opposition between country and city, is crucial to this imagery. Organicism here also implies a low level of technical division of labour. Secondly, the organic community is a social whole. It is a place of immediate, face-to-face communication within a world where everyone knows one other and their social place. It is a world of unproblematic identity because it is a world of durable social order and values. Organic community is not the liberal aggregation of individuals into a mass, but a community as an actual entity, a living thing. Thirdly, the organic community is organic because it is based in continuity over time: it is ruled by tradition, not individual choice or will. In social terms, this links the ideal of culture to romantic celebrations of nation and ethnicity, in which language and folk culture, or national character, become the bearers of the truth and authenticity of the community, transmitted down the generations from time immemorial.

Against the neo-liberal slogan that 'There is no such thing as society; only individuals and their families', we might cite Burke's romantic conservative rendition of organic community, as epitomized in the link between culture and the state:

> The state ought not to be considered nothing better than a partnership agreement in a trade of pepper and coffee, calico or tobacco, or some other such low concern, to be taken up for a little temporary interest, and to be dissolved by the fancy of the parties. It is to be looked on with other reverence; because it is not a partnership in things subservient only to the gross animal existence of a temporary and perishable nature. It is a partnership in all science, a partnership in all art; a partnership in every virtue, and in all perfection. As the ends of such a partnership cannot be obtained in many generations, it becomes a partnership not only between those who are living, but between those who are living, those who are dead, and those who are to be born (Williams 1985: 29).

It is important to recognize here that the ideal of culture is not just a stand taken by reactionary defenders of feudal obligations and *ancien régime* regulation; it can also be a defence of popular rights and popular culture against the encroachments of liberal deregulation and bourgeois power, one in which aristocracy and lower orders form an unholy alliance. E. P. Thompson (1971, 1975, 1978) has given us the fullest picture of the extent to which 'the making of the English working class' and resistance to capitalist exploitation was focused around the defence of traditional rights against economic 'freedom'. A classic example is the notion of a 'moral economy'. This involved an assertion of moral values rooted in tradition and community against economic deregulation (for example, 'just price' versus free market prices). Richard Hoggart's *Uses of Literacy* (1977 (1957)) similarly defends the traditional values of working-class communities as resources of resistance to a commodity culture ruled purely by profit.

Status, commerce and corruption

That 'organic community' whose passing prompted the idea of 'culture' was traditional society, and its loss was significantly experienced through the notion of consumer culture. The most obvious point about traditional society (though it can be unduly exaggerated) is that it was considered a fixed order: it saw itself as largely unchanging and with an obligation not to change. This is often encapsulated through the idea of the 'great chain of being' (Lovejoy 1936), that *every* thing in the universe had an ascribed place or status, ranked in a continuous line from the lowliest creature to God himself. The chain embraced the whole social order, giving all people not merely a fixed status, but also one that was theologically anchored in a cosmic order and socially anchored in 'blood and soil', birth and land. What later comes to be seen as culture – the values that legitimately regulate a community – was earlier seen as naturally or divinely ordained.

Consumption in traditional society was regulated in relation to status: both are juridically fixed in relation to each other. This takes the form of, for example, sumptuary laws, codified from the fourteenth to the sixteenth centuries, followed by the Waltham Black Acts of 1723, which seek the regulation of food (for example the king's deer), clothing (particularly guild insignia, uniforms and livery) and shelter (housing and mobility). These are all designed to preserve an agrarian society by preventing social and geographical mobility. The divine basis of both status and appropriate consumption is made explicit. 'Until the nineteenth century it was customary for sumptuary laws to be read from the pulpit in every church at least once a year – a daunting task, since ordinances regarding dress alone often ran more than one hundred duodecimo pages. Until the Reformation the legislation against luxury enacted by secular European governments was administered by ecclesiastical courts' (Sekora 1977: 61).

In this world, as Sekora argues, luxury – defined as consumption not just above one's basic needs but above one's station – is a form of sin, rebellion and insubordination against the proper order of the world, and represents moral, spiritual and political corruption, as well as a form of madness in that men become ruled by passion rather than by reason. 'Reason will approve of just so much of them [dress, furnishings, housing] as is requisite for the Distinction of Rank, and the keeping up of that Subordination, which is absolutely necessary to Government.' (John Dennis, 1724, cited in Sekora 1977: 80)

From the late seventeenth century, there is a major revival of discussion of the 'great chain of being', attempts to revive and enforce sumptuary legislation, and (as documented by Sekora) obsessive debate about the nature of 'luxury' (for an alternative account of luxury, see Berry 1994). All three are consciously conservative attempts to buttress the old order in response to the same problem: the patterning of society by cosmic order is being undermined by the power of the money economy which allows people to gain access to goods, positions and social standing purely on the basis of their ability to purchase them, rather than on their right to them based on ascribed status. This is in many respects the fundamental argument of 'culture' against modernity, that legitimacy is conferred by economic power rather than by tradition, birth or breeding. It is money that dissolves the old order.

The gross insubordination of luxurious consumption was clearly related by its opponents to the rise of a money economy, the 'cash nexus', and to new sources of wealth. In Britain, these issues come to the fore in response to the 'financial revolution' of 1688–1756 and the general rise of trade and commerce in the same period. The former, which involves such new institutions as taxes, credit, public funds, stock-jobbing and a paid standing army, seems a final public replacement of feudal dues and obligations with monetary values and contracts. This is vividly dramatized through, among other things, the attacks of the Tory traditionalist followers of Bolingbroke against the new 'moneyed men' of Walpole's Whigs. As Bolingbroke himself put it: 'The power of money as the world is now constituted is real power' (Sekora 1977: 70). The central charge is corruption: social order, political office, social relations, authority are now all regulated by monetary exchange, can be bought and sold and are now rooted not in the traditional soil but in the impersonal market. The same period also sees major debates on 'movable wealth' as opposed to the landed variety; commercial capital, like today's multinational financial instruments, knows no loyalty to (let alone regulation by) organic ties to monarch, nation or people and so corrupts the social order. The cash nexus goes beyond corruption to produce *madness*. For example, the South Sea Bubble scandal crystallized the new money mania in the absence of regulation by either tradition or reason. Dabydeen's (1987) analysis of Hogarth's work shows that the new money economy evoked images of sexual, personal, racial and political disorder and insanity, all sins of luxury. Fielding even argues, in 1751, that it is luxury not poverty that has caused 'the late increase of Robbers': crime is a result of the mobility, idleness and insolence occasioned by prosperity and increased aspirations – a theme pursued by today's conservative traditionalists.

Crucially, luxury as a form of insubordination is identified in terms of emulation, the 'aping of one's betters'. It concerns socially illegitimate claims on culture and lifestyle. New money can buy the marks of status which formerly were tied to birth, breeding and blood. New money buys landed estates, it can wear the clothes of court and 'society', it can indulge in the leisure pursuits of the aristocracy. Few images are as telling as those that arise around Bath in Smollett and Austen. For example, in *Humphrey Clinker* (1771) a character describes a ball at which he was 'extremely diverted' to see

> the Master of the Ceremonies leading, with great solemnity . . . an antiquated Abigail, dressed in her lady's cast-clothes; whom he (I suppose) mistook for some countess just arrived at the Bath. The ball was opened by a Scotch lord, with a mulatto heiress from St Christopher's; and the gay colonel Tinsel danced all the evening with the daughter of an eminent tinman from the Borough of Southwark. Yesterday morning, at the Pump-room, I saw a broken-winded Wapping landlady squeeze through a circle of peers, to salute her brandy-merchant . . . and a paralytic attorney of Shoe-lane, in shuffling up to the bar, kicked the shins of the chancellor of England . . . (Smollett 1985: 78–9).

In a sense, the problem of commerce and consumption is that status itself becomes a consumer good: it can be bought.

'Culture', it could be said then, begins as the battlecry of landed Tories against the new Whig plutocracy, and it is heard above a fray about the proper sources of social legitimacy. Culture comes to be defined as precisely that which money cannot buy: birth, breeding, legitimacy. We can see this in many common meanings of 'culture' in the sense of art. It is defined increasingly by its distance from commerce and manufacture. Culture is not consumed (however much the opera-going bourgeoisie may pay for its tickets), but is rather appreciated by a cultured audience; art is not manufactured, it is *created*. True culture cannot be bought, mediated or ruled by money because it was *defined* that way. But if 'true culture' retreats to higher ground as the tide of commerce floods its banks, consumer culture wallows in its mud, an abomination thrown up from its depths. It is culture that can be bought by anyone with the cash; and it is culture that is produced to be sold. Consumer culture is, by definition, illegitimate; moreover, defined as 'luxury', it is the expression in everyday life of the triumph of economic over social value.

Mass culture

The popularity of consumer culture – its being 'of the people' – is central to the idea of consumer culture as non-culture or debased culture. The domination of economic value over society, the spread of purchasing power to ever 'lower' sectors of the population, the deregulation of all traditional constraints over consumption (free choice) and finally the centrality of democracy and equality as modern values – all of these empower non-accredited tastes and desires. Those who are said to make up mass culture are the same people who are seen as consumers: women, children and the elderly, the working classes, youth, ethnic minorities. Ironically, the same people who (as we saw in the last chapter) are excluded from the liberal domain of 'the rational individual' are also excluded from the romantic domain of 'the cultured individual'.

Hence a litany of complaints that modern consumers constitute a market for cheap thrills, a market which – through their mass purchasing power and democratic voice – reorients cultural production and social values around the base and common. Leavis, for example, argues that mass culture involves a 'psychological Gresham's Law' (1930: 7) whereby bad tastes drive out the good – the taste for culture that represents the cumulative learning of the 'race' and which 'makes you a better person' (5) by allowing one 'to profit by the finest human experience of the past' (5). Mass-consumed culture, in the form of advertising, film, newspapers, formula fiction and radio, 'all offer satisfaction at the lowest level, and inculcate the choosing of the most immediate pleasures, got with the least effort' (Leavis and Thompson 1933: 3); for in order to sustain mass production, firms must 'give the public what it wants', 'appeal to the lowest common denominator' and so on. Hoggart charts the impact of similar developments on the decline of 'authentic' working-class culture when confronted with 'this regular, increasing, and almost unvaried diet of sensation without commitment', which 'is surely likely to help render its consumers less capable of responding openly and responsibly to life, is likely to induce an underlying sense of purposeless in existence outside the limited range of a few immediate appetites' (Hoggart 1977 (1957): 246). He portrays mass consumer culture as an escalating addiction, whose hooks involve the appeal to baser instincts and gratifications. Why read a difficult novel (i.e. a culturally valued one) when advertising offers and encourages cultural experiences based on brevity, simplification, bittiness and a short attention span? As T. S. Eliott characteristically remarked, modern advertising represents 'the influence of masses of men by any means except through their intelligence' (Williams 1985: 227).

Many mass-culture theorists can be derided as reactionary and elitist. Many should be, especially those like Nietzsche, Ortega or Pound whose contempt for the 'masses' is not incompatible with a desire to purify them as a *Volk*. However, in so far as culture is a social ideal, it also forms part of a *social* explanation of the debasement of the individual through social forces, rather than merely an account of the triumph of the modern horde. Leavis at least clearly relates the decline of culture less to the evil of the masses than to that of the industrial order which profits by pandering to their untutored tastes. ' "Civilisation" and "culture" are coming to be antithetical terms' according to Leavis (1930: 26) very largely because culture is now industrially mass-produced in the form of consumer goods for profitable sale: industrialization has 'turned out to involve standardisation and levelling-down outside the realm of mere material goods' (Leavis and Thompson, 1933: 3). Indeed, corporations now take on the 'status and function of a public national organ', for it is they who, through advertising and marketing, define the needs and values of the community (Leavis and Thompson 1933: 30–1). Culture in all its senses, as way of life and as art, is artificially produced and ignorantly consumed because it is detached from organic life. As Denys Thompson put it later: 'The selves we are are to a great extent the product of our social contacts. It may be that these social contacts are being replaced by a synthetic substance that exists only in the media' (Thompson 1964: 16).

Following a parallel train of thought, Adorno and Horkheimer (1979) famously decided to abandon the term 'mass culture', which appears to blame the debasement of culture on the masses, and to replace it with 'the culture industry', which places the blame firmly on the power of rationalized institutions to produce mass culture, and to reduce individuals to members of a mass. For both conservative and Marxist mass-cultural theory, liberal society, which purports to liberate individuals from social authority, actually by this very process leaves them disorganized, disoriented, anomic and isolated. Far from being free and autonomous, they are defenceless against new forms of modern power. Culture is said to be absent in the sense that there is a lack of moral order embodied in everyday experience and social relations. For both Leavis and Adorno, this moral order retreats, in the modern world, into an ever more restricted and rarefied aesthetic realm of authentic values (for Leavis, a realm of authentic and trained 'response' to 'life'; for Adorno, a realm of authentically critical, 'non-identity' thinking based on substantive rather than formal rationality).

Both think through the isolation of the individual in sociological terms. These terms are various: disappearance of community and face-to-face relations, the rupture of tradition by the decline of status, the weakening of the authority of family and particularly of the father (especially in Adorno and in Lasch), the decline (or cooption by power) of the voluntary associations of civil society such as religion, trade unions, political parties and the media. This is buttressed by the general privatization of life under capitalism and the isolation of individuals on the basis of both the division of labour and economic competition. All of this is particularly clear in images of mass media consumption: the isolated couch potato is glued to the box in a relationship of passivity and absorption unmodulated by any face-to-face social relations.

A modern world based on pure individual self-interest ironically leaves the individual in a chronically weak condition. Without a binding collective culture, without solidarity, the individual – isolated, adrift on tides of momentary desires – is open to manipulation and the most subtle forms of unfreedom. Moreover, modernity, based on a massive assault on forms of collective or corporate regulation, ironically throws up new forms of collective and corporate control: bureaucratic state institutions, multinational corporations, the mass media, technocracy. Hence, for example, advertising looms very large in this literature as a model of modern unfreedom. Ostensibly the very epitome of capitalist competition, advertising both presents itself and is attacked as a dominating, even scientific, power which organizes individuals into masses. This is most clearly stated in the myth of the 'hidden persuaders'. Vance Packard's argument (1977) was that advertising possessed scientific psychological technologies which, through knowledge of their unconscious desires and motivations, could compel individuals to act against their wills, buying whatever the advertiser wished them to. The individual confronts these forms of power directly, without mediation by collective values or relations. The individualism of competition leads to the destruction of the individual (and of free competition). Packard himself is writing in the journalistic muckraking tradition of American progressivism, a form of populism which spoke out of fears very similar to the culture and society tradition (and fascism): the 'little man' (particularly the middle classes) is being squeezed between, on the one hand, the proletarian and immigrant mob gathered by industrialization, urbanization and the destruction of traditional order, and, on the other hand, the power of modern corporatism. Consumer culture threatens to slide these good people into the arms of the masses. We might compare Packard's conspiracy theories with Leavis's earlier worry (1930: 12) about the 'unprecedented use of applied psychology' whereby advertising is becoming an 'exact' process (he cites J. B. Watson's application of behaviourism to advertising). Leavis hopes that through (literary) education we might 'train up a public that, fully aware of the buttons that are being pressed, would smile at the idea of responding automatically'. Leavis believes that in this industrial civilization formal education must replace the organic defence against such manufactured influences which would once have been provided by the walls of the organic community. The psychological power of advertising only works where the individual has been expelled from these walls and is wandering, lost and alone, in the modern world.

Affluence and disorder

The idea of culture as a critical social ideal, then, asks questions about the debasement of values under modern conditions. But it does so less in the manner of the aesthete than that of a concerned humanist liberal like Mill or Arnold, for whom the opposite of culture is not bad art but social anarchy and individual anomie. For the basic question posed by the tradition of culture is this: Can there be a society, such as liberal commercial and consumer society is meant to exemplify, based purely on formal rationality and utilitarian individualism? The answer to that question, in turn, involves looking at just what the pursuit of self-interest means on the ground, in everyday life and cultural experience. What happens to the *needs* of the individual in a deregulated and affluent society?

Durkheim: need and anomie

It was Durkheim who most stoutly asserted, against utilitarian individualism, the necessary moral and cultural authority of 'society'. Durkheim was notoriously sanguine that modernity *will* produce a cultural basis for legitimate solidarity, but argued that utilitarianism as a way of life cannot provide it. This accounts for the pathology of western society in its transitional phase from one cultural basis to another that has yet to emerge properly.

The modern division of labour, Durkheim argues, has produced an astonishing density of relations of *functional* interdependence between individuals. However, whereas utilitarianism assumed that this would automatically produce social coordination on the basis of each individual pursuing his or her self-interest (as in Smith's 'hidden hand' of the market), Durkheim argues that binding moral commitments are required even for the orderly honouring of self-interested contracts. Markets themselves, as contemporary economic sociology now agrees, requires moral bonds such as 'trust', a sense of 'just price' and so on (see, for example, DiMaggio 1990; Dore 1983; Etzioni 1988; Gambetta 1989; Granovetter 1985; Hodgson 1988; Hodgson and Screpanti 1991; Kahneman et al. 1987; Lane 1991; Swedberg 1987; Thompson et al. 1991; Zukin and DiMaggio 1990). Premodern society solidified itself through the cultural coherence afforded by the *conscience collective* (an analysis clearly compatible with the idea of embeddedness).

Modernity, too, will ultimately promote a 'cult of the individual' that comprises not only the pursuit of interest but also a substantive moral concern for the value, dignity and rights of individual humans. That is to say, both solidarity and social coordination depend on substantive, not just formal, bonds that can be understood as cultural in character, or which will translate the cultural cohesion of the premodern world into the socio-economic conditions of the modern. While Durkheim's formulation locates modern solidarity at the level of the individual, it also presupposes the individual's recognition of the idea of society as a regulative moral ideal. The pathology of contemporary modernity is attributed to its transitional state, to the existence of a 'forced division of labour' which denies human value through inequalities of power and wealth. For Durkheim, class conflict, for example, is a standing refutation of utilitarianism: where social relations are ruled by contract alone moral solidarity cannot establish itself.

Economic progress, Durkheim writes, 'has consisted mainly of freeing industrial relations from all regulation. Until very recent it was the function of a whole system of moral forces to exert this discipline (1987: 254).' These forces included both religion and systems of guilds and corporations, primary traditionalist targets of the liberal bourgeoisie. They have now lost their moral power and can no longer set commanding social aims: 'the amoral character of economic life amounts to a public danger'. Into this moral gap flows the formal utilitarian rationality:

> nations are supposed to have as their only or principal objective the achievement of industrial prosperity . . . industry, instead of continuing to be regarded as a means to an end which transcends it, has become the supreme end for individuals and society. But then appetites thus awakened are freed from any limiting authority. By sanctifying these appetites, so to speak, this deification of material well-being has placed them above all human law. . . . From the top to the bottom of the scale, covetous desires are aroused without it being known where they might level out (Thompson, 1985: 111).

Thus the pursuit of interest as an end in itself is registered quite significantly in the sphere of consumption, for social deregulation appears in everyday life in the form of anomie: 'One no longer knows what is fair, what are legitimate claims and hopes, and which are excessive. As a result, there is nothing to which one does not aspire. . . . Appetites no longer accept limits to behaviour, since public opinion cannot restrain them' (110).

Indeed, Durkheim puts forward one of the grounding themes of the critique of consumer culture: in premodern societies, economic scarcity went hand in hand with social regulation to limit the range of human wants and needs. Modern deregulation and industrial productivity let loose human desires which are in principle insatiable:

> Human nature in itself cannot set invariable limits to our needs. Consequently, in so far as it is left to the individual alone, these needs are unlimited. Without reference to any external regulating influence our capacity for sensation is a bottomless abyss that nothing can satisfy. But, then, if nothing external manages to restrict this capacity, it can only be a source of torment to itself. Unlimited desires are insatiable by definition, and insatiability is rightly considered a pathological symptom. . . . Society alone can perform this moderating role . . . for it is the only moral power superior to the individual (109).

But society is precisely what liberalism reduces to individuals. In everyday life, the expansion of individual need unconstrained by the moral authority of culture or society is a source of personality disturbance and of the profound confusion of modernity: 'crises of prosperity', like those of poverty, are equally 'disturbances of the collective order' (109). Given the context of Durkheim's discussion, we can even say that it leads to suicide (for a comparison of the sociology of suicide and of consumption, see Warde 1994b).

Durkheim was very far from alone in these concerns, as Cross (1993), Miller (1981) and Williams (1982), for example, demonstrate in the case of France (see, for example, Horowitz (1985) and Fox and Lears (1983) for related American debates). Miller's account of moral concerns about women shoppers at the mid-nineteenth century department stores is particularly apropos: going to the Bon Marché, the female shopper escapes the moral surveillance of patriarchal home and community and enters the unregulated space of the city streets, urban crowd and the store itself, a place of unregulated, indeed hyper-stimulated, fantasy, desire and insatiable need. Moral panics arose about women, addicted to shopping, abandoning husbands and children. This pathology of desire was medicalized from mid-century onwards through the notion of 'kleptomania', which was unsurprisingly classified as a form of hysteria – a disease of the womb – and therefore as a sexual disorder. Just as in Hogarth's time, it is feared that the freedom of the money economy leads directly to the madness of lust through the loss of moral regulation.

Durkheim's analysis foregrounds another long-running theme: if needs are not limited by moral order, then nothing can satisfy them. However affluent the economy, however much it produces, it will always produce frustration, unhappiness and dissatisfaction because its unlimited production of goods is so intimately tied to the unlimited production of needs. Whereas proponents of commercial society identify happiness with prosperity, its critics see it as a 'joyless economy' (Scitovsky 1976, 1986; see also Hirsch (1976); Lansley (1994); Leiss (1976); and chapter 6 below). In the absence of a coherent cultural formation to map out for the individual a legitimated and limited agenda of needs, values and commanding social aims, insatiable need 'can only be a source of torment to itself'. Above all, instead of being able to assess their satisfactions in relation to a desired way of life, consumers are obsessed by *relative* wealth, happiness, satisfaction – with keeping up with the Joneses. This is a quantitative calculation whose substantive content is immaterial – we must keep up with the Joneses whatever they happen to be buying or earning this month. It is also a case of ever shifting goal posts in which every level of satisfaction reached instantly turns into a new experience of dissatisfaction as one's neighbours eventually catch up. Finally, many of these concerns increasingly focus on questions about the ecological limits to insatiable need. Is it the case that the enervating spiral of expanded needs and expanded production will meet its nemesis in the depletion of natural resources and the pollution of the environment?

Rousseau: need and inauthenticity

Modern need is insatiable because it is no longer fixed either by nature or by the traditional social order. Whereas culture might subordinate need to higher values, consumer culture dreams up ever more needs and enslaves people to a vicious circle of unceasing need feeding off perpetual dissatisfaction. Deregulated society, then, far from providing a moral framework for meaningful individual and collective life, now exercises a deep form of corruption and compulsion over its disoriented members.

The most profound and influential attack on the pathology of affluence and deregulated need stems from Rousseau, for whom the problem of need, corruption and social progress was central. Rousseau, famously, reverses the central terms of the entire liberal tradition. This tradition, from Hobbes onwards, argues that men's needs are *naturally* insatiable: needs, wants and 'luxury' cannot be distinguished in the state of nature. The urgency of individual desire – greed really – is in fact the engine of progress. Hobbes was probably the first to equate the absence of desire not with virtue but with personal and social death ('felicity' does not consist 'in the repose of a mind satisfied. For there is no such *finis ultimus*, utmost aim, nor *summum bonum*, greatest good, as is spoken of in the books of the old moral philosophers. Nor can a man any more live, whose desires are at an end, than he, whose senses and imaginations are at a stand. Felicity is a continual progress of the desire, from one object to another . . . ' (Hobbes 1972 (1651): 121; also see Xenos (1989: 4)). However, he also argues at great length that unlimited needs are the basis of violence, of the 'war of all against all' and of the nasty, brutish and short lives led *in the state of nature*. Social contract theory equates the formation of civil society and the state with the creation of regulatory frameworks in which men can safely pursue their desires, though not with the regulation of desire itself. Civil society and the state therefore come into existence *in response to* the naturally unlimited desires of individuals and the violence this produces in the state of nature.

Rousseau completely inverts this argument. The man of unlimited greed whom Hobbes is describing is not man in a state of nature but rather man as he has been produced by modern society (Rousseau 1984 (1755): 92, 98–9). For Rousseau, insatiable needs are a product of society, above all of social inequality institutionalized through property rights (the cherished foundation of *equality* for liberalism), and they are both a means and an end for social domination. Rousseau argues this through a distinction between real needs and social needs: 'it is easy to see that all our labors are directed upon two objects only, namely, the commodities of life for oneself, and consideration on the part of others' ('Discourse on inequality', quoted in Hirschman (1977: 109)). Man in the state of nature is characterized by *amour de soi*, 'self-love', a proper regard for one's own interests, in which people act on the basis of finite, real needs. In this state, the abundance of nature and the limits of need complement each other. No man is hungry, both because all he wants are berries, and because nature provides enough of these to pick easily off the bush. (Compare Sahlins's (1974) 'original affluent society'.)

It is human *association* and specifically the comparison with others that brings about an awareness of inequality and thus a motive for competition. Desire becomes associated with possession. There is a social pressure to *have*, as opposed to *enjoy*, the pleasures of the earth. The increasing refinement and sophistication of desire proceeds in a vicious spiral with the development of social competition. The healthy, because limited and therefore satisfiable *amour de soi*, is replaced by the unending pathology of *amour-propre*, desire for 'consideration on the part of others'. Needs are no longer anchored in nature but are linked to the approval and admiration of others, and therefore have no limit. Liberalism promised autonomy – needs and interests defined by individuals for themselves. It actually delivers heteronomy – man's needs are determined by the fashions, opinions and scrutiny of society, or (to use a phrase we will explore later) he becomes 'other-determined'. 'Behold man, who was formerly free and independent, diminished as a consequence of a multitude of new wants into subjection, one might say, to the whole of nature and especially to his fellow men ... ' (Rousseau 1984 (1755): 119). Rousseauian solutions to the problem of needs in modern society therefore revolve around the restraint of both need and culture (see for example Talmon's (1986 (1952)) discussion of Babeuf), for 'the real world has its limits; the imaginary world is infinite. Unable to enlarge the one, let us restrict the other' (cited in Xenos 1989: 26).

In some respects, Rousseau is utterly opposed to the culture and society tradition from which we started. Whereas for that tradition *high* culture is a refuge for the higher values chased out of everyday lived culture by industrial civilization, Rousseau sees *all* forms of culture as based in luxury, artificial refinement and social emulation. Firstly, it is imagination which 'extends for us the measure of the possible ... and which consequently excites and nourishes the desires by the hope of satisfying them' (cited in Xenos 1989: 25); hence Rousseau's famous desire to ban the theatre (Sennett 1977). Secondly, culture represents not only the falsity of society but also its special tool for enslaving men. Princes desire the spread

> of taste for the arts and for superfluities ... For, besides fostering the spiritual pettiness so appropriate to slavery, they know well that the needs that people create for themselves are like chains binding them. . . . The sciences, letters, and arts . . . wind garlands of flowers around the iron chains that bind [the people], stifle in them the feeling of the original liberty for which they seemed to have been born, make them love their slavery, and turn them into what is called civilized people (quoted in Williams 1982: 43).

Thirdly, Rousseau's attack on culture partly targets aristocratic consumption, which is divorced from enjoyment and used cynically to exercise power in court society and over the upper bourgeoisie and salons, both of whom ape chateaux manners (Williams 1982: 33). Whereas the ideal of culture tends to laud aristocracies of taste, intelligence or birth, castigating both popular coarseness and bourgeois materialism, Rousseau appears as the defender of bourgeois propriety, soberness and restraint against luxury, which he defines in terms of aristocratic corruption.

As we have seen, Sekora argues that eighteenth-century conservatives regarded luxury as a vice of the poor and middle classes, who strive above their station; the aristocracy have a culturally legitimate right, through their breeding and status superiority, to refined and excessive consumption. By the nineteenth century, luxury was redefined: it was now the vice of an aristocracy with too much money and idleness. Working-class consumption then came to be seen as akin to aristocratic luxury, and often allied with it (drinking, gambling, horses, boxing and so on are debauched entertainments of both upper and lower classes (see Cunningham 1980)). On the other hand, middle-class consumption above basic needs had been relabelled as 'comforts' (Appleby 1993: 168) and 'conveniences' (a favourite word of Smith's) and is quite respectable: a happy mean between necessity and luxury. Rousseau, attacking the vices of aristocratic luxury, might be seen as an early advocate of bourgeois sobriety. Laclos's vision of Rousseau's hell, *Les liaisons dangereuses*, clearly attacks the way in which society, exemplified in aristocratic debauchery, alienates humans from all natural feeling.

Despite these oppositions, Rousseau and the tradition of culture take their places side by side within romantic attacks on consumer culture and liberal society because they are both concerned with the authenticity of human values and human being, an authenticity they associate with an organic society (based, respectively, in nature and tradition) which is ruptured by the material abundance and individualistic, competitive basis of modern society. We can appreciate just how completely Rousseau reversed the terms of liberal-utilitarianism by looking more closely at the way in which he, as opposed to Smith and Hume, evaluates the relation between 'society' and 'insatiable need' (see Berry 1994; Ignatieff 1984; Xenos 1989).

For Smith (and Hume) limitation to basic needs is neither morally nor economically good:

> the whole industry of human life is employed not in procuring the supply of our three humble necessities, food, cloaths, and lodging, but in procuring the conveniences of it according to the nicety and delicacey of our taste. To improve and multiply the materials which are the principal objects of our necessities, gives occasion to all the variety of the arts (Smith, in Xenos 1989: 11).

Progress in both culture and civilization depends on the expansion of desire. This argument goes back to Hobbes, as we have seen, to debates in the 1690s concerning the importation of luxury goods (see especially Appleby 1993), and above all to Mandeville. 'Luxury' may be relabelled as 'conveniences' of life, but the central point for Smith is that the arts are both product and catalyst in a virtuous circle with commerce. The arts produce desire; greater material prosperity enhances the arts.

The basis of this virtuous circle is not a desire for utilities which, being related to the needs of the body, are finite. Rather,

> it is chiefly from [the] regard to the sentiments of mankind that we pursue riches and avoid poverty. . . . From whence . . . arises the emulation which runs through all the different ranks of men and what are the advantages which we propose by that great purpose of human life which we call *bettering our condition*? To be observed, to be attended to, to be taken notice of with sympathy, complacency, and appreciation, are all the advantages which we can propose to derive from it. It is the vanity, not the ease or the pleasure, which interests us (from *Theory of Moral Sentiments*, in Hirschman 1977: 108).

Amour-propre, social competition, the imagined needs produced by culture and human association – these are not, as for Rousseau, a new form of slavery, or simply a spur to keep us on the treadmill of economic growth. They are necessary to the general advancement of human civilization. Indeed, as Hume puts it, 'perhaps the chief advantage which arises from a commerce with strangers' is not economic exchange but the cultural intercourse through which we are exposed to new possibilities, new needs. 'Commerce with strangers' 'rouses men from their indolence; and presenting the gayer and more opulent part of the nation with objects of luxury, which they never before dreamed of, raises in them a desire of a more splendid way of life than what their ancestors enjoyed' (cited in Xenos 1989: 11–12).

But Hume and Smith go much further than this, in the very opposite direction to Rousseau: 'consideration on the part of others' is not a form of moral corruption but the very basis of morality and social solidarity, and the basis of emulation is to a very large extent an innate human desire for aesthetic pleasure, a drive to culture. Their arguments are based on the notion of 'sympathies': it is through the human imaginative capacity to place ourselves in the position of the other, and to view self and other 'from the standpoint of a "spectator", a hypothetical Other embodying the values and customs of a given society' (Xenos 1989: 14) that we can see, and desire and aspire to, the satisfactions which various goods (forms of wealth) can offer. Yet this capacity for sympathy is also the basis of all moral behaviour and social solidarity. The *Theory of Moral Sentiments* gives Smith the moral psychology which allows the competitive individualistic world of *The Wealth of Nations* to hold together. Thus, whereas from Bentham onwards solidarity and economic growth arise automatically from the isolated hedonic calculus of monadic individuals, Smith and Hume still anchor both morality and self-interest itself in an innately *social* sentiment, a desire to be approved of by others.

For Rousseau, as we have seen, emulation does not represent social solidarity but social tyranny and artificiality: 'The savage man lives within himself; social man lives always outside himself; he knows how to live only in the opinion of others, it is, so to speak from their judgement alone that he derives the sense of his own existence' (Rousseau 1984 (1755): 136). Human authenticity resides in natural feeling and sensibility; man's innate moral sentiment is 'pathos' and compassion (hence the Rousseauian 'cult of sensibility' displayed its authenticity by shedding tears (Campbell 1989; Schama 1989: 145–62; Todd 1986). Emulation replaces that authenticity with mere appearances: with the rise of society, 'to be and to appear became two entirely different things, and from this distinction arose ostentatious display, deceitful cunning, and all the vices that follow in their train' (Rousseau 1984 (1755): 119).

Tocqueville: need and political freedom

The idea of 'the consumer' conjoins the ideas of 'freedom' and 'desire'. These terms were traditionally opposites. For example, in both classical philosophy and in neo-classical revivals during the eighteenth century (neo-Stoicism, civic humanism), desire makes slaves out of men because passion destroys reason. Moreover, national and civic freedom, like individual freedom, can only be guaranteed by the good government provided by men free from material want or greed. Desire spelled out a vertiginous descent into corruption and slavery.

In the formation of responses to consumer culture, the themes of civic humanism and neo-stoicism were crucial (see Burchill 1991; Hirschman 1977; Pocock 1975, 1985). The argument here is about the relation between private and public virtues, echoing Aristotle's distinction between *oikos* (the domestic economy) and the public virtues of the citizen: if the good life is a life ruled by reason rather than desire, the public good too depends on a clarity of mind derived from the restraint of desire (self-mastery). The citizen is concerned with the public good rather than with private gain (though this depends on being wealthy enough in property, slaves or women to be free of personal need and greed). As Hirschman (1977) argues, while early arguments for capitalism held that commerce (the pursuit of private gain) promoted peaceful interdependence, there is also an early and mounting concern that it will also erode civic virtue. Even Hume and Smith – despite all we have said about them so far – share this very old-fashioned worry: private wealth and luxurious living, accomplished through commercial prosperity, may corrupt the virile, martial strength on which the defence of that prosperity ultimately depends. One 'bad effect of commerce is that it sinks the courage of mankind, and tends to extinguish martial spirit . . . By having their minds constantly employed on the arts of luxury, they grow effeminate and dastardly' (Smith, in Hirschman 1977: 105). The association of luxury with a decline in military virility is no doubt part of the general association of consumer culture with feminization.

This whole line of thought is most powerfully transmitted through Tocqueville, whose work has been particularly influential in American critiques of consumer culture, particularly those discussed below. Summarizing his life's work in 1856, in the foreword to his history of the French Revolution, he writes:

> For in a community in which the ties of family, of caste, of class, and craft fraternities no longer exist people are far too much disposed to think exclusively of their own interests, to become self-seekers practicing a narrow individualism and caring nothing for the public good. Far from trying to counteract such tendencies despotism encourages them, depriving the governed of any sense of solidarity and interdependence; of good-neighborly feelings and a desire to further the welfare of the community at large. It immures them, so to speak, each in his private life . . . (de Tocqueville 1955 (1856): xiii).

Tocqueville believes in freedom, but in a very different sort from the personal liberty of liberalism, in a freedom that promotes solidarity through social intercourse in a rather Durkheimian way, by making men aware of their common interests and thus 'lifting men's minds above mere mammon worship and the petty personal worries which crop up in the course of everyday life, and of making them aware at every moment that they belong each and all to a vaster entity, above and around them – their native land.' Individualistic equality, embodied in the pursuit of private gain, inevitably undermines itself and turns to despotism when, obsessed with private desires, men turn over the reins of power, and with it their freedom, to political professionals. Despotism (and Tocqueville is concerned with the corrupt sham of the French second empire under Louis Napoleon) arises when men abandon the public sphere for private wealth; the greatest weapon of despotism is the further encouragement of desire, greed, luxury and consumption.

The self in consumer culture

Thus consumer culture, which to liberalism seemed to be exemplary of individual autonomy, comes to stand for all sorts of slavery: to desire and insatiable needs, to social scrutiny and competition, to political as well as cultural despotism and tyranny. Liberation from social restraint really means the loss of natural feeling and of stable social values and therefore the weakening, disorientation and subjugation of the individual. Society comes to dominate the individual, not least through the material world of objects and interests, which are now essential not merely for meeting needs but for being or finding a self. For the tradition of 'culture', consumer culture is part of a loss of the self brought about by modernity rather than an efficient way of satisfying the needs of autonomous selves. It is precisely this loss of self in a post-traditional world, a society without a culture, that informs many of the most influential twentieth-century accounts of consumer culture.

The post-traditional self

'Post-traditional society', to which the idea of culture is a response, is marked by *pluralization*. In place of a secure order of values and social positions there is a bewildering variety and fluidity of values, roles, authorities, symbolic resources and social encounters out of which an individual's social identity must be produced and maintained. Giddens (1991: 84) usefully summarizes this in four themes. Firstly, modernity is a post-traditional order in which fixed identities are neither ascribed nor unambiguously indicated.

Increasingly unanchored in tradition, religion, law etc., identity can only emerge from choice. Secondly, modernity involves a 'pluralization of lifeworlds' in which each individual has to negotiate multiple and contradictory identities as they traverse different public and private spheres, each with their different roles, norms etc. Thirdly, modernity replaces traditional authority with 'methodological doubt' (rather than the 'certainty of reason' for which it had originally hoped). Truth is contextual; authority and expertise are provisional. Finally, modernity places 'mediated experience' at the centre of social life. Through commerce, the city, the mobility of travel and communications, through the mass media, ever more 'lifeworlds' are made visible to us, become possible choices of identity. Through marketing and advertising, and their commercialization of mediated experience, this plurality of modern life is directly translated into consumer choices.

We can add a fifth theme, commercialization itself. The modern dynamic of pluralization is intensified by subordinating culture to economic ends. On the one hand, consumption is regulated by purchasing power rather than socio-cultural rights and privileges, thus allowing a great fluidity in the use of goods to construct identities and lifestyles; on the other hand, cultural values and meanings are ever renewable resources for economic competition as advertising indicates every day.

Modernity, then, involves the vertiginous production, display and interaction of myriad possible ways of life, none of which has indisputable cultural authority or value. It is a recipe for identity-crisis on a mass scale. There are no naturally or divinely ordained social places and individual selves. Individuals must, by force of circumstances, choose, construct, maintain, interpret, negotiate, display who they are to be or be seen as, using a bewildering variety of material and symbolic resources. A range of recent authors such as Giddens (1991), Bauman (1983, 1988, 1990, 1991, 1993) and Beck (1992) place consumer culture in this context, charting the implications of the destruction of the traditional order for the process of character-formation, for identity and for the nature of intimacy and authenticity (see also Warde's (1994a, 1994b) reviews of this literature). They also link to a range of authors whom we shall review in the next sections.

The contrast with liberalism is, as ever, instructive. For liberalism, choice is a hard-won freedom, wrested from the social order. For the works under discussion here, choice is a requirement and compulsion, something we are forced into by the absence of a stable social order. 'We have no choice but to choose' (Giddens, 1991: 81) because no identities are unproblematically assigned to us. Moreover, liberalism assumes the existence of coherent individuals who make choices, individuals who know their needs and pursue them rationally. Yet coherent identity seems to be precisely the main *problem* of modern existence and is itself something to be chosen and achieved. We have already seen this issue posed by Foucault and Rose (whose work converges in some respects with these authors): liberal society appears as a social space which requires and produces a 'choosing self', rather than one in which a naturally choosing self is liberated.

The characterization of modernity as mass identity crisis connects with consumer culture in several major ways. Firstly, the metaphor of individual choice dominates our sense of the social. Social action and structure are increasingly understood in terms of individual choices undertaken in relation to the needs of, or *for*, a self. Modern identity is best understood through the image of consumption. We choose a self-identity from the shop-window of the pluralized social world; actions, experiences and objects are all reflexively encountered as part of the need to construct and maintain self-identity. Secondly, identity itself can be seen as a saleable commodity. Self is not an inner sense of authenticity but rather a calculable condition of social survival and success. We have to produce and 'sell' an identity to various social markets in order to have intimate relationships, social standing, jobs and careers. Thirdly, the resources – both material and symbolic – through which we produce and sustain identities increasingly take the form of consumer goods and activities through which we construct appearances and organize leisure time and social encounters. Conversely, the quest for identity in post-traditional anomie is arguably the greatest market of all, or the motivation which underlies all markets: marketing, at least, assumes that we want goods primarily for the meaningful or desirable identities with which they might endow us. Consumerism simultaneously exploits mass identity crisis by proffering its goods as solutions to the problems of identity, and in the process intensifies it by offering ever more plural values and ways of being. Consumer culture lives and breeds in the cultural deficits of modernity.

That the self must be a project is dictated to us by a pluralized world and must be pursued within that pluralized world. This entails a high level of anxiety and risk. In terms of consumer culture, there is high anxiety because every choice seems to implicate the self: all acts of purchase or consumption, clothing, eating, tourism, entertainment, 'are decisions not only about how to act but who to be' (Warde 1994b: 81). The things I consume in some sense *express* my identity, my values, tastes, social membership and so on. But if I have to choose my identity and means of expression, I am involved in 'qualitatively new types of personal risk ... the risk of the chosen and changed personal identity' (Beck 1992: 131). Consumer culture (particularly typified in the form of advertising) increases the individual's experience of risk and anxiety by offering ever more choice and images of different identities and by increasing the sense of social risk involved in making the 'wrong choice'. This is particularly unjust as consumer culture also speeds up and dislocates, through the fashion system, planned social obsolescence and so on, any sense of what a 'right choice' might be today as opposed to last week or next week. Again, this is an extension of general modern developments in which modernity 'confronts the individual with a complex diversity of choices and, because it is non-foundational, at the same time offers little help as to which options should be selected' (Giddens, 1991: 80). Post-traditional society is non-foundational both cognitively (through methodological doubt and relativism) and socio-culturally (its values are not perceived to be anchored in an organic social world).

In theorizing pluralization and identity crisis, two terms keep appearing: 'expertise' and 'lifestyle'. Both denote features of modern life which manage, assuage, and organize anxieties about modern identity and at the same time can be used to exploit and intensify them. Despite its 'methodological doubt' in relation to all forms of knowledge, modernity is an expert culture. As in Weber and the Frankfurt School, modernity approaches all problems, including those of identity, as technical matters to be solved by technical means. Consumer culture 'technicizes' the project of the self by treating all problems as solvable through various commodities (Bauman 1990: 200–5). Firstly, commodity culture creates and solves problems in the production and maintenance of the self: for example, cosmetics advertising divides the woman's face into a series of 'problems' (bags under the eyes, thin lips, no cheek bones . . .) each of which can be 'cured' by a commodity, and all of which are depicted as 'essential' to a socially desirable (and even ethically responsible) self. Secondly, the entire idea of the self as a project involves forms of expertise and ignorance which are addressed by commodities: hence, these writers, as well as Rose and authors like Sennett, Lasch and Bell, whom we shall consider in a moment, focus continually on the rise of self-help books, courses and programmes, the proliferation of therapies and a 'therapeutic culture', and recipes for developing self-esteem, assertiveness or whatever other values seem necessary for carrying out the project of the self. These offer 'authoritative' guidance. The skills required to construct a self are themselves sold in the form of commodities (cf. Lears 1983). Thirdly, consumer culture offers extensive guidance on the relation between the expanding domain of meaningful consumer goods, services and experiences and the project of maintaining a self. This comes in the form, for example, of consumer magazines and consumerist editorials in more general magazines, but also in the form of advertising itself. For authors such as Marchand (1986), Leiss, Kline and Jhally (1986) and Schudson (1981, 1984) advertising provides 'maps of modernity', authoritative (if unstable) 'discourses through and about objects' which allow us to orientate ourselves to the social meanings of things in a commercial world. Advertising thus replaces traditional authorities about such meanings (e.g. religion and custom) with a modern information system.

All these aspects of expertise connect up the project of the self with commodity exchange. Lifestyle can also be seen as a way in which the pluralism of post-traditional identity is managed by individuals and exploited (or organized) by commerce:

> Lifestyles are routinised practices, the routines incorporated into habits of dress, eating, modes of acting and favoured milieus for encountering others; but the routines followed are reflexively open to change in the light of the mobile nature of self-identity. Each of the small decisions a person makes every day . . . contributes to such routines. All such choices (as well as larger and more consequential ones) are decisions not only about how to act but who to be. The more post-traditional the settings in which an individual moves, the more lifestyle concerns the very core of self-identity, its making and remaking (Giddens 1991: 81).

Lifestyle orders things into a certain unity, reducing the plurality of choice and affording 'a continuing sense of "ontological security" that connects options in a more or less ordered pattern' (81). The way in which these authors connect this patterning to the commercial system is fairly conventional and relates to depictions of Fordism and post-Fordism (see chapter 7). Social reproduction is transferred from traditional culture (which is seen as a brake on modernization) to the market for goods and labour. The notion of individual wants becomes central to the whole system, and standardized consumption patterns become central to economic growth and stability. They reduce risk for the individual, but also for the corporation (which has to face market competition on the basis of unpredictable effective demand) and for the state (which has to balance productivity, political order and consumption for stable growth). 'The project of the self becomes translated into one of the possession of desired goods and the pursuit of artificially framed styles of life . . . The consumption of ever-novel goods becomes in some part a substitute for the genuine development of self' (Giddens, 1991: 198).

Lifestyle is different both from the traditional status orders it replaces and from modern structural divisions (such as class, gender and ethnicity) in at least two crucial respects. Firstly, lifestyle tends to indicate a purely 'cultural' pattern: it is made of signs, representations, media and is as mutable and unstable as they are. Secondly, one can in theory switch from one lifestyle to another in the move from one shop-window, TV channel, supermarket shelf and so on to another. The instability of the modern self is thus partly understood as an aspect of the instability of modern forms of social membership. Bauman (1990), for example, employs Maffesoli's concept of neo-tribalism (see also Boorstin's (1962, 1973) notion of 'consumption communities'): lifestyle groupings and patterns do not reflect communities with well-policed social gates, with obligations to long-term commitment or to extensive social learning processes. Moreover, lifestyle groups are 'elective communities', memberships which we choose rather than have ascribed or allocated to us. Social membership is reduced to identities one puts on and takes off at whim, a transience which moves us beyond even the solidarity of subculture to 'the supermarket of style' (Polhemus 1994). Identity is literally skin deep. (It is interesting to note the current fascination with tattooing and body-piercing. Especially when related to subculture, they involve etching onto the body permanent signs of identities and memberships that are essentially transitory or even faddish.)

The 'other-directed' self

In modernity, the individual casts off from traditional society only to be cast adrift in a turbulent sea of sociability without a paddle or an anchor. A dominant modern concern is that, lacking a coherent self and authoritative cultural values, lacking character and depth, the individual is determined by society in the most trivial sense: individuals *conform* to the expectations of their immediate social surroundings, accept the authority of transient public opinion, media, advertising, peer groups, the Joneses. 'Americans', claimed Riesman, 'have always sought [the good opinion of others] and have had to seek it in an unstable market where quotations on the self could change without the price-pegging of a caste system or an aristocracy' (Riesman 1961: xx). The further worry is, as Sennett (1977) argues, that consumer culture has developed, along with modernity, from simple social emulation and conformism, in which individuals used goods for social advancement and security, to a far more dangerous condition (narcissism), in which they seek their *real* selves in their consumption, appearance and social performances.

The key terms of this issue were laid out as early as the 1750s, as we have seen. For Hume and Smith, seeing oneself through the eyes of the other is the basis both of our moral sense and of economic and cultural progress. Conviviality does not imply social conformism but autonomy and dynamism. For Rousseau, on the other hand, the other-regarding self is inauthentic and enslaved by social expectations. The society to which he or she seeks to conform is itself artificial. Certainly the idea that the modern self is constructed in its immediate social circumstances – rather than from authentic internal or transcendental sources of selfhood – runs clear through modern thought from this period through to twentieth-century social and psychological theory, especially in America and often in close connection with theorizing consumer culture. Thus, for example, symbolic interactionism (Mead, Cooley, Goffman) emphasizes a self that is constructed by adopting and internalizing the point of view of (significant) others, a 'looking-glass self', a 'performative self' in a 'dramaturgical' social world, and indeed an 'over-socialized self'. In a related vein, 'role-theory' and Parsonian sociology in the mid-century see the pluralism of modern society in terms of individuals having to conform to roles and role expectations, institutionally or structurally defined positions with norms of required behaviour and belief attached to them. Ewen (1976: 34–8) notes that Floyd Allport's notion of 'the social self' ('My idea of myself is rather my own idea of my neighbor's view of me') was ideologically useful to vanguard American advertisers of the 1920s. Whether or not they directly applied his social psychology, similar thinking seems to inform advertising copy which runs, 'You will be amazed to find how many times in one day people glance at your nails. At each glance a judgment is made . . . ': if their self is immediately social, then fear of social disapproval will bring consumers to market. Similarly, J. B. Watson, doyen of the kind of behaviourist psychology that reduced 'conformity' to 'conditioning', to a pure stimulus–response relation of self to environment, left academia for advertising in 1922, proclaiming the latter to be the effective modern replacement for family, religion and other traditional socializing agencies.

The clearest and most popular explorer of this theme was David Riesman. His sociological concern in *The Lonely Crowd* was in line with the structural-functionalism of his day – the question of how social order is established at the level of the individual by socializing them into roles, the role being the point at which systemic order and individual personality must meet, and meet happily. Riesman proffers a typology of modes of achieving social conformity. In traditional society, kinship relations and the sanction of *shame* (the bad opinion of a close and immediate community) ensures the individual's external behavioural conformity to a fixed social order.

By the age of liberal capitalism, however, this order has splintered into plurality and 'too many novel situations are presented, situations which a code cannot encompass in advance. Consequently the problem of personal choice, solved in the earlier period . . . by channeling choice through rigid social organization, . . . is solved by channeling choice through a rigid though highly individualized character' (Riesman 1961: 15). Hence an 'inner-directed' character type emerges: 'The source of direction for the individual is "inner"' (15) in the sense that, early in childhood, parents implant internally maintained norms which can govern choice and behaviour throughout life. Bad behaviour incurs the sanction of *guilt*.

'Other-directed' personalities emerge in a world that looks rather like the post-Fordist world (see chapter 7). The world is more plural and we encounter more of these pluralities through the media and social mobility. In the worlds of work and bureaucracy, social mobility 'depends less on what one is and what one does than on what others think of one – and how competent one is in manipulating others and being oneself manipulated' (45). In the world of work (and Riesman is writing in the same vein here as Whyte (1957) and Mills (1951)) *'the product now in demand is neither a staple nor a machine: it is a personality'* (46). To maintain a career one must market one's personality through the same kind of 'product differentiation' that characterizes commodities. Socialization is now directed not towards maintaining inner standards but towards developing 'an exceptional sensitivity to the actions and wishes of others' (22) so that the individual can be 'at home everywhere and nowhere, capable of a rapid if sometimes superficial intimacy and response to everyone' (25). Instead of being sanctioned by guilt, the other-directed character is driven by 'a diffuse *anxiety*' about measuring up to the transitory expectations of others. Where the 'control equipment' of the inner-directed personality is like a 'gyroscope', that of the other-directed is more like 'radar' (25).

With this kind of sensitivity and anxiety, the individual is obsessed with preferences, tastes, appearances, norms. In dealing with this kind of world, 'safety consists . . . in mastering a battery of consumer preferences and the mode of their expression . . . The proper mode of expression requires feeling out with skill and sensitivity the probable tastes of the others and then swapping mutual likes and dislikes to maneuver intimacy' (73). The self becomes dominated by fashion since 'to escape the danger of a conviction for being different from the "others" requires that one can be different – in look and talk and manner – from *oneself* as one was yesterday' (75). This has always been true, but now fashion has spread through all classes, and has speeded up in time. The possibilities are readily grasped by commodity producers able to 'accelerate swings of fashion as well as to differentiate goods by very minute gradients' (75). This endless splitting of marginal distinctions requires consumers to possess vast amounts of information and a capacity to make the most minute distinctions, which is precisely what the other-directed character is built upon: 'narcissism with respect to minor differences' (Freud, cited in Riesman 1961: 46).

Significantly, in his introduction to the second (1961) edition of *The Lonely Crowd*, Riesman insists that the book's aim – appearances notwithstanding – was not to condemn other-direction, and he is indeed sympathetic to both consumerism and popular culture. In an almost postmodernist sense he praises the 'considerateness, sensitivity and tolerance that are among the positive qualities of other-direction' (xxi) and which are due to 'a general tendency, facilitated by education, by mobility, by the mass media, toward an enlargement of the circles of empathy beyond one's clan, beyond even one's class, sometimes beyond one's country as well' (xxi) – an argument that we have seen stretch back to Montesquieu or Hume's praise of commerce. Moreover, Riesman argues that *all* the character types he is describing are modes of ensuring conformity. The other-directed character is no more 'conformist' than any other, and has its own mode of being autonomous. In fact, 'other-directed autonomy' looks very like contemporary notions of reflexivity, for it 'depends ... upon the success of [the individual's] effort to recognize and respect his own feelings, his own potentialities, his own limitations' (259).

The cult of the self

Paradoxically, the other-directed self of post-traditional society, perpetually hanging on everyone else's good opinion, is at the same time *self-obsessed*. At the limit point – 'narcissism' – other people and social relations are perceived only in terms of their implications for maintaining a coherent self-identity. In a post-traditional society, attention to immediate social expectations is the nearest equivalent available to that erstwhile social solidarity or 'culture' on which having a coherent identity depends.

For Giddens (1991), the instability of identity in the post-traditional world demands that we be inescapably involved in a '*reflexive* project of the self': this project is reflexive because it involves unremitting self-monitoring, self-scrutiny, planning and ordering of all elements of our lives, appearances and performances in order to marshal them into a coherent narrative called 'the self'. We have to interpret the past and plan the future in relation to an identity we are attempting to constitute in a particularly immediate and transient social present.

Consumerism is central to this self-obsession. This is partly because we not only have to choose a self, but (as Foucault's line of argument also indicates) have to constitute ourselves as a self who chooses, a consumer. One implication of this is that we are deemed personally responsible for every aspect of ourselves: we could always choose to do something about our appearance, health, manners. At the same time, everything we do has implications for the self, implications that we obsessively monitor; wearing this, eating that, looking like this are all read as reflections of the self (see, for example, Finkelstein 1991). As a result, all aspects of our existence are monitored and scrutinized as objects of instrumental calculation in the creation of the self, and the self is itself as much a thing one must produce as a person that one is. And consumer industries stand ready with things one can buy in order to address all these technical problems in the production of ourselves. Moreover, advertising and the media routinely offer aspirational narratives of the self – images of lifestyles, goods, advice – with which the viewer can identify. Most crucially, much like Foucault's ethical technologies, they offer up the very idea of the self as a narrative form, something to be constructed through individual choice and effort.

The modern relation to the body has provided a well-worked example of this (see, for example, Featherstone 1991a, 1991b; Gaines and Herzog 1990; O'Neill 1985; Shilling 1993; Turner 1985). The state of the body is seen as a reflection of the state of its owner, who is responsible for it and could refashion it. The body can be taken as a reflection of the self *because* it can and should be treated as something to be worked upon, and generally worked upon using commodities, for example intensively regulated, self-disciplined, scrutinized through diets, fitness regimes, fashion, self-help books and advice, in order to produce it as a commodity. Overweight, slovenliness and even unfashionability, for example, are now *moral* disorders; even acute illnesses such as cancer reflect on the inadequacy of the self (Coward 1989; Sontag 1983), and indeed of its consumption. One gets ill because one has consumed the wrong (unnatural) things or failed to consume the correct ('natural') ones: self, body, goods and environment constitute a system of *moral* choice.

The crucial point about this intense conjuncture of self-obsession and consumerism is not that it produces superficial social conformity, but the very opposite: unfortunately we are *not* simply keeping up external appearances. As Riesman points out, inner-directed characters were concerned with maintaining respectability, decorum and esteem through external appearances. The other-directed person is original in that this conformity reaches deeply into the *internal* life: 'The other-directed person wants to be loved rather than esteemed.' (1961: xx) The game has become deadly serious because the consumer's very soul is at stake in the management of consumerist conformity for, 'though he has his eye very much on the Joneses, [he] aims to keep up with them not so much in external details as in the quality of his inner experience' (24).

For Giddens, and to a great extent Riesman, the reflexive project of the self and its commodification constitute modern normality, however undesirable in certain respects. For others it is a pathological condition: narcissism. The idea of narcissism clearly connects modern self-obsession to the weakness of the self in the post-traditional society and indicates how consumer culture can both intensify and exploit this dynamic. Narcissism does not mean self love, as in its everyday usage, but close to the opposite. It stems from an inadequate sense of the self and its boundaries. Freud postulates a 'primary narcissism' in which the new-born exists in an amorphous world, unable to distinguish 'self' as source of need from 'other' (parents, carers) as source of gratification. Lacan theorized this as the 'imaginary', a 'condition in which we lack any defined centre of self, in which what "self" we have seems to pass into objects, and objects into it, in a ceaseless closed exchange' (Eagleton 1983).

In Freud, this imaginary unity breaks up – and the sense of a self distinct from others begins to emerge – when needs are not gratified and the infant becomes aware of itself as dependent, thus also arousing fears of abandonment, incompleteness, ungratified need. Narcissism as a pathology (secondary narcissism) occurs when the infant attempts to annul the pain of disappointed object love (frustration, lack of gratification), and its 'rage against those who do not respond immediately to its needs', attempting 'to re-establish earlier relationships by creating in his fantasies an omnipotent mother or father who merges with images of his own self' (Lasch, 1979: 36). That is to say, the individual fails to acknowledge the autonomy of others (parents, people and objects) as satisfiers of need. The narcissist is utterly self-absorbed, obsessed with the relation of every person and event to his own needs, unable, as Sennett puts it, to understand 'what belongs within the domain of the self and self-gratification and what belongs outside it' (1977: 9). The narcissist is driven by a desire for endless gratification, experience, and impulse, but with no possibility of any commitment; for any object, human or other, is desired not for its own sake but as part of the dialectic of a self strung out between omnipotence and impotence. And no object – human or other – has any real existence independent of the narcissist's fragile ego. Identifying the self alternately with 'grandiose objects' and with inner emptiness, the narcissist is 'neurotically dependent on others, especially for the maintenance of self-esteem, yet possesses insufficient autonomy to be able to communicate effectively with them . . . ' (Giddens 1991: 178).

Lacan's version develops along a different route but to the same conclusion. The infant, existing without a self in the undifferentiated world of the imaginary, sees its image in a mirror. This image shows the child as 'unified', a discrete and integral object, and thus an autonomous and whole being. This image is pleasing: the child both identifies with it as an (ideal) image of the self, yet also recognizes that it is not-I, is something alien and outside. 'As the child grows up, it will continue to make such imaginary identifications with objects, and this is how its ego will be built up. For Lacan, the ego is just this narcissistic process whereby we bolster up a fictive sense of unitary selfhood by finding something in the world with which we can identify' (Eagleton, 1983). The self is only perceived and loved from an external vantage point, through a gaze, as an object with an imaginary unity; and, for Lacan, all desire is related to the denial or confirmation of this precarious selfhood: 'narcissism envelops the forms of desire' and renders all need and desire insatiable because they are all overwhelmed by the need for one's self to be loved. Lacan, according to Harland (1987: 41) associates this kind of desire directly with consumerism: 'For western culture puts a special emphasis upon individuality and selfhood, and derives therefrom a special dynamism and drivenness. What could be more conducive to expansion and achievement and aggression than a kind of desire that nothing can ever truly satisfy?'

For Lasch and Sennett, narcissism is the pathology at the heart of a consumer society in which the boundaries between the private and the public world – like the narcissist's boundaries between the self and the other, inside and outside – are dangerously blurred. In Lasch's more conventional analysis, the public world is able to invade the private through consumerism and other forms of power because of the decline of organic bases for a strong self (above all, the decline of the patriarchal family). Consumerist concern with the self and consumerist promises of the ability to produce a desirable self merely disguise the total powerlessness of individuals and the invasion of their private world by 'forces of organized domination' to the extent that 'personal life has almost ceased to exist' (Lasch 1979: 30), and what there is is dominated by 'murderous competition for goods and position'. Capitalism, Lasch argues apropos of de Sade (1979: 69), reduces individuals to interchangeable objects that relate to each other as pure objects (things that can potentially gratify the needs of the self). In the resulting social anarchy there is nothing left but the pursuit of pleasure, but pleasure which is pure aggression. He concludes, much like Durkheim (or Rousseau), that:

> In a society that has reduced reason to mere calculation, reason can impose no limits on the pursuit of pleasure – on the immediate gratification of every desire no matter how perverse, insane, criminal, or merely immoral. For the standards that would condemn crime or cruelty derive from religion, compassion, or the kind of reason that rejects purely instrumental applications; and none of these outmoded forms of thought or feeling has any logical place in a society based on commodity production.

Sennett, on the other hand, is concerned that the obsession with the private self has taken over the public world. Rather in the vein of Riesman, he argues that the 'performative self', conformism and the pressures of social expectation are hardly new developments. At the birth of modernity and consumerism, the eighteenth-century (male) member of the bourgeois public sphere was certainly expected to perform through emulative consumption, adoption of fashionable manners, expressions and activities and so on. Figures like Smith and Hume identify the self with the ego, with the ability to carry out sociable performances in public, rather than with the content of those performances. The content could be playful, arbitrary, whimsical, inconsistent – it did not need to be authentic. He was *not* expected to believe that this public behaviour expressed, or even should express, his true self: it was a performance, and a performance carried out 'at a distance from the self'. Private and public behaviour did not call each other into question and need not coincide; they were separate issues. 'Seeming' and 'being' could live in comfortable discordance. For Sennett, it is a combination of forces – romanticism, the sanctification of bourgeois privacy and respectability, religious control over public ethics – that produces the fundamental problems of modern consumer culture, that we must really be what we seem and must appear as we really are. We must, in a word, be sincere or authentic. In the words of mid-century sociology, role-distance must be overcome by assimilating self to social role. This is a difficult or impossible task in a pluralist world and one that requires increasingly intrusive strategies for making a self which is fragmented across the social world cohere into a single, authentic story, and one accurately reflected through one's appearance back to that social world. At the very least, the demand for authenticity, launched by romanticism, entails that in everyday life we are scrutinized not only for our fashionability but also for our consistency (as a mark of our truth). The task is insupportable and unjust.

The romantic self

Romanticism, like the ideal of culture, addresses the cultural deficits of modernity, but does so through a desire for organic and integral forms of being. Performance 'at a distance from the self', a knowing split between being and seeming, was precisely what Rousseau would not suffer; it represented for him a state of inauthenticity and enslavement to social pressures. Yet, Sennett argues, it was precisely the romantic insistence that we really be what we seem, that we merge private and public, inside and outside, that makes us obsessed with the self and prey to a consumerism which constantly vaunts promises of a coherent, authentic and valued self.

In fact, romanticism and the ideal of culture have a double and ironic relation to consumer culture. On the one hand, the romantic view of culture is a critique of the material civilization which produces consumers. On the other hand, consumer culture – like the elite culture which supposedly opposes it – constantly promises precisely those values that romanticism believes were destroyed by civilization. As Colin Campbell (1989) points out, we can see this in most advertising. It is about feeling, imaginative desiring and longing, rather than reason; it is about collective values, social acceptability and identity as much as about individual choice; it tends to hide mechanism and manufacture, rather showing its products either as immaculate conceptions or as linked to a mythical history (Williamson 1978, 1979); it deploys images of the exotic, the natural, the surreal and the unconscious rather than empirical facts or rational arguments. As Raymond Williams (1980: 185) said, it is not 'sensibly materialist' but profoundly idealist, offering emotional and spiritual rather than utilitarian gratifications.

It is as if romanticism and culture, rather than rationalism and utility, furnished the language of modern consumption; a language meant to critique the cultural deficits of modernity was adopted to fill them, inauthentically. This is largely Campbell's argument: modern consumerist hedonism, as he defines it, is not about the satisfaction of need (which limits the experience of pleasure) but about the pursuit of the experience of pleasure for its own sake. This is associated with a focus on the intensification of emotional experiences, which are understood as located in the internal world of the self. In modern hedonism emotions are stimulated, incited, made into an obsession, through the use of imagination, the production of 'longing' and imaginative dissatisfaction, along the model of the day-dream. The basic motivation of modern consumers is a 'longing to experience in reality those pleasures created and enjoyed in the imagination, a longing which results in the ceaseless consumption of novelty' (Campbell 1989: 205). (There are affinities with the narcissistic personality's thirst for experiences to fill out the empty internal world of the self.)

Campbell traces this modern hedonistic ethic back to a 'romantic ethic' which has its roots in the same social classes and the same period (the middling orders of early modernity) as the Protestant ethic. If one follows the story of the Protestant ethic beyond the early seventeenth century, where Weber left it, one finds, Campbell argues, that it splits between the rationalistic Calvinist strain and a Pietism which fostered the stimulation, examination and above all the display of certain powerful emotions (for example melancholy, sympathy and benevolence, self-pity) which developed into the cult of sensibility and then romanticism. This focus on the emotions also created a link between aesthetic and moral aspects of the self. The capacity to react with strong emotions to artistic beauty or to the sublime and the picturesque in nature is a mark of moral worth, a theme we have already encountered in Hume's and Smith's grounding of morality in the imaginative capacity of 'sympathy'. The display of emotional capacities has the same status in the romantic ethic as the calling and wealth have in the Protestant ethic: a mark of moral election.

Nineteenth-century romanticism continues the association of moral worth with emotion, passion, imagination, the ideal as opposed to the factual, and above all with the self ('the Romantic is one who discovers himself as centre' (184)), not with the conscious ego of the utilitarian individual but rather with the unconscious and natural forces within the individual that constitute the authentic sources of the self. This set of valuations opposes both the emotionally restrained, calculating and status-driven consumption of the aristocracy and the self-interested hedonic calculus of utilitarianism. In the process:

> The romantic ideal of character, together with its associated theory of moral renewal through art, functioned to stimulate and legitimate that form of autonomous, self-illusory hedonism which underlies modern consumer behaviour. ... The romantic world-view provided the highest possible motives with which to justify day-dreaming, longing and the rejection of reality, together with the pursuit of originality in life and art; and by so doing, enabled pleasure to be ranked above comfort, counteracting both traditionalistic and utilitarian restraints on desire (201).

If Campbell is right, then 'culture' and 'consumer culture' are less opposed and more deeply connected than either thinks: they are connected through the romantic concern to make up for the deficits of modernity by revaluing the emotional, aesthetic and spiritual notions of the self which have no place in a utilitarian society. For many of the authors discussed here, however, it is a cure which renders the disease ever more chronic.

Culture versus society

It might be useful to conclude by looking at Daniel Bell's *The Cultural Contradictions of Capitalism* (1979). In Bell's argument culture and consumer culture are openly complicit in late capitalism and both are profoundly dysfunctional, not so much for the individual as for the social order itself: ideals of 'culture' fill in the cultural deficits of modernity but in a way that undermines the society itself. Bourgeois society, he argues, has two cultural sources. The first, the puritan work ethic, was distinctly functional: it provided a 'transcendental ethic' (21) otherwise missing from the utilitarian world, which held the unlimited and open-ended nature of economic self-interest and needs in check by emphasizing not just work but also 'the formation of *character* (sobriety, probity, work as a calling)' (81), and by subordinating the individual to the authority of society.

However, the second cultural source, familiar from our discussions of liberal-utilitarianism, 'was a secular Hobbesianism, a radical individualism which saw man as unlimited in his appetite, which was restrained in politics by a sovereign but ran fully free in economics and culture' (81). The Protestant ethic has been ravaged by mass consumption, was 'sundered from bourgeois society' and persists into the modern world only in the form of 'the crabbed, small-town mentality' obsessed with respectability. It was, instead, 'the secular Hobbesianism [which] fed the mainsprings of modernity, the ravenous hunger for unlimited experience' (21). However, hedonistic individualism cannot provide the 'transcendental ties' that arose in the work ethic; 'society fails to provide some set of "ultimate meanings" in its character structure, work, and culture' (21).

In place of 'ultimate meanings', there is now only an explosion of individual desire and self-obsession, fed by and feeding into mass consumption and gradually moving beyond matters of manners and taste to affect social structure. For mass consumption brings to everyday life something implicit in liberalism (secular Hobbesianism) and developed through romanticism: a cult of the hedonistic self, individuals defined through their desires. Modern culture takes an essentially anti-bourgeois form from early in its history in the sense that it attacks the Puritan ethic as repressive and personally stifling. The axial principle of modern culture is not restraint but rather 'the expression and remaking of the "self" in order to achieve self-realization and self-fulfilment. And in its search, there is a denial of any limits or boundaries to experience. It is a reaching out for all experience; nothing is forbidden, all is to be explored' (13). This theme dominates modernist artistic culture, is evident in the use of Freud to argue that unhappiness results from self-control and the repression of instinctual gratification, and enters everyday life through popular culture which is built around hedonism and a 'fun morality'. 'Whereas gratification of forbidden impulses traditionally aroused guilt, failure to have fun now lowers one's self-esteem' (Wolfenstein, quoted in Bell, 1979: 71).

Most authors pursuing these themes are concerned to show that this hedonistic culture is dysfunctional for the individual (it feeds off their modern insecurity) but functional for the system (it produces insatiable consumers). Bell, on the other hand, argues that it is dysfunctional for the system itself: culture and consumer culture undermine the economy and polity, for there is now a fatal contradiction 'between a social structure that is organized fundamentally in terms of roles and specialization, and a culture which is concerned with the enhancement and fulfillment of the self and the "whole" person' (14). In more lurid terms, 'In the 1950s and the 1960s, the cult of the Orgasm succeeded the cult of Mammon as the basic passion of American life' (70).

Conclusion

We have been looking at one of the most powerful and enduring themes in the study of consumer culture, an attempt to understand it as a social pathology intrinsically bound up with modernity. Modernity dismantles a stable social order which provides fixed values and identities, reducing the social to the individual, the transcendental to the calculated, the rational, the material. In these conditions, it is argued, the individual's boundaries, sources of meaning, social relations and needs become blurred and uncertain. This is the context of consumer culture: it floods modernity with a torrent of values, meanings, selves and others, both filling in the cultural deficits of the modern world and constantly intensifying and exploiting them. Underlying such a perspective is an ineradicable nostalgia or lamentation: consumer culture can never replace the world we have lost, or provide us with selves we can trust, or offer a culture in which we can be truly at home. Consumer culture comes to epitomize a sense that the sources upon which modernity draws for selves, values and solidarity are somehow wrong from the start.

4

The Culture of Commodities

Introduction

Much critique of consumer culture revolves around a brutal paradox: that
modernity's world-historical production of material abundance does not
promote happiness, or even satisfaction. Firstly, alongside the production
of wealth – indeed as its price – has come the production of obscene levels
of poverty, exploitation and insecurity, whether absolute or relative, whether
at home in the metropolis or abroad in the developing world. The second
counterpart of massive wealth, experienced even by the most privileged, is
summed up by 'alienation': this world of goods, and the world that produces
those goods, is a place in which we find it hard to be at home (even when
consumer culture is loudly promising us all manner of homes, identities,
values), over which we have little control, in which we are isolated
individuals passively facing an architectonic structure of *things* in relation to
which we can do little more creative or active than choose. Our alienation
is evident in an endless oscillation between feverish, frustrated, overstimulated and somewhat desperate desire and an utter boredom and
indifference to all these new things which are somehow always the same.

Common sense associates greater wealth with the satisfaction of needs.
Consumer culture, on the other hand, associates satisfaction with socio-
economic stagnation: there must be no end to needs. The question arises as
to who needs all these needs. The answer proposed by critiques of alienation
is that it is the system of production that requires our needs both to be
insatiable and yet always to look to commodities for their satisfaction. Hence
the core of the critical paradox of consumer culture: that a system which has
the material power to liberate humans from want and provide the basis for
human development instead subjugates them to the logic by which material
goods are produced and exchanged. 'Alienation' is a meditation on how the

modern world of goods holds dominion over the world of men and women, both in their everyday life and in the global processes which structure it.

The dialectic of consumption: subjects and objects

One way of putting all this is that modernity has introduced a massive objectivity into the world, in two senses. Firstly, more things are produced; secondly, more of social life is produced in a thing-like form ('reification'). The central issue is how, under modern social conditions, we relate to things and the thing-like nature of much social life. We can of course define the very idea of 'consumption' in exactly the same terms, as a question of object relations: consumption is a question of how human and social subjects with needs relate to things in the world which might satisfy them (material and symbolic goods, services, experiences).

To think about modern consumption in terms of the relation between subjects and objects connects it to the central philosophical preoccupations of modern western thought. And this is precisely what is at stake in the material reviewed in this chapter. Figures like Marx, Weber, Simmel, Lukács, the Frankfurt School theorists and the Situationists develop, in relation to the philosophical concern with subject–object relations, sociological propositions about modern subjectivity and structure which lead directly to theories of consumer culture. (See Miller (1987) for a lucid review of the Hegelian tradition and a powerful argument for how to use it in theorizing consumer culture.)

The entire problematic of subjects and objects in modern western thought is conventionally, if crudely, traced to Descartes' *cogito*, which sees the world in terms of, on the one hand, human subjects (a mind or consciousness which thinks, knows, believes and ascribes meanings and values to the world) and, on the other hand, objects (the world seen as 'matter in motion', as a collection of things which interact, which can be observed and grasped in the form of facts, but which are in and of themselves devoid of subjectivity, of mind or spirit, of meaning or essence).

Having split subject from object, how do humans assimilate the world of objects into their subjective experience? This idea of assimilation is very general indeed and incorporates many different kinds of relations between subjects and objects. Pre-eminently, western philosophy (epistemology) has been preoccupied with the assimilation of objects into subjective experience through a relation of 'knowledge'. How can subjects know the world of objects, how can they assimilate it intellectually, and how can they know that their knowledge is valid? However, if we think about knowledge in the practical, social forms it takes – common sense as well as science, technology, exploration, discovery and invention – we can see that assimilation can also mean the appropriation of objects by subjects in a very concrete sense. Objects are assimilated into the subjective experience of individuals – or of the collectivity, in the form of culture and production – by appropriating them to human ends. We collect, use, make, own and transform objects according to the aims, goals, desires and needs posited by human subjects. In a sense, this can be one clear meaning of consumption: we view the world and assimilate it both intellectually and practically in the light of subjective projects and desires.

This view of the world leaves subjects and objects as entirely other to and different from each other. Subjects are pure consciousness or reason, and external to nature and the material world. The latter, in turn, is emptied of mind or consciousness. This is the disenchanting or demystifying mission of modern science and reason, which empties nature of all supernatural forces and of all inherent meaning. However, this project of disenchantment is also a project of subjugation. Stripped of their own intrinsic powers and meanings, objects come to have meaning purely in terms of the uses to which they may be put by human subjects. Objects are perceived solely in terms of their 'useful properties', the utility they may possess for subjects. Hence, in liberal-utilitarian thought, 'I' – a self-defining subject – define my own needs and then go to nature and the market, the world of things and goods, to find something that satisfies my already defined desires. Such a perspective is distinctively modern, and for those who endorse it consumer culture constitutes the most dramatic practical proof of its superiority: industrial technology and rational calculation have so efficiently assimilated the objective world to subjective desires that every conceivable whim can be catered for.

While liberal modernity regards this objectification and appropriation of the world as 'other' in terms of the march of progress, others regard it as a pathological alienation of humanity from its own being and its own world. If the world has become pure object to human subjects, how can they ever be at home in it? As we have seen, the stress on organicism, integral being, one-ness with nature, on solidarity and authenticity achieved through culture, all permeate the responses to consumer culture of romanticism and the tradition of culture. Similarly, the critiques of alienation, rationalization and reification regard the split between subject and object as one that needs healing; subject and object must be reconciled and this must be accomplished through real social and historical processes.

The profoundly influential insight of Hegel, who solidified this train of thought, is that the relation between subject and object is *in reality* dialectical and interrelated, not external and mechanical. It is a relationship or process of mutual constitution of subject by object and object by subject. At the heart of this dialectic is labour or practice, the fact that human subjects actively engage with the object world, transforming, moulding and creating it through their intellectual and practical efforts. In working on the world, individuals and societies recreate it in relation to their needs and projects. Their needs – their subjectivity, their meanings *for* the world – are 'objectivated', take material form, in the objects they produce. The object world is human subjectivity made manifest by remaking the world in its own lights. However, in contrast to non-dialectical (roughly speaking liberal and positivist) views, humans do not simply transform or use objects according to their self-defined needs. Rather, the world they have made is indeed objective and becomes the new environment in which they live, by which their subjective experiences are formed and constrained and in which they define and refine their needs, desires, projects and plans. The world they have made is a world they have to know and appropriate, but also one that determines them as subjects who know and appropriate. In transforming the world, we transform ourselves.

In this tradition, consumption cannot be reduced to 'subjects using objects', because the two are not independent but integrally linked, whether they are aware of it or not. The world of things is really culture in its objective form, it is the form that humans have given the world through their mental and material practices; at the same time, human needs themselves evolve and take shape through the kinds of things available. From this perspective consumption is the process 'by which society reappropriates its own external form – that is, assimilates its own culture and uses it to develop itself as a social subject' (Miller, 1987: 17).

Differentiation and refinement

From this perspective arise two central themes which are decisive for looking at consumer culture. The first point is that human nature – needs, ways of knowing and doing, consciousness – is not fixed but develops in line with the objectivated world it has created. Above all, as human-made 'nature' gets more complex and differentiated, so does human subjectivity. It has to assimilate a more complex environment through increasingly complex knowledges and needs. At the most obvious level, my knowledges and needs will be altogether different depending on whether I am dealing with an environment in which I hunt and gather (I construct the world into edible versus inedible, dangerous versus easy prey, in relation to the need of hunger) or an environment in which I can eat out or have a take-away, microwave a prepared meal, insist on organic ingredients and so on. The point is that I do not simply have more options for satisfying the same need (hunger); I have vastly more needs.

Hegel, Marx and Simmel all associate human progress with this dialectical relation between the increasing differentiation of the objective world and the refinement of subjective experience. Indeed, for this reason, Marx places the concept of need at the centre of his work, particularly of his early *Economic and Philosophical Manuscripts*. Firstly, the authentic human being towards which Marxian social theory strives is the one who is 'rich in needs'. The truly 'rich man' is not the possessor of money wealth but 'the man in need of a totality of vital human expression' (Marx 1975: 355) and for whom praxis has become a richly differentiated process of self-development. Secondly, the development of a richness of needs depends on the development of objective culture, for 'only through the objectively unfolded wealth of human nature can the wealth of subjective *human* sensitivity . . . be either cultivated or created' (353). Capitalism is a progressive force for Marx precisely in so far as it explosively develops the technical forces (industry) that can produce a material basis for people who are 'rich in needs' (though in its present alienated form it merely supports a few 'rich men' and lot of very poor ones).

Distance and alienation

The second theme is the problem of alienation. In order to assimilate this objective world into subjective experience we must be able to recognize that world as indeed having been *made by us*. If we do not recognize it as the product of human labour (mental and material) we see it as literally alien, as a natural environment that is beyond our control – which is how the world of objects appears, for example, in Cartesian dualism, positivist science and liberal economics. We lose the connection – and control over the connection – between the transformation of objects and the transformation of ourselves. This is the state of 'unhappy consciousness', as Hegel calls it, and it is a state into which human history periodically plunges. Indeed, this provides the narrative pulse of the Hegelian philosophy of history: an oscillation between recognition and distance, between self-determination through knowing transformation of the world and domination by objects and objectified social processes.

Modernity can appear as the height of 'rich' differentiation but also of distance and alienation. The object world of consumer culture, for example, seems to demand astonishing refinement and differentiation of needs and subjectivity but generally in the form of merely *choosing* among given objects: individuals are unable to recognize these objects as the products of their own labour and therefore as externalizations of their own subjectivity. They can *choose* between pleasurable things but cannot *assimilate* them into a process of self-development. The industrial transformative powers of modern society, Marx argues, should be 'the *open* book of the essential powers of man, man's psychology present in tangible form'; instead, all the things of consumer culture appear in estranged form, as merely '*sensuous, alien, useful objects*' (1975: 354).

The same themes can be pursued through the work of Simmel, who views modernity (and at times life itself) through a pervasive and intensifying contradiction between objective and subjective culture (Frisby 1988; Miller 1987; Simmel 1950, 1990, 1991a (1896), 1991b (1896); Turner 1986). Simmel argues that the production of objective culture has far outstripped our capacity to integrate it subjectively within our personal and social development. He too associates modern productivity with increasing differentiation of goods and increasing refinement and discrimination in tastes, needs and experiences. Indeed, the intense fragmentation and monotony of the industrial division of labour and specialization on which productivity depends is compensated for and complemented by 'consumption and enjoyment through the growing pressure of heterogenous impressions, and the ever faster and more colourful change of excitements . . . the many stimuli . . . are the ways in which the human soul . . . seeks to come alive' (Simmel 1991a (1896): 120). However, in modernity – especially in the city, in the metropolitan experience which he takes as emblematic of modernity – our capacity for assimilating this richness is strained to a breaking point defined on the one hand by 'neurasthenia' and on the other by the 'blasé attitude'. The individual is confronted with a bewildering sensorium of ever changing stimuli, which produces a nervousness, restlessness and unease. At the same time the individual defends against this deluge by a countervailing response, the blasé attitude, in which a psychological cut-off point triggers a general indifference and a sense that all this variety is somehow all the same. In a final twist, however, it is precisely this exhaustion that prompts the individual to demand ever greater stimulation in order to overcome indifference.

In the broadest philosophical terms, then, the contradiction between abundance and dissatisfaction that consumer culture can so dramatically produce arises from the conflict between refinement and alienation, differentiation and distance, as society produces an increasingly complex world which it cannot internalize as its own creation. Consumer culture, however materially rich or poor and whatever it produces, is therefore intrinsically an instance of the 'unhappy consciousness'. And, unlike liberal thought but in many ways like romanticism and the tradition of culture, the entire aim of this perspective (certainly in Marx's work) is to reconcile subjects and objects, not just in philosophy but in history and practice.

Commodity culture

Alienated labour

Marx's whole work is a meditation on the unhappy consciousness peculiar
to capitalism and a rigorous effort to see how this unhappiness is sustained
in and through practical, social life. The dialectic of subject and object
presumes that production and consumption, the mutual construction of the
environment by humans and of humans by their environment, should be
organically and transparently related. The unhappy consciousness arises
when production and consumption become separate processes, as in
consumer culture.

The basic outlines of Marx's account of this separation are clear. Under
capitalist social relations, people do not produce directly for their own needs.
Having been deprived, by various social developments, of ownership of or
control over the means of production, they must submit to wage-labour in
order to gain the money to purchase consumption goods on the market. This
is a process of commodification. Primarily, there is the commodification of
labour, of people's transformative capacity (in the Hegelian tradition their
very essence) in the form of 'labour-power'. People's creative relation to the
material world becomes something to be sold – literally alienated – on the
market-place.

This means, firstly, that labour no longer represents a qualitatively rich
and substantive relation to the world and one's needs (using one's skills to
make this or that), but rather something entirely abstract and formal: I sell
my capacity to labour *in general* (indeed I sell a quantity of abstract labouring
time) for a sum of money. My labour-power has no particular qualities *for
me* and I do not even use it to produce the specific things I need. Rather,
I sell my labour-power and produce goods I do not need in order to get the
cash to buy goods I need but did not produce. Being unrelated to my own
transformative work on the world, these goods must appear to me as alien
and objective, as is my own labour.

Secondly, the sale of labour-power is not an exchange between two equal
parties. Though formally free to dispose of my precious commodity, I am
actually compelled to do so in order to obtain the very means of existence
– cash to buy commodities. And in selling my labour-power, I surrender
control over it. I am entirely at the disposal of the capitalist and am integrated
as a cog in the wheels of productive forces: technology, systematic
organization, rationalized discipline. As part of a technical division of labour
my praxis is fragmented into meaningless acts (screw in that bolt, fill in that
form) whose relation to the final product is opaque to me. I cannot relate

to the product of combined labour from the point of view of my very fragmented place within it. This fragmentation and alienation is intensified by the division of labour between head and hand, mental and manual labour. Consciousness and control are structurally separated from work.

Given that, in this tradition, creative labour is the human essence or 'species-being', work should be an end in itself, the satisfaction of the intrinsic human drive to fashion the objective world. Alienated labour, however, is 'a mere means to satisfy needs outside itself' (Marx 1975: 326). 'The result is that man (the worker) feels that he is acting freely only in his animal functions – eating, drinking and procreating, or at most in his dwelling and adornment – while in his human functions [i.e. labour] he is nothing more than an animal' (327). When labour is alienated as a commodity, consumption is split from production, labour from its objects, and both sides take on estranged forms.

Thirdly, separation from the means of production produces class exploitation. The price for which I sell my labour-power is not related to the value it produces. The difference is profit. When selling their labour-power, workers reproduce a social relationship that is of its essence exploitative. Moreover, as we shall see in chapter 7, Marx argues that it is structurally impossible for the combined wages of the working class to purchase all the value – all the goods – that it has produced. In the philosophical terms of alienation, subjects cannot assimilate objects into their everyday life in the very simple but outrageous sense that most of them cannot afford to buy and use what they have made. My alienated labour, used by others to produce wealth, produces my own poverty and reduces my needs to 'basic needs', needs below the level of refinement, discrimination and self-development of which I could be capable given the bounteous potential of modern technological power.

All this defines a state of alienation. I relate to myself and my labour, to the products of my labour and to other people abstractly and as entirely 'other' to me. In a very strong sense, I become a consumer the moment I become a worker, for my subjection to commodities is intrinsically bound up with having myself become a commodity in the form of labour-power. Commodified labour produces commodities, things that are produced for sale and therefore for consumption by someone other than the person whose labour produced it. Instead of being organically and transparently linked within praxis, the relation between production and consumption is indirect and mediated through markets, money, prices, competition and profit – the whole apparatus of commodity exchange. This separation is reflected in the very form of the commodity as Marx defines it, a form comprising 'use-value' and 'exchange-value'.

Marx argues that *every* society must allocate its scarce resources of labour and materials in such a way as to produce the specific things it needs in order to reproduce itself. For an economy to continue from one year to the next, for human bodies and human cultures to survive over time, particular things with specific qualities must be made in sufficient quantities: enough wheat or rice, enough skilled workers, enough women to manage domestic reproduction, enough cars to get labour and materials to work. These 'things' are 'use-values': they are the substantive side of economy and culture.

The need for particular use-values is as pressing in capitalist society as in any other, but it is mediated rather than direct. Instead of people directly producing the use-values they need (and thus being simultaneously producers and consumers), capitalists enter production and buy labour-power in order to make profits and accumulate the capital necessary to produce on an ever expanding scale. Marx's capitalists are economic amoralists in precisely the sense we used in chapter 2: they are utterly indifferent to the specific use-values they produce, be they heroin or hospitals, so long as they can be sold on the market, realize 'exchange-value' and be changed back from specific things into money, the 'general form of wealth'. The capitalist economy is therefore radically formal and disembedded with respect to the substantive world of use-value.

This is definitely not to say that use-value and need become irrelevant to capitalists. Quite the contrary. For them to realize exchange value, their goods must possess a use-value for someone – indeed must possess use-value for enough people with enough purchasing power to buy up their output at a decent price. The point, however, is that use-value is not an end in itself but merely the means and necessary condition for the capitalist's goal of securing a profit. More precisely, human need has become an inconvenient and unpredictable but necessary condition for moving from one quantity of capital to a larger one (Marx's famous M-C-M′). The relation between needs and goods, between subjects and objects, is not part of a dialectic of self-development but an object of calculation and exploitation.

Alienated needs

Marx penned some of the most powerful hymns of praise to capitalist modernization ever written. This praise is based on the kinds of social potentialities for future happiness that are built up in the belly of the capitalist beast: above all, the socialization of production (through both the division and the concentration of labour) and the development of technical forces of production (machinery, scientific knowledge, industrial organization). Competition between capitalists inevitably sends them on a forced march towards the abolition of scarcity, control over the material world and therefore a potential intensification of the dialectical development of subjects and objects. The whole process may be driven by the thirst for abstract exchange value, but it fundamentally depends on use-value (all these things need to be *sold*). Therefore the productive apparatus that produces this astonishing expansion of objective culture

> requires the production of new consumption ... The exploration of the earth in all directions, to discover new things of use as well as new useful qualities of the old ... the development, hence, of the natural sciences to their highest point; likewise the discovery, creation and satisfaction of new needs arising from society itself; the cultivation of all the qualities of the social human being, production of the same in a form as rich as possible in needs, because rich in qualities and relations – production of this being as the most total and universal possible social product, for, in order to take gratification in a many-sided way, he must be capable of many pleasures, hence cultured to a high degree – is likewise a condition of production founded on capital. ... a constantly expanding and more comprehensive system of different kinds of labour ... to which a constantly expanding and constantly enriched system of needs corresponds (Marx 1973: 408).

One point to be drawn from this peroration is that by the force of its inner logic, capitalism must drive society out of the realm of nature and natural necessity and into (the possibility of) culture. The enrichment of needs and use-values, the creation of people 'rich in needs' represents a state in which 'natural necessity in its direct form has disappeared; because a historically created need has taken the place of the natural one' (1973: 325). A person who is 'rich in needs' is the subject of human culture rather than the object of natural necessities, one driven by basic ('animal') wants. The titanic productivity of modern capitalism, whose 'ceaseless striving towards the general form of wealth drives labour beyond the limits of its natural paltriness' (325), will reduce to a minimum the 'realm of necessity' – the subjugation to basic needs, the need to 'wrestle with Nature to satisfy his want, to maintain and reproduce life' (Marx 1959: 820). And 'beyond [the realm of necessity] begins that development of human energy which is an end in itself, the true realm of freedom ... '

However, the Moses of capitalism will never reach this promised land of freedom. The exploitative relations on which the refinement of both productive forces and human needs is being accomplished ensures that the 'system of needs' is inherently warped. Needs themselves become abstract: since the development and satisfaction of needs depends on access to commodities, the only real need is the need for money, the abstract form of wealth. The needs of those who *have* money are not ends in themselves but merely a means by which capitalists realize exchange value. Their needs simply constitute effective market demand and an incitement to the capitalist to produce more needs, not in the interest of humane development of a rich individuality but simply with a view to extracting more money from rich individuals. Marx's opinion of this relationship is worth quoting at length:

> We have seen what significance the wealth of human needs has, on the presupposition of socialism . . . A fresh confirmation of human powers and a fresh enrichment of human nature. Under the system of private property their significance is reversed. Each person speculates on creating a new need in the other, with the aim of forcing him to make a new sacrifice, placing him in a new dependence and seducing him into a new kind of enjoyment and hence into economic ruin, each attempts to establish over the other an alien power, in the hope of thereby achieving satisfaction of his own selfish needs. With the mass of objects grows the realm of alien powers to which man is subjected, and each new product is a new potentiality of mutual fraud and mutual pillage. Man becomes ever poorer as a man, and needs ever more money if he is to achieve mastery over the hostile being. . . . The need for money is . . . the real need created by the modern economic system, and the need it creates . . . Lack of moderation and intemperance become its true standard. Subjectively this is manifested partly in the fact that the expansion of production and needs becomes the inventive and ever calculating slave of inhuman, refined, unnatural and imaginary appetites – for private property does not know how to transform crude need into human need. Its idealism is fantasy, caprice and infatuation. No eunuch flatters its despot more basely or uses more infamous means to revive his flagging capacity for pleasure, in order to win a surreptitious favour for himself, than does the eunuch of industry, the manufacturer, in order to sneak himself a silver penny or two or coax the gold from the pocket of his dearly beloved neighbour. (Every product is a bait with which to entice the essence of the other, his money. Every real or potential need is a weakness which will tempt the fly onto the lime-twig.) (1975: 358)

So much for consumer culture. On the other hand, for those *without* money – the proletariat who produce the goods – the proceeds of their sale of labour-power cannot sustain any such 'refinement'. In fact, it can only fund a style of life below the level of animal needs, let alone the realm of necessity:

> the refinement of needs and of the means of fulfilling them gives rise to a bestial degeneration and a complete, crude and abstract simplicity of need . . . Even the need for fresh air ceases to be a need for the worker. . . . Light, air, etc. – the simplest *animal* cleanliness – ceases to be a need for man . . . It is not only human needs which man lacks – even his *animal* needs cease to exist. The Irishman [at the time of the famine] has only one need left – the need to *eat*, to eat *potatoes*, and more precisely, to eat *rotten potatoes*, the worst kind of potatoes (1975: 359).

Obviously, an analysis of working-class consumption in terms of absolute immiseration has not looked particularly plausible to later theorists of the 'affluent society' and of the Fordist high-wage, high-productivity economy. The earlier quote looks rather more promising. What is nevertheless powerful in this aspect of Marx's work is the connection *between* the two quotes. Both the exploitation of needs and the exploitation of labour (at whatever level of poverty), both the cunning by which desires are stimulated and the injustices by which they cannot be satisfied, are for him aspects of the same process of alienation in which 'the multiplication of needs and of the means of fulfilling them gives rise to a lack of needs and of means' (1975: 360). Thus, Marx argues against Malthus, who advocates greater luxury consumption in order to balance the capitalist books, and against Say and Ricardo, who advocate thrift that the latter

> refuse to admit that production is regulated by caprice and fancy; they forget the 'refined needs' and forget that without consumption there can be no production; they forget that through competition production inevitably becomes more extensive and more luxurious; they forget that it is use which determines the value of a thing, and that it is fashion which determines use; they want only 'useful things' to be produced, but they forget that the production of too many useful things produces too many *useless* people [i.e. unemployment]. Both sides forget that prodigality and thrift, luxury and privation, wealth and poverty are equal (1975: 361–2).

Commodity fetishism

At the centre of the critique of alienation is the problem of recognition and distance. Can we recognize as our own the world we have made? It is unsurprising therefore that Marx was at times preoccupied with 'modes of representation'. How are social relations and commodities represented? How do they appear to modern social subjects in everyday life and in the realm of thought? How are they made to appear alien and 'other' to us? The broad framework for these preoccupations is the theory of ideology; a more specific analysis emerges from Marx's critique of commodity fetishism.

In many respects, Marx's famous chapter on commodity fetishism had a rather narrow aim, to offer a critique of contemporary political economists and to explain how they could get things so wrong. Basically, political economists confined themselves to analysing the immediately visible appearance of an already alienated world, to observing the behaviour of its alienated objects as if they represented the truth of society. They observed the market-place, in which commodities already circulate independently of the labour which produced them. If we look only at the market, commodities appear to have value in relation to each other (or in relation to money, which abstractly represents all commodities). The true source of their value – human labour – is not visible. We therefore perceive value in 'the fantastic form' (Marx 1976: 165) (or 'the phantasmagoric form', Rose 1978: 47) of a relation between things rather than as arising from relations between people (relations of production: labour, wage-relations, structural class divisions). In doing so, we replicate the alienation that constitutes the world of objects in the first place, as well as the forms it takes (the commodity-form, wage-labour, capital). We perceive them as forces beyond human making or changing, as frozen into static, ahistorical forms, as natural rather than socially produced. The fantastic form taken by value 'transforms every product of labour into a social hieroglyphic', which people then have to decipher in order 'to get behind the secret of their own social product' (Marx 1976: 167). The process is 'fetishistic' because – as in the case of religion, which (in Feuerbach or Durkheim) involves the projection or externalization of human powers and social values onto the image of an independent 'God' or totem – the object-world is endowed with intrinsic powers, properties, values and meanings.

This train of thought is developed from a critique of political economy into a general account of commodity culture along a number of interrelated lines (including the concept of 'reification' to be discussed later). Firstly, the idea of commodity fetishism can be extended so that not only does economic exchange-value appear to be a natural property of the thing itself, but so too may a whole range of social and cultural values. This is the natural mode of representation in, say, advertising, which depicts a car not as a social product of human labour endowed with sensuous properties that are of use to people's practical life, but rather as something naturally endowed with masculinity, excitement, status and modernity, which is endowed with the power to confer these qualities onto its consumer, but which is accessible only through the mystical and abstract relations of buying and owning (the magical mediation of money) rather than through the organic relations of doing and making (through praxis). As we shall see in the next chapter, semiotic theory could be considered a methodology for investigating precisely this process (for example, Barthes's investigations of ideology and 'mythologization' by which arbitrary cultural values are fetishistically transformed into natural ones).

As Richards (1991: 66) argues, a figure like Adam Smith regards the commodity as purely a neutral form or 'featureless channel of exchange, and separates the cultural and economic worlds into entirely different realms' (67). As we have seen, the substantive cultural form of individual commodities is irrelevant to him. With Marx, we begin to see in the commodity structural and practical possibilities for transforming the entire way the world appears, both the outer world of things and the inner world of needs. Richards himself traces the ways in which, over the nineteenth century, through exhibitions and advertising, through modes of displaying things, the commodity-form develops 'forms of representation', along the lines of fetishism, for the presentation of objects as mystical, as independent things endowed with life and as apparently objective. This is very much in line with the work of Walter Benjamin, much of which centres precisely on the re-enchantment of the modern scientific and industrial world through the magical properties of alienated things.

W. F. Haug (1986) produced a more conventionally Marxist account of this process. As we have seen, the sale of alienated goods through market exchange depends on the buyer's self-acknowledged need for the good in question: use-value is a necessary, if not sufficient, condition of sale. However, at the moment of exchange, the commodity is not yet a use-value to the consumer: it is still a promise of certain satisfactions yet to be experienced. It is the promise of use-value that is sold, and this promise is established through the commodity's appearance. Haug therefore investigates the development of 'commodity aesthetics' – the representation of the commodity's promise not only through advertising, but through salesmanship, brand names, design, packaging and display – all those elements of the product's appearance through which it promises satisfactions. The production of the appearance of use-value has become a specialist technology within advanced capitalism, an alienated one in that it develops its commodity aesthetics, the commodity's 'second skin', independently of the commodity's material body. The commodity aesthetic is, moreover, rigorously subordinated to 'the valorization standpoint' in that every aspect of the commodity's appearance is calculated in relation to increasing sales. Later theories recognize the extent to which this 'second skin' is designed into the body of the commodity and governs decisions about what goods to produce and how they should function, as well as about their appearance. For example, Wernick (1991) argues that modern objects are produced as 'promotional objects' or 'commodity-signs': they are designed so as to be simultaneously both objects and advertisements, use-values and promotional tools for their own sale, advertisements for themselves. The logic of promotion has invaded the production process and the product to such an extent that 'the promotion of mass-produced consumer goods transfigures what it ostensibly helps only to sell' (18). Modern commerce has in a sense itself been transfigured into a science of fetishization or, in Haug's terms, a 'technocracy of sensuality', a 'domination over people that is effected through their fascination with technically produced appearances' (Haug 1986: 45).

A second theme: commodity fetishism and the modes of representation developed around the commodity-form work a fundamental mystification into modern life in that people mistake the appearances of society for its reality or essence. This 'false consciousness', it is argued, has political as well as intellectual consequences. People are mistaken about the social conditions that determine their existence and therefore falsely identify their real material interests with the market and commodities, with consumption and the quantitative standard of living. Judith Williamson (1978), to give but one example, argues in the case of advertising that

> in our society, while the real distinctions between people are created by their role in the *process* of production, as workers, it is the *products* of their own work that are used, in the false categories invoked by advertising, to obscure the real structure of society by replacing class with the distinctions made by the consumption of particular goods. Thus instead of being identified by what they produce, people are made to identify themselves with what they consume ... The fundamental differences in our society are still class differences, but use of manufactured goods as a means of *creating* classes or groups forms an overlay on them. This overlay is ideology (13).

Consumer culture is false in a double sense. As in 'false consciousness', it is untruth or misrecognition of social relations (as in the Althusserian formulations which Williamson relies upon); and it consists of 'fantastic' or 'phantasmagoric' forms – the social relations depicted in advertisements exist (only) in and through cultural images, the modes through which the commodity is represented, unlike class, which has a structural and material reality.

Thirdly, Marxist theory (though Simmel too) has been crucially concerned with the relation between the particular and the general, fragment and totality, social moments and the social whole. Commodity fetishism as a mode of representation presents capitalist modernity as fragmentary and fissiparous, a welter of individual experiences, actions, items. Commodity exchange breaks down social experience into minute and discrete calculations and into calculating (and competing) individuals; it abstracts all social phenomena from their substantive context, transforming them into movable, transformable, alienable objects; the imperatives of the cash nexus dissolve all social ties so that 'all that is solid melts into air'. This appearance of fragmentation and flux, of modern experience as 'the fleeting, the ephemeral and the transitory', is both exciting and terrifying (Berman 1983) and a major stimulus to modernist aesthetic practices. Thus, Baudelaire's *flâneur* who 'goes botanising on the asphalt' (i.e. observing, visually consuming the myriad variety of the modern street and crowd) becomes a metaphor for the modern consumer in Benjamin's work: all of modern social experience is in some respect reduced to the 'consumption' of chance, isolated events much like the commodity, which when fetishized seems to come from nowhere in particular and is experienced through a predominantly aesthetic mode as surface or appearance without depth or historicity (see Bauman 1993; Benjamin 1989; Buck-Morss 1989; Frisby 1988).

Yet a major impetus behind this theoretical modernism (as documented in the cases of Simmel, Kracauer and Benjamin by Frisby (1988)) has been to relate the fragmentary appearance of consumer and popular culture back to the underlying forces that generate it, to place the fragments back into an analytical (or dialectical) totality. A major resource for this project comes back to commodity fetishism as a mode of representation: modern capitalism involves the extension not of real diversity but rather of a single dominating form, the commodity form, which renders all diversity *equivalent*, that is to say all equal as discrete exchangeable or calculable objects. Hence Benjamin's stress on the Nietzschean theme of the 'eternal return of the ever-same'. Hence, too, part of Simmel's stress on the blasé attitude as a defence against overstimulation. The theorist's job is to unearth the unchanging pattern beneath the constantly renewed 'brand newness' of consumerism. This is the force of Benjamin's notion of the dialectical image: the attempt to see, against the grain of commodity fetishism, the totality of capitalist social relations as they are filtered through each of its commodified fragments. (And it is this stress on totality and on explanation that makes it rather hard to swallow the attempted recuperation of figures like Simmel and Benjamin by contemporary postmodernism.)

Alienation and romanticism

If we take the Hegelian origins of Marx's critique of alienation and commodity fetishism seriously, then a society that reduces human praxis to the commodity 'labour-power' must represent a tragic fall from grace. And the resulting consumer – one who chooses amongst a selection of ready-made objects and who acts on that choice through a disposal of abstract quantities of money rather than through concrete acts of making and doing – must represent for Marxism a profound brutalization and indignity of the person, however ostensibly affluent the individual. Consumer culture marks a closure of their capacity for human development. Stunted human subjects confront overpowering objects. Yet this is what capitalism produces as its fundamental principle: by virtue of the separation of workers from the means of production and the consequent reduction of labour to a commodity, capitalism necessarily produces these *consumers*. They may be poor or rich, but their capacity to transform the world has become a mere means to the end of buying goods; whereas their own needs and desires, the basis of their relation to the world, have become a mere condition for the making of profit.

This entire tradition traces the fall from grace and seeks out forms of theory and practice by which a new and even better state of grace can emerge out of the carcass of capitalism. The state of grace is represented by the reconciliation of subject and object. In sociological terms, it is represented by a direct, immediate and transparent relation between production and consumption, humans in society producing directly for their own needs and using this capacity to develop ever richer needs and things. Such a hope is inscribed in the ideas of use-value and 'concrete labour', concepts that stand for a kind of natural relation between human and nature, the use of concrete skills to transform objects with specific properties into things which serve particular needs that are experienced organically, as their own, by individuals.

There is a powerful romanticism at work here, very closely related to the attacks on formally abstract, utilitarian society, which we looked at in the last chapter, a stress on organicism, unity, authenticity and integral being in opposition to separation and to analytical and calculating objectivity, a stress on the substantive values lost or buried in a formally rational world (see also Miller 1987: 32). Indeed, Marx, like many critics of culture, sometimes explicitly romanticizes premodern and post-capitalist societies as worlds governed by use-value and concrete labour (craftsmanship rather than industrial manufacture), as worlds not governed by the cash nexus and made abstract by economic value. Primitive peoples, peasants and craftsmen (the myth goes) transform materials in direct relation to their needs, unmediated by market exchange. The non-modern world, as Marx (unlike conservatives and romantic reactionaries) clearly recognizes, is a world of material scarcity, and it is therefore also limited, and governed by its own forms of oppression, injustice and expropriation. But it is not *alienated*.

Moreover, in contrast to the organicism of pre- and post-capitalist society, capitalism is for Marx *totally* alienated and *entirely* governed by abstraction, formal rationality and calculation. As a basis for constructing a theory of consumer culture, it falls prey to the same problems we investigated in the debate between Polanyi and liberal economics. Was the premodern so utterly substantive and embedded? Is the modern so entirely formal and disembedded? (See, for example, Godelier 1986.)

Finally, the entire romance of reconciliation is founded on the notion of labour (as opposed to 'culture'). This can appear deeply problematic. As Baudrillard (1975) argues in *The Mirror of Production*, Marx's hopes are pinned on precisely that human aspect which modern society itself most desperately fetishizes. It may very well be transformed labour that Marx desires for us, but it is still the labour of transformation, the capacity to turn the world into objects of utility, which defines our essence for him. Baudrillard himself offers an equally romantic basis for the reconciliation of subject and object ('symbolic exchange'), but the point is well taken that by making labour fundamental Marx is still bound up with that same relation of *mastery* of subject over object that most clearly characterizes industrial and rationalizing modernity. This same point also takes us (but not Baudrillard) back to feminist critiques of mainstream economics, for the labour that concerns Marx is *productive* labour rather than *reproductive* labour: for all the talk about 'social relations' or 'relations between men', the heart of his concern is the relation between subject and object, culture and nature, *men* and *things*.

Rationalization and reification

Much of the subsequent development of western Marxism, and certainly its engagement with consumer culture, has involved extending and generalizing the model of commodity fetishism. This has proceeded along two interrelated paths. Firstly, an argument that, because the commodity form has spread to all aspects of social life, the model of commodity fetishism can be generalized into an account of capitalist culture and consciousness in general, from the everyday to the philosophical. Secondly, an argument that the modern world is increasingly dominated by rationalization and instrumental rationality and that this orientation reduces both people and things to the status of manipulable, calculable objects (cf. Ritzer (1993) for an interesting application of this perspective to consumer industries). This theme entered the tradition through the influence of Weber and Simmel, particularly on Lukács: he used the term 'reification' to synthesize the two themes into an image of capitalism that moves beyond the alienation of labour to the generalized production of a world that is systematically constituted as objective, natural and independent of human action, and which comes to regulate human life as an all-encompassing power.

Rationalization

Weber and Simmel were both concerned that modernity is increasingly characterized by formal and objectifying systems of administration, control and calculation, by quantification, methodicity and rules. At its most general level, the idea that social life is governed not by individual whims and subjective impulses but rather by formal, impersonal calculation is obviously related to the idea of objectification and alienation. For example, a bureaucracy is an organization made up of individual actions, but it takes the form of something objective and implacable in which the impersonal nature of rules and law takes on the appearance of laws of nature. Weber's specific emphasis is on the way in which methodical calculation of the world takes the form of instrumental rationality, in which everything can be treated as a calculable object rather than as a meaningful, intrinsically valued subject. In the hands of Adorno and Marcuse, this becomes an account of modern social life as an 'administered world': as we shall see, mass and consumer culture have an instrumental relation to individuals, an impetus to integrate them functionally as elements within a system. The marketing of consumer goods and cultural products involves, as Marx argued, treating people's needs as means to ends, and the concept of rationalization can shed light on the way in which this is carried out by, for example, target marketing, the quantification of need through market research and the overcoming of consumer resistance by advertising. Consumer culture then fits into a general image of modernity in which domination is effected through rational planning rather than through arbitrary power: 'domination is transfigured into administration' (Marcuse 1964: 39). For example, in the work of the non-Marxist Galbraith, technocratic corporations have as their main aim the reduction of market uncertainty and therefore the elimination of such risky elements as competition (through monopoly power) and insufficient demand (through advertising and marketing). In a dystopic realization of Saint-Simon's hopes for industrial society, the rational administration of things comes to include the rational administration of people.

In Simmel, the idea of rationalization is bound up with the extension of 'objective culture' in modern society; this in turn is – at least in *The Philosophy of Money* – clearly to be accounted for through monetarization and the generalization of exchange which promotes impersonality in social relations, objective interdependence, calculation and the 'intellectualization' of everyday life. The objectivity of the modern world comprises treating the contents of that world as objects: impersonal, calculable and law-like in their social circulation. This is not a purely negative development for Simmel. Following a rather Smithian argument, commerce is capable of linking people into prosperous interdependence; at the same time, it also offers 'wide scope to individuality and the feeling of personal independence' because of the impersonality of money, its indifference to individuals (and to moral and ethical rules) (Simmel 1991b (1896): 21). All of these features are due to the abstraction of money, whereby it reduces all qualities to equivalence and promotes quantitative calculation and 'the necessity for continuous mathematical operations in everyday life. The life of many people is filled out with . . . reducing of qualitative values to quantitative ones. This certainly contributes to the rational, calculating nature of modern times against the more impulsive, holistic, emotional character of earlier epochs' (28).

Lukács

Lukács, in this respect more closely aligned with Simmel than with Weber, treats rationalization as a product of the dominance of commodity relations. In line with Marx's early writings (which he could not have read when he wrote 'Reification and the consciousness of the proletariat'), Lukács starts from the premise that the objectification of the products of people's labour (their material and intellectual culture) arises from the objectification of that labour as a commodity. Specifically, Lukács is concerned with the intensive calculation and rationalization of that labour-power once it has been sold and neither labour nor its product is under the worker's control: 'a man's activity becomes estranged from himself, it turns into a commodity which, subject to the non-human objectivity of the natural laws of society, must go its own way independently of man just like any consumer article' (Lukács 1971: 87). The estrangement and objectivity of labour are intensified by the systems of rational planning and administration that gather steam under advanced capitalism. The scientific rationalization of the labour process – as, for example, in Taylorism, which so preoccupied the inter-war left (Trotsky, Lenin, Gramsci) – produces an ever more intensely calculated division of labour, in which the human must conform to the laws of a mechanical system that is 'already pre-existing and self-sufficient', that 'functions independently of him' (90). Workers appear as 'mere sources of error' in relation to an autonomous technical logic of production.

Rationalization of the work process reduces the person to an 'isolated particle in an alien system' of production, and 'destroys those bonds that had bound individuals to a community in the days when production was still "organic". In this respect, too, mechanisation makes of them isolated abstract atoms whose work no longer brings them together directly and organically ... ' (90). Reification, like alienation in Marx, is a destruction of the transparent social and object relations that typified pre-capitalist modes (however brutal Lukács acknowledges them to have been). Thus, under a regime which mediates all needs through commodity exchange,

> consumer articles no longer appear as the products of an organic process within a community (as for example in a village community). They now appear, on the one hand, as abstract members of a species identical by definition with its other members and, on the other hand, as isolated objects the possession or non-possession of which depends on rational calculations (91).

Lukács thus echoes the very early Marx for whom capitalism transforms social relations from a situation in which people *are* by virtue of what they *do* into one in which they simply *have* or do not have.

The rationalization of industrial labour is central to reification, but it is only one part of a general rationalization of society, of the production of that fixed, stable, predictable universe of calculation which capitalism needs to inhabit and which characterizes modernity in general. Thus, for example, law and bureaucracy, just like production, must be 'rigid, static and fixed' in order to allow for 'exact calculation'. On the basis of fetishism, society takes on a law-like character – money and power circulate through the economy and polity in predictable ways according to 'laws' (of value, of political action and so on), which can be discovered and calculated by people in their pursuit of self-interest but which are no longer perceived as being the results of their labour or interaction, which are no longer seen as social rather than natural and which are no longer, therefore, perceived as alterable by collective action.

Consequently, everyday life, work and leisure (as well as high and philosophical culture) in the reified capitalist world are all characterized by the same 'contemplative', rather than active or creative, attitude to the world: by observation and calculation of the social order unconnected to a sense of action to change that order, to a sense of its historicity. Calculation, for example, is contemplative in that 'the essence of rational calculation is based ultimately upon the recognition and the inclusion in one's calculations of the inevitable chain of cause and effect in certain events – independently of individual "caprice" ' (98). The sense of inevitability arises from the objectification of human practice in a law-like social world. One lives within the social order as if it were a natural environment rather than one produced by human action. One can only contemplate this objective nature: observe given laws, functionally conform to them or calculate within their framework in order to further one's self-interest.

Modern capitalism, then, transforms all objects into commodities which are viewed contemplatively, appropriated through possession rather than praxis. So, too, all the qualities and capacities for acting or feeling that a human possesses 'are no longer an organic part of his personality, they are things which he can "own" or "dispose of" like the various objects of the external world' (100). Consumer culture – a contemplative attitude based on having rather than doing or making or being – arises directly from the rationalization of the life world under the impetus of capitalist economic relations.

Marcuse

Precisely because these authors so fundamentally believe that human development depends on the recognition of the objective world as a human reality, as a world made by humans, they are necessarily preoccupied with understanding the appearance of modernity. By the same token, they must be concerned with *critique* and *critical consciousness*. What forms of knowledge and theory can penetrate these false appearances? How can a critical theory promote critical *practices* that relate to the world as a human product rather than as a natural structure? To use Lukács's term, how can we break out of the 'contemplative' attitude? What prevents this critical consciousness and practice from emerging? Consumer culture typifies the absence of critical consciousness in the modern world, but it is also a major force preventing its emergence. Moreover, a central aspect of all these attempts to theorize alienation, fetishism and reification is a methodological concern to avoid reification in theory itself. Critical thought must not be produced as another commodity, as an objective entity to be passively consumed. This is the case with positivism and its mass production of facts and data. Avoiding this takes the form of historicizing and sociologizing our conceptual categories, returning them to a dialectical relation with the world from which they emerged.

The Frankfurt School of Critical Theory developed these lines of thought furthest and with the notoriously deepest pessimism. Critical consciousness depends on an oppositional culture, one that has sufficient autonomy from the commodifying and rationalizing forces of modernity to exist in a state of critical tension with it, to act as its negation. Culture acts as a negation when it expresses the repressed potentialities for freedom inherent in modernity, and by expressing them to the fullest it can constitute a critique of capitalist reality.

However, culture as a whole has become consumer culture. All culture is now produced, exchanged and consumed in the form of commodities. It has therefore lost all oppositional content and all critical distance from capitalist society with which it is now totally identified. It is produced on a rationalized and exploitative basis and for mass sales, just like any commodity; and it is consumed within alienated social relations. It is part of the system − an 'affirmative culture' − rather than its negation. All consumption, but above all cultural consumption, has become compensatory, integrative and functional. It offers the illusions of freedom, choice and pleasure in exchange for the real loss of these qualities through alienated labour; it integrates people within the general system of exploitation by encouraging them to define their identities, desires and interests in terms of possessing commodities; and it is functional in that consumer culture offers experiences ideally designed to reproduce workers in the form of alienated labour.

Thus television, for example, offers to the worker, who is deprived of any real individuality by rationalized production systems, a wide choice of easily consumed images of 'pseudo-individuals'. These images, moreover, do not encourage reflection on this contradiction, they do not provoke a critical distancing from these capitalist realities, but rather provide entertainment: merely an escapist vehicle for recuperation, for renewing one's energies and morale in order to return tomorrow morning to precisely that alienated labour that exhausted one mentally and physically the day before. The image conjured up is undeniably the male factory worker returning home from a day on the assembly line only to collapse into a chair with a six-pack of beer, a TV dinner and a baseball game on the box. The image is made more complex by an account of the disorganization of subjectivity under capitalism (as discussed in chapter 3), which allows such fertile ground for alienated consumption: for example, the loss of civil society and those institutions that formerly mediated between individuals and power, the decline of the patriarchal family and the authoritative role of the father at home or in public life. Lowenthal summed up the whole arrangement with his brilliant if cryptic remark that mass culture was a process of 'psychoanalysis in reverse': analysis aims to bring to light the conditions that make a person neurotic and to decipher his or her neurosis as a personally unsatisfactory and self-defeating adaptation to contradictory circumstances; popular culture aims to bury this potential awareness ever deeper and to intensify the neurosis by encouraging the individual to find solutions to unhappiness in precisely the system that caused it, the system of commodities.

In more philosophical terms, consumer culture is, for Adorno, just one aspect of that 'identity thinking' which pervades modern consciousness. Like similar notions in Lukács and Marcuse, this phrase goes back to the original Hegelian problem of subjects and objects. Subjects and objects are neither identical and reconciled (that happens only at the end of history, when all contradictions are resolved) nor entirely different and unconnected (since they mutually constitute each other, albeit in highly mediated ways). Consumer culture promotes the false sense that subject and object, individual and consumer good, audience and culture perfectly match and are reconciled now, under present social conditions. In fact, this identification is true in so far as individuals have actually been reduced to objects themselves, to functional, administered units within systems of production and consumption. Mass and consumer culture, in this sense, both reflect (or 'have a homologous relation to') reality and play a crucial role in reproducing that reality. They are false, however, in that things do not have to be this way, yet consumer culture – in being identical with the system rather than critically distanced from it – forecloses any vision of or even desire for an alternative. Critical friction and dissatisfaction are reduced to zero.

Yet on what basis should we be critical or dissatisfied when consumer culture appeared to offer, as the twentieth century progressed, both freedom of choice and unprecedented material satisfaction? The critical methodology proposed by the Frankfurt School is that of 'immanent critique': to judge the system by its own declared promises and its intrinsic potential. The system, for example, promises freedom and appears to deliver it in the form of consumer choice, yet denies the most basic form of freedom: non-alienated labour and a creative relation between subjects and objects, people and their world. However, such an argument, uncomfortably for contemporary thinking, requires us not only to accept but to expect that people (in fact a whole population) can be 'falsely conscious', can think that they are satisfied when 'really' they are not, can feel free and yet be economically and bureaucratically dominated. In a word, this argument requires us to distinguish – as liberalism (and postmodernism) will not allow – between what people think they *want* and what the analyst thinks they really *need*. And in order to make this distinction one also needs to provide a sociological account of how the discrepancy arises, how it is maintained, how the theorist has managed to perceive it when no one else has, and must also, hopefully, indicate which actual social groups might be moved to adopt a critical consciousness on the basis of their material circumstances.

The most developed form of this account was probably that of Marcuse, and it is worth pursuing in detail. As we have seen, Marx argues that the enormous development of productive forces under capitalism is in contradiction with alienating social relations. For Marcuse, this contradiction has become potentially explosive, because society now has the technical capacity to meet the total material needs of society with a fraction of the labour it currently deploys. Why should we continue to submit to the exploitative conditions under which capitalist production is carried out? The realm of necessity – that labour required to secure the means of mere existence – could be reduced to a minimum, and thus the real human need for non-alienated praxis could at long last be met: the need for human activity to be a conscious project of self-development rather than a struggle for material survival. This of course is in principle utterly incompatible with the capitalist mode of production, which directs resources not to the development of real needs but only towards the realization of abstract wealth: a reduced need for commodities spells economic death. (Note that this theme is also extensively developed by 'post-scarcity' theorists; see, for example, Frankel 1987; Gorz 1982, 1989.)

Marcuse argues, following Marx, that all societies contain an irreducible 'realm of necessity' and therefore require their members to work. The key issue is how capitalism manages to keep expanding this realm in order to maintain the dynamic of alienated labour and capitalist profit. Marcuse takes up this issue at the level of the individual and in terms of Freud. The necessity of labour is defined by an historically variable 'reality principle'. The reality principle always indicates limits to the 'pleasure principle' (immediate, instinctual gratification) and indicates that human needs cannot be satisfied without restraint, renunciation and delay, and that humans must enter into 'more or less painful arrangements and undertakings for the procurement of the means for satisfying needs: i.e. work' (Marcuse 1973 (1955): 43). Thus, there is always a minimum social requirement for repression and for sublimation (the diversion of libidinal energies into work).

Marcuse however distinguishes this necessary repression from 'surplus-repression'. This is the imposition of restrictions and sublimations – and therefore the perpetuation of work – in the interest of social domination rather than in the pursuit of the reproduction of human society as such. Domination and surplus-repression are evident in capitalist society in that 'the distribution of scarcity as well as the effort of overcoming it, the mode of work' is not equal nor is it organized 'with the objective of best satisfying the developing needs of the individuals'. Rather, it has been imposed by the logic of capitalist social relations, and in their interests. Capitalism has a vested interest in expanding the realm of alienated labour (because it yields surplus value) and of alienated needs (because it sells more commodities). It has a vested interest in extending the realm of necessity way beyond what is now technically required.

Surplus repression is accomplished through a variety of means, but centrally by a restructuring of the individual at the level of their needs. They come to identify their needs so utterly with the system of commodities that they 'cannot reject the system of domination without rejecting themselves' (Marcuse 1973 (1969): 26). Needs are never fixed for Marcuse; they vary historically and develop (as for any theorist within the Hegelian tradition) through a dialectic of subject and object. Marcuse defines 'biological needs' simply as 'vital needs, which, if not satisfied, would cause dysfunction of the organism' (20). In this sense even the most whimsical of cultural needs can be installed at the 'biological' level, as 'second nature', when their satisfaction is understood as vital and natural. And this is what has happened on a systematic scale:

> The so-called consumer economy and the politics of corporate capitalism have created a second nature of man which ties him libidinally and aggressively to the commodity form. The need for possessing, consuming, handling, and constantly renewing the gadgets, devices, instruments, engines, offered to and imposed upon the people, for using these wares even at the danger of one's own destruction, has become a 'biological' need in the sense just defined. The second nature of man thus militates against any change that would disrupt and perhaps even abolish this dependence of man on a market ever more densely filled with merchandise – abolish his existence as a consumer consuming himself in buying and selling. The needs generated by this system are thus eminently stabilizing, conservative needs: the counter-revolution anchored in the instinctual structure (Marcuse 1973 (1969): 20).

This counter-revolution does not operate through repression and sublimation, through the ever delayed gratification of oppressive labour. Capitalism could not survive the restriction of need. In the material abundance of advanced capitalism, neither the worker who sees prosperity and productive power all around nor the system which needs to sell its commodities could long survive on the basis of a puritan asceticism which channels (sublimates) all desire into yet more labour. Instead, consumer culture operates on the basis of 'repressive desublimation'. Consumer capitalism unleashes, positively whips up, libidinal energies in general and sexual ones in particular; it demands instant gratifications under the pleasure principle and seems to provide them. However, both desire and satisfaction are allowed only to take their most limited and repressive forms: the lust for commodities, satisfaction *within* the system. The broad sensuality, the 'polymorphous perversity' of unalienated sexuality, is reduced to sex appeal and the purchase of cosmetics, the commodification of the body as a sexual object, to 'competitive performances and standardized fun, all the symbols of status, prestige, power, of advertised virility and charm, of commercialized beauty' (1973 (1969): 26). Identified so utterly with the commodities on offer, modern subjects cannot see alternatives or perceive the limited nature of satisfaction within the commodity system. Most crucially, however, in being convinced to find their satisfactions in commodities, they are unable even to perceive their most fundamental need, the true need whose denial produces all the 'false ones', the need for non-alienated labour, the need for their relations with the object world to be based on praxis, on creativity, on play, pleasure and the development of their own proper needs. With bitter irony, Marcuse calls this false reconciliation of subject and object their identification within consumer culture, the 'Happy Consciousness'.

Consumer culture, then, is alienated because it develops needs according to the logic of commodity production rather than the logic of human development. It therefore structures individual needs in line with the system's needs: economically, to sell more goods and secure a docile and hard-working labour force that accepts the stick of alienated labour in exchange for the supposed carrot of (alienated) consumption; politically, to secure social order by getting people to identify with the system that oppresses them. At the same time, the most fundamental need of the commodity system is also the one most fundamentally opposed to the *real* human need, the need for non-alienated activity: capitalism needs labour to take the form of the commodity labour-power. Consumer culture is basically a lot of false compensations for the fundamental loss of human authenticity in the form of praxis.

Marcuse – and most of the rest of the tradition – are conventionally accused of taking a 'manipulationist' view of modern consumers: their needs are entirely imposed on them by the functional requirements of the system. This ignores, indeed snubs in a wholly patrician way, the creativity, consciousness and rebelliousness with which people deal with goods, the extent to which the meanings of things are contradictory (not functionally determined by the system or by rationalized commodity aesthetics) and the extent to which human subjects continue to assimilate consumer goods into their everyday life *on their own terms.* We will discuss this further in the next two chapters.

This line of criticism has some force. At the same time, I think it is a mistake to interpret even Marcuse's notion of 'false needs' to mean that needs are now mechanically and automatically imposed, inserted or 'hypodermically injected' into entirely passive human objects. A central and still valuable dimension of this work is the stress on analysing those modern social forces by which human subjects are increasingly disorganized, disoriented and confused about their needs and identities while living in a system that is structurally impelled to produce ever more goods and values which claim to solve the individual's problems (which the system caused) but only in the system's interests (economic, social and political reproduction). The individual's problems and needs are very real ones for the Frankfurt School (and they have been analysed, at least in the School's early days, in some empirical detail); so too are the constraints under which they seek to solve them. The danger in consumer culture is its ability to offer false satisfactions to real needs – not necessarily 'real' in the sense of universal or basic or biological, but needs really generated both by the potential of modern society for subjective and objective development and by the inability of modern social relations (most fundamentally the alienation of labour) to deliver this potential. These needs themselves become false when they are experienced as needs for more commodities rather than less alienation, unfreedom, injustice. As Haug puts it in the specific case of advertising and commodity aesthetics, 'An innumerable series of images are forced upon the individual, like mirrors, seemingly empathetic and totally credible, which bring their secrets to the surface and display them there. In these images, people are continually shown the unfulfilled aspects of their existence. The illusion ingratiates itself, promising satisfaction: it reads desires in one's eyes, and brings them to the surface of the commodity' (Haug 1986: 52). This only makes sense if we can meaningfully talk about a society which produces real needs that it cannot fulfil, needs aroused by the promises of commodities that cannot possibly satisfy them, which can 'offer only an illusory satisfaction, which does not feed but causes hunger' (Haug 1986: 56). The distance between the aesthetic illusions of the commodity and the needs of people in an alienated society make the thirst for commodities insatiable and absorb the individual through his or her psychic structure ever deeper into the system.

Spectacular society

The authors we have been dealing with tend to produce highly totalized images of consumer society: consumers face an objective and alien reality systematically produced in order to absorb them. Indeed, modern subjects are all essentially consumers in the sense that both their desires and the means of fulfilling them are structured by a system in which the most individuals can do is make choices. The system itself does not appear as a matter of choice or change but has a law-like nature which is beyond challenge, taken for granted by the contemplative attitude.

For Marcuse, the system is largely successful. Our needs have become utterly identified with commodities. Those who are marginalized by this system may produce oppositional needs, but there is little indication of how this opposition may lead to radical social challenges. However, a quite different possibility emerges from the notion of alienation as developed through Lefebvre, Gorz, the Situationists and Baudrillard: that we are *bored*. For example, in the Situationists' concept of the 'society of the spectacle' all of reality has become alien and objective; we observe everyday life as a spectacle that unfolds without our participation, activity or involvement. Everything has been deprived of its proper reality by being turned into signs and images on the basis of their commodification. Because everything can be commodified and objectified – including all forms of opposition (the very idea of 'revolution' can be packaged as a subcultural style, an advertising slogan, an urban guerrilla clothing fashion) – everything can be absorbed into the spectacle. Alienation, then, has spread from the work-place to absorb all of life, above all the free spaces of leisure, consumption and culture in everyday life. This analysis is closest to Lukács: an account of a completely reified society. On the other hand, the stress in Situationism is on the capacity of individuals to get really irritated by the sheer meaninglessness of the whole show, its meaninglessness in relation to the kinds of desires, spontaneity, creativity, impulsiveness, play etc. that real humans can spark. Rather like Marcuse, they appeal to a kind of libidinal self and body still lurking under the many layers of commodification and passivity (Plant 1992).

Another point of comparison is the work of Baudrillard, which, as we shall see, takes the Situationist vision of total reification through commodity-illusions to its ultimate conclusion: not only does rationalization order the world and reality, but codes, models and cybernetic systems take precedence over reality itself by constituting the 'hyperreal'. The fate of the modern consumer, the true modern citizen, is not manipulation, as in Marcuse, but complete passivity, to be turned into a bored 'black hole' onto which the spectacle is meaninglessly projected.

Consumer culture and critique

Scary visions emerge from the critique of alienation: the unhappy consciousness, one-dimensional men and a totally administered world, a society of the spectacle. In all these visions, human consciousness is dominated and circumscribed by a totalized system of objectivity. We march (or sleep) to the beat of the commodity. Moreover, we can imagine no other tune, since our consciousness is limited to the factuality of the contemporary commodity world and we have lost the capacity for critique.

The source of this deep pessimism (which in itself is no argument against this perspective) can be understood in terms of the problem of needs. The critics of alienation and reification make it clearer than anyone else that the concept of need is one of the most fundamental critical and political categories of modern thought and everyday experience. When talking about the needs of individuals or of humans in general, we are putting forward critical standards by which a society may be judged. When Marx (or Marcuse or Debord) argues that man's fundamental need is to produce and to produce freely, he is saying that this need is rooted in the essential nature of the human ('species-being'); for a society to be judged good, just, true, it must provide the conditions under which this need is satisfied and humans can thus be true to their nature. Conversely, society is judged false precisely by tracing the ways in which this need is unfulfilled, warped, mystified or transformed into something other than itself by commodity culture. The concept of 'needs' states those substantive values which *should* govern a society and judges it by whether they do.

In many respects, the reason why someone like Marcuse describes society as total and one-dimensional is precisely that, in a consumer and commodity culture, the concept of need no longer provides this independent and substantive standard of critical judgement. The very concept has been made a functional part of the system, and we have therefore lost our independent critical vantage-point, both in theory and in everyday life. For example, as we saw in chapter 2, liberal society and consumer culture do not easily accommodate the concept of need at all, but rather are concerned with preferences and effective demand. The latter are matters of entirely individual, subjective choice; they are a matter for the sovereign consumer and cannot be judged by external standards or by reason. On this basis we can only judge society in terms of its formal rationality (its quantitative efficiency in delivering *the goods*), for there is no concept of human need which could justify a substantive critique (what *good* does society deliver?). Moreover, the next step in the argument is that because modern society is characterized by commodification and rationalization, people's needs (their preferences and choices) are themselves the targets of intensive social pressure, both as to their form (needs must always be needs for commodities) and content (status competition, advertising and marketing, life-style imagery and so on are brought to bear). If the needs of the individual are defined by society and are defined as needs for its products, then people will simply identify with society and find it satisfying, not because it satisfies their needs but because it has defined their needs in terms of the satisfactions it offers. Without a perceived contradiction between an independent criterion of need and the satisfactions on offer, the very idea of and impetus towards critique cannot arise, people are entirely identified with the system, and the only 'political' questions that are asked are not really political at all: they are technical, formally rational questions about the efficiency with which society produces both needs and satisfactions.

The problem is that substantive and critical concepts of need (such as a need for non-alienated labour) are necessary, but they are also untenable or dangerous. The Frankfurt School theorists were the most honest about the dangers and difficulties of the entire project of critique: when one defines a 'real need' as a standard by which the 'false ones' experienced by modern consumers can be judged as false, one is making statements about the 'real' or 'essential' nature of the human (one is engaging in philosophical anthropology). To do so, however, is to engage in precisely the kind of reified thinking that the whole tradition is devoted to challenging. One is producing definitions of the human outside society and social relations (the Robinson Crusoe myth, for example), as ahistorical, essentialist, unchanging and even ideal. This is also the purest form of ideology: one states one's own values and politics (which is what statements of need are) in the form of universal statements about the nature of the human, about human nature; one tries to pass off one's politics in the form of science, one's 'oughts' in the form of an 'is'. The danger in all this is not particularly abstract, and it is one consistently pointed out by liberals (and more recently by post-structuralists and postmodernists). When social institutions and discourses proclaim themselves to be authorities about people's needs, and moreover when they try to legitimate their authoritative knowledge of needs through science, reason or truth, they can constitute themselves as a particularly insidious form of totalitarian social power: the state, the welfare system or health service, the command economy which claims to know its citizens' real needs better than they do, and on a scientific basis, is anti-democratic in the most threatening sense and has the social power to impose its definitions of needs on the individual in practical everyday life.

It is in this context that Marcuse's position can be rather worrying. 'In the last analysis, the question of what are true and false needs must be answered by the individuals themselves, but only in the last analysis; that is, if and when they are free to give their own answer' (1973 (1969): 20). Yet two sentences later he is declaring that 'no tribunal can justly arrogate to itself the right to decide which needs should be developed and satisfied'. Indeed, the entire project of Frankfurt School theory and its critique of consumer culture both acknowledged the dangers inherent in the concept of needs and yet perpetually danced with it, recognizing the necessity of this concept for any possibility of critique. They therefore attempted to justify a particular substantive rationality (a set of values) through formal reason, but to do so immanently, through an examination of processes and potentialities within real historical developments rather than through the simple positing of reified and ahistorical absolutes.

I am not concerned here with assessing the success of this project. However, the question it posed has been utterly fundamental in dealing with consumer culture. How do we *judge it* (as either everyday participants, political citizens or social theorists)? And given that our necessary standards of judgement are precisely those needs which consumer culture so intensively operates upon, how can we be sure that we are possessed of a properly independent standard – our own standard – rather than of a self-legitimating ideological sleight of hand?

The Hegelian tradition running through Marx and his descendants certainly provides the most creative solution to these modern conundrums. None of these authors reify human nature in the form of a fixed set of basic needs. They do not provide a universal human shopping list of specific human needs, such as food, clothing, shelter, nurturance etc. (compare for example Maslow's influential 'hierarchy of needs'; see also Geras's (1983) attempt to propound a notion of basic needs within the Marxist tradition). As we have seen, need unfolds and expands, becomes richer and more differentiated, through a *process*, through the dialectic of subject and object, of expanding technical control over the object world and of a historically variable capacity to assimilate objective culture into subjective experience. However, at the centre of this process, as its presupposition, the tradition installs one fundamental and non-negotiable need, on which is founded human dignity, freedom, reason and hope: the innate need for non-alienated praxis, the need to engage in the creative transformation of the world in relation to humanity's unfolding needs, and to do so in a state of consciousness. It is by its failure to satisfy *that* need – as a result of the separation of production and consumption through the commodity form and of the ensuing alienation and reification of both the human productive capacity as well as its products – that consumer culture stands judged by these authors as false and wrong.

Whether *their* standard of judgement – non-alienated activity – 'works', whether it can legitimately ground our ethical and political life, must itself remain a matter for argument, discussion, reasoning and – unfortunately – choice.

5
The Meanings of Things

Introduction

All the perspectives we have discussed so far share one assumption: that consumption is a *meaningful* activity. Humans do not consume like animals in that our relation to our needs and environment is neither instinctive and programmed nor confined to the physical survival of the individual or species. Rather, it is assumed that people understand their relation to things in the world – their needs – in terms of projects and goals, social conventions and norms, concepts of what being a human or human society involves.

It is time to examine this assumption. In this chapter, we will look at how the meaningful nature of consumption in general and consumer culture in particular have been conceptualized. In the first instance this involves dusting off some old conceptual issues about needs and things. Secondly, it involves looking at the broad tradition of semiotics as a way of thinking about 'consumption as meaningful'. In the process we will raise a number of issues about the relation betweem semiotics and social theory, between the meanings of things and the uses of things within social practices by social agents. These will be developed in chapter 6.

Cultural reproduction

When you eat, you do not eat simply in order to reproduce yourself physically, by taking in a quantity of nutrients and calories required to keep a physical body alive at a certain level of activity. On the contrary, you probably do not eat many six or eight-legged creatures or domesticated four-legged ones like dogs or cats. And there are some fuzzy categories, such as rabbits and horses, which are problematic for the British but not, say, for the French. You combine and prepare foods in specific ways, which can be mapped out as forms of ethnic cuisine. Your eating, moreover, takes place within rituals of sociability – when you eat and with whom, the utensils you use and the etiquette you follow. In sum, the activity of consuming food does not involve you just in physical reproduction, but also in cultural reproduction. By knowing and using the codes of a particular ethnic cuisine you reproduce both that ethnicity and your own identity as a member of it.

In fact, *all* consumption is cultural. This statement signifies several things. Firstly, all consumption is cultural because it always involves *meaning*: in order to 'have a need' and act on it we must be able to interpret sensations, experiences and situations and we must be able to make sense of (as well as transform) various objects, actions, resources in relation to these needs. At the very least, in order for an object to be 'food' it must undergo a cultural sifting of the 'edible' from the 'inedible', as well as cultural practices of transformation (collecting, selecting, preparing, cooking).

Secondly, consumption is always cultural because – as against liberal-utilitarian thought – the meanings involved are necessarily shared meanings. Individual preferences are themselves formed within cultures. It is not that all members of a culture are unanimous and uniform in their consumption (this is impossible, especially as all cultures involve differentials of power, wealth and status). The point is that when we meaningfully formulate our needs in relation to available resources, we draw on languages, values, rituals, habits and so on that are social in nature, even when we individually contest, reject or reinterpret them.

Thirdly, all forms of consumption are culturally specific. They are articulated within, or in relation to, specific meaningful ways of life: no one eats 'food'; they eat a sandwich, *sushi*, a chip buttie (and all of these are not just 'eaten' but eaten for 'lunch', a 'snack', a 'school meal'). So too with needs: 'the hunger gratified by cooked meat eaten with a knife and fork is a different hunger from that which bolts down raw meat with the aid of hand, nail and tooth', as Marx rather ethnocentrically put it (1973: 92).

Finally, it is through culturally specific forms of consumption that we produce and reproduce cultures, social relations and indeed society. To be a member of a culture or 'way of life', as opposed to just 'staying alive', involves knowing the local codes of needs and things. By knowing and using the codes of consumption of my own culture, I reproduce and demonstrate my membership of a particular social order. Moreover, I *act out* that membership. My identity as a member of a culture is enacted through the meaningful structure of my social actions – the fact that I *do things* in this way rather than that. Not only my identity but the social relations themselves are reproduced through culturally specific consumption (and by changing or rejecting the consumption codes of my culture I negotiate both identity and aspects of the culture). For example, it is evident that between a household that sits down to a 'family meal' every evening and one whose members 'graze' (individually raid the kitchen at random points of the day for food consumed in their own rooms while consuming their own TV or computer game), altogether different families and family relations are being reproduced.

Basic needs

The idea that consumption is cultural can take several forms. One argument is that humans have basic needs but that these take on different cultural forms in different societies (the desires for Chinese or French food are different forms of the basic need of hunger). Another is that consumption is 'influenced' by culture: for example, that individuals normally act on their own private desires but are sometimes pressured in other directions by cultural forces. In both cases, culture is an addition to consumption. Thus many accounts (for example Leiss 1976; Leiss et al. 1986) argue that consumer culture (as opposed to earlier modes of consuming) is the product of affluence, rather than of capitalism or modernity. Once the satisfaction of basic needs has been materially secured, the meaningful or cultural aspect of consumption comes to predominate, and people become more concerned with the meanings of goods than with their functional use to meet a basic or 'real' need. In many such formulations not only consumer culture but also the cultural nature of consumption are bound up with the idea of 'luxury'. To take one example of very many, Waters (1995: 140) writes that 'in a consumer culture the items consumed take on a symbolic and not merely a material value', and that this arises when 'powerful groups . . . encourage consumers to "want" more than they "need" '. Yet it is difficult to imagine any society in which objects are purely material and without meaning, let alone to argue that the symbolic use of goods should be primarily understood as arising from manipulation.

The stronger argument is that culture does not 'influence' consumption or give specific forms to a basic need, but rather that culture *constitutes* the needs, objects and practices that make up consumption. It is not an added extra, let alone a frivolous, superficial or luxurious decoration painted over natural desires by affluent civilizations. Culture, in this view, represents the fact that all social life is meaningful and that needs and uses can arise only within a particular way of life: it is only by virtue of the cultural nature of social life that we can have needs in the first place or identify objects which might satisfy them (see, for example, Sahlins 1976).

One powerful counter-argument brings out the difference quite starkly. It is often said that we know what basic needs are because we know what needs have to be filled in order for *any* kind of culture to be sustained, or for any individual to be able to participate (have 'membership' and 'identity') in a culturally specific 'way of life'. Individuals need first to be alive, healthy and possessed of sound mind in order to be part of any culture. The way in which they define and achieve life, health and sanity may vary culturally, but even for this variety to exist the underlying needs must be satisfied (Doyal and Gough 1991; Sen 1985, 1987a, 1987b; Slater 1996). This argument is also politically and morally powerful: to tell a starving or homeless person that 'all consumption is cultural', that 'ways of life' take conceptual precedence over 'staying alive', is obscene. Moreover, against such basic need, for *any* kind of food, clothing and shelter, the 'cultural' wants and preferences of consumer culture, its endless discrimination of meanings (a need for nouvelle cuisine versus McDonald's as opposed to needing *food*) stand condemned as deeply trivial and warped.

However, the central problem for these basic needs arguments is their assumption that we can identify basic needs such as hunger independently of the specific cultural forms they take, or that it is in any way meaningful to do so. We experience all needs (including physical ones) *within* cultures. We can only identify basic needs (or the basic form taken by need when stripped of its 'cultural forms') by abstracting from any and all particular and observable forms of life. Yet we certainly cannot observe basic needs – the needs 'before' or 'beneath' culture – *empirically*. It is rare, perhaps impossible, for people to be entirely reduced to pre-cultural basic needs, for example to a point of starvation, where any food will do because the cultural person has been reduced to a 'natural' body. It is only at the most horrific extremes of inhumanity, economic catastrophe, war, when social and cultural life has broken down, when – as we say in these circumstances – 'people have been reduced to animals', that 'basic needs' might emerge. Even then, however, it is brutally but often heroically obvious how catastrophic things must be before 'trivial' and 'superfluous' culture gives way to 'basic need'. Even in concentration camps or slave ships people were not entirely reduced to basic needs (a central issue of, for example, Primo Levi's *If This Be a Man*). People starve to death in their own culturally specific ways (for example refusing culturally prohibited or even distasteful foods, sacrificing themselves because they put social solidarity above physical survival, carrying out the rituals and cultural activities by which they socially define themselves as fully human (Fine and Leopold 1993)). Indeed, this is what we call human dignity. And even if a breaking point comes at some degree zero of human existence at which 'basic need' emerges, this is surely no basis on which to define human need, for what we observe in these catastrophic conditions is not the 'truth' of need, but the extremes of social failure.

Finally, it is evident that people do not take such a degree zero of existence as the baseline for assessing *their own* needs, nor do they prioritize staying alive over living a meaningful life, nor do they treat culture as secondary to physical reproduction when considering their own case. Such standards are left to international aid, relief and charity, where we can regard others' consumption as a question of bodies and materials rather than of selves and cultures. In our own case, we invariably assert a right to more than a basic body.

In fact, Doyal and Gough's (1991) argument – that we can define basic needs as those that are necessary conditions of cultural participation – clearly acknowledges that these needs will always take particular cultural forms in any empirical case. However, they argue that they can rationally abstract from this diversity and assert a universal right to the necessary underpinnings of meaningful life as such: sound bodies and minds. Yet even here we get into problems. Different societies set different 'entry requirements' for social participation. They not only meet the needs for sound bodies and minds in culturally specific ways but also define this soundness itself in quite different ways. For example, we need only look at debates about disability to know that the threshold of health required to be a full member of the community is set socio-culturally: a bit more wheelchair access, some changes in attitudes and bureaucratic structures, and there will be more participation, not by filling an invariable basic need (giving everyone a 'normal' body physically capable of social participation) but by refusing to make social participation contingent on having a 'normal' body.

Just as in the discussion of real needs in chapter 4, there are intellectual and political problems with both basic needs and 'culturalist' approaches. Critical concepts of need seem both necessary and dangerous (see especially Soper 1981, 1990). For example, if Doyal and Gough put forward a particular definition of basic health they can be accused of cultural imperialism; if they do not, they revert to cultural relativism and lose the ability to judge and compare the need-satisfying abilities of particular societies. One important point is that although social theorists may be unable validly to define 'basic needs', it is evident that the distinction between basic needs and luxuries has been fundamental to western society (and many others): it is used to define baselines of entitlement, participation, individual variation, moral standing and so on (Berry 1994). Perhaps theorists should be less concerned with defining, or refusing to define, our basic needs and more concerned with the social conditions under which the process of defining need is carried out in different societies. For example, whether needs in consumer culture are *really* basic or trivial, true or false, may be quite beside the point; the more important point is how modern societies go about defining people's needs and their relative importance. Perhaps the central issue is that the mediation of needs by market exchange and corporate interests is undemocratic and gives people little opportunity to publicly discuss and collectively control decisions about what their real needs are and, therefore, about how social resources should be used and allocated. Perhaps the issue is whether 'consumer choice' is the best way for a society to go about defining, let alone filling, its basic needs (Slater 1996).

Basic objects

The counterpart to the idea of basic needs is 'basic objects'. For example, many argue that consumer society is somehow *more* cultural in its consumption than other societies because advertising and marketing attach extraneous meanings to basically functional objects (the perfume does not just smell nice, it signifies or promises sexuality, femininity, prestige, getting a partner). The cultural meanings of things appear not only superfluous but mystifying and exploitative. They draw us into a realm of commodity-signs in order to get us to buy more, rather than leave us to a realm of use-value or utility in which we use the 'real' properties of objects in order to *do* things.

Conversely, consumer culture – some argue – could be demystified by removing the extraneous cultural meanings from the 'basic object'. Baran and Sweezy (1968: 139–41), for example, equate the meanings of things entirely with the needs of commodity exchange, as an aspect of fetishization. Outside of capitalist social relations, objects – in their example the car – would not require the enormous economic cost as well as social mystification involved in advertising, marketing and constant style changes (with costs of retooling factories, new spare parts and so on). They argue that the real cost of producing the commodity car, the difference between it and a rationally designed and distributed car, amounted to 2.5 per cent of American GNP in the late 1950s. This is a powerful critique: they measure the 'cost of capitalism', the waste of social resources against a baseline of rational production. However, they arrive at this figure by comparing contemporary automobile production with the cost of producing a 'basic' car, one that is not conceived as a commodity requiring meanings, but rather is rationally designed in terms of how best to carry out its intended function.

However, if we argue that all consumption is cultural we are also arguing that all objects are culturally meaningful and indeed that no object can be simply functional. It would be as hard to find an example of a purely functional object 'without meaning' (without even the meaning of 'being functional' as opposed to, say, 'being merely decorative') as to find a basic need separable from its cultural form. But even more importantly, functions themselves are culturally defined. The idea that any object is useful or has useful properties depends on the existence of a particular way of life in which there are particular things to be done and ways of doing them. As Sahlins put it, 'the decisive quality of culture ... [is] not that this culture must conform to material constraints but that it does so according to a definite symbolic scheme which is never the only one possible. Hence it is culture which constitutes utility' (Sahlins 1976: viii).

From this point of view, the difference between consumer culture and other modes of provisioning is not a difference between regimes that produce meaningful objects and regimes that provide rational or functional objects, but rather one between different systems for defining, producing, distributing and organizing meaningful needs and goods and their relations: that is to say different ways in which cultural reproduction is organized. The dominant mode through which this reproduction is carried out in a consumer culture is through commodities. If consumer culture is trivial or mystifying or exploitative, it is not because it is cultural (whereas a truer form of provisioning would be rational or functional in its use of things) but because of the *kind* of culture and cultural processes, the *kinds* of power over culture and meaning, that are involved in commodity relations.

Semiotics

How then are we to understand 'consumption as cultural', the way in which needs, things and uses are organized or constituted through social meanings? And, most crucially, how are we to relate all these meanings to social actions, relations, processes and institutions? The most influential approach to these questions has been semiotics. Semiotics generally labels a very broad tradition deriving largely from Saussure's structural linguistics, which entered social theory through structuralism and post-structuralism, cultural studies and some branches of anthropology and literary studies.

What holds these diverse strands together is the model of language. Semiotics looks at all elements of culture as if they were elements of a language, and with tools derived from the analysis of language systems and texts. Elements of a culture – including consumer goods and events – are treated metaphorically as texts that can be read (and less often as statements that have been spoken). We can read these texts by understanding them as a particular organization of signs drawn from language-like systems and codes of signs. The text makes sense, and is made sense of, in terms of the systems of signs from which its elements are drawn and which give them their meaning.

The foods we eat are neither simply 'objects which provide nutrition' nor are they naturally or inherently recognized as food. The notion of an ethnic cuisine or culture of food organizes objects into oppositions such as edible and inedible, sweet and savoury, ordinary and special, fruits and vegetables and so on. Each is understood, and has meaning, in relation to the other: meaning therefore depends on the system of signs rather than on the objects in themselves or even on their functional place in social practices. It is the classificatory order that matters. Moreover, we can also talk about the organization of foods into a kind of grammar. There is an order of what follows what (sweets after the main course) and what goes with what (Europeans may balk at smothering turkey with a chocolate and chilli sauce, as in the Mexican *molé*).

The ability to talk about consumer goods in this way comes from the way in which Saussure defined language in developing his project of structural linguistics. The basic linguistic unit, the sign, is divided into three components: the signifier (the material form, the spoken or written word or, in the case of consumer goods, the object itself or a representation of it); the signified (the meaning of the thing); the referent, the object to which the sign refers, which has a somewhat shadowy existence in semiotics and eventually disappears. This is basically because in semiotics the referent in no way determines the meaning or 'value' of the sign; their relation is arbitrary. For example, there is nothing about a four-legged furry animal which meows that demands it be called a 'cat', and it is not in other languages. Moreover, we could conceivably not distinguish between furry animals that meow and those that roar, as when we refer to lions as 'cats'; or we might find Persians to be so different from Burmese or your average alley-cat that we will not include them all in the same category. Semiotics is generally concerned with these culturally specific ways in which sign systems divide up the world (*découpage*), and these are not generated by the referent but by the system of signs.

Semiotics can then talk about the way different organizations of things and their meanings arise from systems of meanings, and therefore talk about fashion systems, food systems and so on. This can be a limited intellectual project. We might simply go on to describe how things are meaningfully organized in a particular culture and produce a kind of catalogue or dictionary of a material culture, documenting, say, different organizations of domestic space, eating or whatever. As a *social* account of consumption, the biggest gain is in recognizing that things do not have inherent meanings: meanings and things are socially organized.

Myth

Things get more interesting, sociologically, when we look at the range of meanings that signs can accommodate and the status these meanings are given. Roland Barthes's *Mythologies* (1986) stands at the centre of this discussion, providing a methodology for examining the wider universe of meanings that everyday objects – steak and chips, wine and milk – can invoke as well as the way meanings can be ideologically restricted. I might take as an example the hamburger, which can refer to a particular kind of food, in relation to other items in a food code, such as frankfurter, bun, chips, ketchup. But it also seems capable of signifying rather broader meanings, such as American culture (in opposition to *sushi* or roast beef), or even McDonaldization, American cultural imperialism, modernity as a fast-food culture. In his early work, Barthes reinterprets the Saussurean distinction between denotation and connotation to account for this. The word (or image of) 'hamburger' can 'denote', can have as its signified, a perceptually identifiable thing in the world – a slab of grilled minced beef. However, this sign as a whole can also act as a signifier within another system, or level, of signification, in which the world is divided up into, for example, national cultures and the kinds of values they represent (American commercial dominance as opposed to European elite culture or indigenous local cultures). 'Hamburger' can therefore connote Americanism, modernity or other values which are not in any literal sense perceptible in the object. It is denotation which gives mythological power to the connotated values: the latter appear to be natural properties of the former.

Judith Williamson (1978: 25) offers an example widely taken as paradigmatic. A press advertisement for Chanel No. 5 simply juxtaposes two images – a bottle of the perfume and the face of Catherine Deneuve. There is of course no inherent connection between the two, between a smelly liquid and a woman's face, but their being placed within the same frame leads us to assume one. The connection is made in terms of what Deneuve's face means: within conventional codes and constructions of femininity, Deneuve stands for a classical, elegant, French ideal of female beauty. These meanings are transferred to the bottle of Chanel so that the latter comes to connote (and indeed promise) this kind of beauty: indeed, Deneuve-style femininity comes to appear as a property of the perfume itself. Moreover, a contemporary advertisement for Babe perfume, using the same technique, juxtaposes a bottle with the judo-kicking figure of Margaux Hemingway. Hemingway's image derives its meaning – brash, confident, American, 'women's lib' femininity – from its difference to images such as Deneuve's within contemporary codes of the feminine. By associating them with these two different signs within the code of femininity, the two bottles are able to be meaningful, to mean different things (and thus to differentiate themselves as commodities) and to make these meanings appear as their natural properties.

The latter point is the crucial one for Barthes and Williamson, neither of whom is particularly concerned with how connotation helps sell things. Rather, their interest is in how the selling of things promotes the social hold of ideology. In these examples, elegant and brash femininity, as well as the codes of femininity themselves, appear to be natural rather than cultural because, through the rhetoric of the image, they appear to be natural properties of the object. Perfume (magically) seems to possess femininity. Connotation turns cultural categories into seemingly natural elements of the material world, a process Barthes calls 'naturalization'. Sign systems, at whatever level, are distinctly cultural in the sense that they are ways in which particular societies divide up and organize the world, and they are arbitrary with respect to the real world: there is no more reason for smelly liquids to signify femininity than for bat dung or the evening star to do so. However, signification appears capable of making femininity appear to be a natural property of perfume, as natural an attribute of it as its smell or liquid state. In a sense, then, this aspect of semiotics is providing an account of the mechanics and internal operation (a 'phenomenology') of commodity fetishism: how, through signification, relations between people (culture) can appear as a relation between things (nature).

Social theory

Semiotic concepts and methods have had an enormous impact, particularly on two of the frameworks most closely associated with theorizing consumer culture: cultural studies and postmodernism. It is therefore important to understand some of the ways in which it has structured the field. We need to be more precise about which questions it asks and which it seems to ignore. Specifically, we have seen that semiotics directs us to look at how systems of meaning are internally organized. The next question is how, or whether, it relates those signifying systems to 'the social'.

We can start by asking, what *kind* of project Saussure launched. Saussure's central aim was to establish the study, indeed the science, of language, as an independent discipline, one that could not be reduced to its traditional component parts, psychology and history. This aim is identical to Durkheim's ambitions for sociology, and Saussure, influenced by him, adopts a Durkheimian strategy. He defines his science in terms of its object – language – which, like Durkheim's 'society', he establishes as a *sui generis* phenomenon. That is to say, language, like society, has its own internal dynamic, relations, laws, which can be studied without reference to anything outside itself. However, in order to make the study of language like the study of society, Saussure ironically has to detach language *from* society. (See, for example, Anderson 1983; Timpanaro 1980.)

He does this by deciding on three major methodological distinctions. Firstly, although language always takes the form of enunciations by particular people (statements, texts, utterances), he believes it should be studied as a system of signs that exists independently of particular individuals and is not to be explained in terms of their intentions or understanding (the *langue/parole* or performance/competence distinction). Language is a Durkheimian 'social fact' which is external to individuals and constraining on their behaviour. Secondly, although language, like society, happens in history, over time, it can be studied not as a sequence of historical actions and processes but rather as the relation between elements of a linguistic system at a single point in time (diachronic versus synchronic analysis). This model draws on Durkheim's organicist and functionalist notions of the relation of parts within a whole. Finally, although linguistic units appear to refer to objects in the world – to label, name, point to objects – Saussure argues that their meaning does not arise from this relation but rather from their relation to other units within the language-system (sign/referent, the arbitrary).

Thus, in order to establish linguistics as an autonomous discipline, Saussure makes a series of *methodological* distinctions that define and constitute his subject matter. All of these are designed to prevent language from being explained by anything other than itself (its internal systematic relations), that is by social action, historical social processes or 'the real'. What Saussure is left with is the project of *describing* the internal structure of systems of meaning, and in answer to a rather new kind of question, not '*Why* did she say that?', '*Why* are BMWs a status symbol?', '*Why* in our society does technology connote masculinity?', but rather '*How* does the structure of a sign system make possible, offer certain resources for, certain statements, meanings and associations, and in reliable ways?', '*How* is orderly and intelligible meaning sustained?'

This is an interesting and very important kind of question. But it is not a project of social explanation: answers to these *how* questions cannot add up to an answer to the *why* questions. As Anderson put it (1983: 48), 'Language as a system furnishes the formal *conditions of possibility* of speech, but has no purchase on its actual *causes*.' For example, to say that Chanel No. 5 connotes a certain kind of femininity by virtue of its association with the face of Deneuve and her position in a system of femininity that includes alternatives such as Hemingway, gives an account of *how* the various parts function together within a system, but does not explain *why* advertisers might choose this kind of imagery, why they chose Deneuve's face rather than, say, Sylvester Stallone's, why (or indeed *whether*) actual social readers of the text will read it the way Williamson has read it, and so on (Slater 1989). The association between smelly liquid and femininity might well be ontologically arbitrary (that is there is no inherent connection between them in nature); it is certainly not *socially* arbitrary. There is a very complex history of social actions and motivations through which they have been connected (patriarchy, commerce, etc.) but which cannot be investigated by looking only at how their results (sign elements and systems) are connected within a text.

The how questions are undeniably crucial. Problems arise only if answers to them are mistaken for social explanations, if 'conditions of possibility were systematically presented "as if" they were causes' (Anderson 1983: 49). For example, it is interesting to note that Chanel and Babe, Deneuve and Hemingway can be systematically related. It is quite another thing to treat one's systematic analysis of a text as if it were a social fact that *explains* contemporary advertising as well as cosmetics use, patriarchal ideologies of femininity, the interpretative practices of both advertisers and consumers and so on. For example, Williamson does not relate the meanings she finds in advertisements to the actions of people interpreting texts. Rather, in her account texts 'interpellate' subjects: the objective structure of the advertisement, she argues, assumes and requires that the bottle of Chanel and the face of Deneuve be connected and addresses its readers as subjects who will indeed make that connection. They and their reading are inevitable 'effects of the structure'. The structure is therefore treated as a cause, an answer to a social why question rather than a structural how question.

These confusions were deeply consequential for studies of consumer culture, particularly through the influence of structuralism. Firstly, many semioticians felt that they did not have to look at social practices (for example those of advertising agents or consumers): these could be 'read off' the structure of the text or sign system, for example by analysing advertisements (Slater 1989). Secondly, these structures could be treated as objective (as if they exist in the world and can be scientifically known by analysts). One consequence of this was a kind of theoretical arrogance. By using semiotics to unearth the deep structure of a text, the analyst can know both the true meaning of the advertisement or consumer object (a meaning of which the actual consumer may be unconscious) and the kind of subjectivity it will produce in the consumer. And yet it is unclear why their analysis of the advertisement is any more scientific or objective (as opposed to simply different) than any produced by the consumer (Leiss et al. 1986).

Thirdly, semiotic accounts can look very like mass cultural theories of consumerism. Especially in their structuralist form they are highly deterministic. Consumer culture comprises systems of signs or codes which determine the meanings of all goods for all people (generally through advertising) and indeed 'constitute' the people themselves through the subjectivities produced in the readings of these texts, through their positioning within discourses. As in Marcuse, it is hard to imagine any social basis for opposition, or indeed any sort of social agency: the codes are all-determining. Baudrillard, as we shall see, provides the most extreme version of this determinism, in which all of social reality is swallowed up by the omnipotent code. However, whereas Marcuse posits, wrongly or rightly, a notion of human need that can be used to criticize the social subjugation of people by codes in today's capitalism, structuralism rejected this as another mythology: 'humanism' (Soper 1986). For structuralism, domination by codes is not a pathology of capitalism but a universal condition. Human agents are *always* an effect of structures, not just when capitalist rationalization and reification are in operation.

Post-structuralism represents the opposite pole of the same set of problems caused by treating sign systems as social facts. Post-structuralism deconstructed this deterministic view of social meaning very radically. Texts – for example films, tourist experiences, television and so on – should be seen as contradictory and ambiguous structures rather than as objective and coherent. They always involve an excess of meaning, individuals can come to wildly different readings of them, there is no authoritative semiotician or structuralist science which can claim to know their real and objective structure, and the meanings of items within a system never stand still so that they can be pinned down to something like a dictionary definition. Precisely because meaning is relational, the chain of meaning goes on and on, final meanings are eternally 'deferred' (Derrida), never to be solidified into fixed synchronic structures.

However, as we shall see more clearly below, the result of this thinking, especially in theorizing consumer culture, seems to be a move from the total determinacy of structuralism to a state of complete indeterminacy and something close to the complete impossibility of any *social* explanation of consumer culture. Humans are still entirely constituted within semiotic processes, but these are now understood less as solid and reified structures than as boundless, endlessly fluid and indeterminate flows, networks and libidinal economies. Finally, given that, on the one hand, the idea of all-determining structures has broken down, and that, on the other hand, humanist concepts of agency are still inadmissible, there are few analytical resources left with which we can make sense of the social processes through which meaning is made. What is left tends to be rather mystical notions of agency such as the body, desire, pleasure, power and so on.

In response to how questions about meaning, post-structuralism certainly offers better answers than structuralism. Both however suffer from the same problems when they try to produce social explanations: they treat descriptions of the social organization of meaning (which are produced by bracketing both social agency and historical process) as if they were social facts that explain how those meanings came to be. What is missing is an account of social practice as opposed to social texts. We shall look at attempts to connect meaning and practice in the next chapter.

Function and meaning

The central problem in looking at the 'meaning of things' in consumer culture is how to maintain the position that all consumption is cultural (to avoid naturalizing needs and things) without allowing culture to become an abstract idea (autonomous sign systems divorced from social practice and history). In a sense, we are still caught up with the problem of basic needs and basic objects. We need to be clear that meaning is not a separate, systematic something that is *added* to consumption by modern consumer culture. We might summarize the problem through yet another distinction: between meaning and function.

Here again methodological distinctions become confused with social ones. For example, Douglas and Isherwood's (1979) point of departure is: 'Forget that commodities are good for eating, clothing and shelter; forget their usefulness and try instead the idea that commodities are good for thinking; treat them as a nonverbal medium for the human creative faculty.' The problem lies in interpreting this to mean that one can sensibly talk about functions and meanings independently of each other. That is to say that one can talk about either functions (or basic needs or basic objects) that are defined independently of particular cultures; or cultural meanings that are defined independently of social practices, for example by arguing that they are defined within sign systems (Slater 1987). As we shall see in the next chapter, Douglas's work is in fact much more grounded than this.

We can understand some of the conundrums this distinction can produce by looking at how Barthes and Baudrillard use it. Barthes, in extending Saussurean linguistics to culture in general, recognizes that consumer goods, services and experiences, unlike signs in a language, have a place not only in systems of meaning but also in structures of practice or practical action. A piece of meat does not just signify; it is also, in fact, eaten. He therefore makes a rather dangerous distinction between a utilitarian order of practice (of function without meaning) and an order of signification (of meaning independent of function). For example, an item of food, he argues, can simultaneously occupy two quite different systems, one governed by 'the utilitarian' principle, the other by the 'signifying' principle (1977: 41). He calls such signs, 'whose origin is utilitarian and functional, *sign-functions*'. His intentions are fairly commonsensical: a filet mignon can give the body necessary nutrients, but it may also signify the connoisseur's prestigious knowledge of the choicest cut of the cow. But this way of putting the distinction seems to imply that there can be functions determined purely by the utilitarian as opposed to the signifying principle, that the function of an object can be defined independently of signification. As we argued earlier through the idea of basic objects, this position seems untenable.

On the other hand, Barthes also argues that 'as soon as there is a society, every usage is converted into a sign of itself' (41; see also Eco 1979: 21–8). In this sense, the function of an object is just another meaning and therefore can be analysed in terms of semiotic systems rather than social practices. For example: 'Once a sign is constituted, society can very well refunctionalise it, and speak about it as if it were an object made for use: a fur-coat will be described as if it served only to protect from the cold' (42), whereas we semioticians know that it *really* serves to distinguish very wealthy women from their status competitors. The function of the fur coat – to protect from the cold – is (as Baudrillard puts it) merely an 'alibi', a way of naturalizing the cultural order, of making something as culturally arbitrary as a status symbol appear to have a natural and rational function (protection), and one that is motivated by reality. 'Function' therefore mythologizes; it is ideological. In this case, Barthes is treating function as just another meaning and therefore as something constituted within semiotic process rather than social practice (hence his analysis of 'the fashion system' does not consider how people wear clothes; it is about the organization of meanings about clothes within various discourses on dress).

Thus Barthes's final position seems to be that the function of an object, far from being independent of signification, can be entirely reduced to ideology. The very idea of function is merely an ideological strategem to anchor culture (erroneously) outside the system of signs, in nature. (At least this is the case in bourgeois consciousness under capitalist consumerism; in *Mythologies* Barthes takes a fairly romantic view about the closeness of the proletariat to real functions and needs, and therefore about their exemption from mythology and ideology.) Baudrillard carries this argument to its ultimate conclusion, that we now consume only signs rather than things. Goods make sense not in terms of their functional place in the order of social practices but rather as 'sign-values', which are semiotically linked into systems of meaning: aesthetic, functional, hierarchical and so on. The modern fridge-freezer of the post-war kitchen, Baudrillard argues (1968), had meaning in terms of a composite system including, say, functional Scandinavian furniture and tract housing, which all together signified the modern affluent consumer democracy of the 1950s. In buying one part of the system, one buys (into) the sign system as a whole: in more contemporary terms, one buys into a life-style, since buying any one sign function invokes the entire system of meaning. This systematic semiotic relatedness gives the underlying dynamic of contemporary consumer culture, as production, marketing and retailing are increasingly oriented to provide consumers with coherent, coordinated and appealing life-style concepts, life-style shopping, life-style advice and so on, which give both consumer and consumer good a firm social identity within a meaningful universe. It is in this sense that Baudrillard argues that the consumption of signs has replaced the consumption of goods.

Baudrillard is in fact putting forward two arguments here. Firstly, he is making the conventional semiotic point that meaning arises from relations between elements in a code – in this case the elements are things. Secondly, he argues that concepts such as 'need', 'function' and 'usefulness' are ideological notions – 'alibis'. They appear to be 'finalities', endpoints or realities that exist outside the systems of signs. As in the case of the fur-coat, we can rationalize and repress the arbitrary nature of semiotic difference by seemingly grounding our choices in nature, in the necessity or functionality of the thing itself. Hence, he argues (1981: 63–87), what is needed is not a theory of needs, but a theory of the ideology of needs in capitalist modernity, a theory of how the cultural arbitrary of consumerism has been grounded in the system of objects through the concept of need.

In many respects Baudrillard, basing himself on Barthes and (as we shall see in the next chapter) Veblen, is launching an acute attack on liberal economic theories of consumption:

> The origin of meaning is never found in the relation between a subject (given a priori as autonomous and conscious) and an object produced for rational ends – that is, properly, the *economic* relation, rationalized in terms of choice and calculation. It is to be found, rather, in difference, systematizable in terms of a code (as opposed to private calculation) – a differential structure that establishes the social relation, and the subjects as such (1981: 75).

Both human needs and functional objects are the fictions of bourgeois economy; only 'the Code', the logic of social differentiation, is real. At the same time, Baudrillard appears to give a historical account of this reduction of things to signs and to argue that it is peculiar to a capitalist society that is able to liberate things (as commodities) from all social determinations except for the logic of meaning. For example, in contrast to gifts and symbolic exchange, 'the object-become-sign no longer gathers its meaning in the concrete relationship between two people. It assumes its meaning in its differential relation to other signs ... Thus, only when objects are autonomized as differential signs and thereby rendered systematizable can one speak of consumption and objects of consumption' (1981: 66). As object of consumption, the object 'is released from its psychic determinants as *symbol*; from its functional determinants as *instrument*; from its commercial determinations as *product*; and is thus *liberated as a sign* to be recaptured by the formal logic of fashion, i.e., by the logic of differentiation' (1981: 67). Thus, in some of his earliest work, Baudrillard documents the way in which modern objects, divorced from their traditional contexts (for example custom, family, religion) are freed to be organized through a *code* of modern functionality: through signifiers like streamlining they signify domestic modernity. For Baudrillard, semiotics, the rigorous restriction of accounts of meaning to the internal structure of sign systems, is not just a methodology; it is rather a *description* of consumer society, of an extreme point in the development of the commodity at which objects are given an entirely new and perverse ontological status, a point at which both objects and social practices – society – can be reduced without residue to 'the Code'. We will pursue this logic further in chapter 7.

Conclusion

To argue that things, needs and uses are not natural but culturally defined (as we did at the start of this chapter) is one thing: it is to argue that we have to look at how they are defined and enacted within particular practical ways of life. On the other hand, to argue in a semiotic mode that the only real use of a thing is to signify is to say that we need not look at the complex ethnographic worlds in which we use goods in a variety of everyday practices but only at the systems of meaning, the social classifications of difference within which things signify. Social practice is properly acknowledged as cultural, but then disappears entirely into the sign system. We will see in the next chapter how various theorists have attempted to recapture consumer culture at the level of meaningful social practice.

6

The Uses of Things

Introduction

The meaningfulness of goods is only a starting point. Understanding consumer culture is a matter of social rather than textual analysis, not an enterprise of reading but rather of explaining and accounting. It is a matter of understanding the ways in which the meanings of things are part of the making of social relations and social order. In this chapter we will be looking at various attempts to produce such understanding, most of which start from a similar intuition, that the meanings of things are not socially arbitrary but deeply related to, or even reflect and represent, the underlying social divisions of a community. In the exemplary case of the status symbol, social stratification is directly mapped onto a division between kinds of goods and consumers. Moreover, by using goods in accordance with their meanings we experience the social order as a compelling moral order and reliably reproduce it in everyday life.

Consumption, then, is part of the cultural reproduction of social relations, a rather concrete process carried out through social practices in mundane life. This view of things can be mechanical, can imply that consumption is inevitably conformist as well as an agent for ensuring social conformity. Yet precisely because consumption is an everyday practice in which actual social agents skilfully use cultural resources (language, things, images) to deal with their needs, it necessarily involves reinterpretations, modifications, transgressions – and can be used to culturally challenge as well as culturally reproduce social order. As we move from Durkheim to Bourdieu and finally to cultural studies, the reliability of this cultural reproduction can be brought into question and more focus can be placed on disruption and agency, less on order and structure. Through our 'symbolic labour' (Willis 1990) in everyday acts of consumption, we go to work on, we can work through, we can even disrupt the contradictions and conflicts surrounding our position in the social order.

Mapping the social

Rather ironically, much of this perspective derives, just like semiotics, from the work of Durkheim. Like Marx, Durkheim bases much of his analysis of social representation on the idea of the fetish, or totem. The 'tribe' projects its sense of being a society onto a sacred animal and its represented form; in turn, the spirit of the animal or its image, mediated through social rituals, inhabits the members, acts on their behalf, gives them ancestry and identity, and so on. For Marx, this is mystification; for Durkheim, essential to solidarity. Modern collective leisure and consumption rituals such as sporting events, feasting, the arts – all of which descend from religious ritual – may be similarly essential to 'moral remaking' and social solidarity (Rojek 1985: 50–4). Goods and rituals make social order both visible and effective: in a sense, patterns of consumption are like a map of social order, along which can be traced the classifications and categories that constitute it.

This theme is explicit in Mauss's work *The Gift*. In trying to answer the apparently simple question, what 'compels the gift that has been received to be obligatorily reciprocated?' (Mauss 1990: 3), he investigates the social organization of gift-exchange into complex networks of circulating goods, reciprocal and competitive consumption rituals (feasting, destruction of goods) and competitive generosity. In each case goods are consumed and exchanged as part of the construction of social bonds and moral obligations. The flow of goods maps out along the ley lines of social relationships and simultaneously reproduces and represents those relationships. The exchange of goods may create a spiritual bond in so far as the good is believed to possess a spirit, as in the classic case of the *hau* in Polynesia. The *hau* originates in the original giver's self, clan and territory; in possessing the *hau* the gift object possesses something of the giver, and this spiritual something wishes to return to its birthplace. It is the *hau* that compels the receiver to return something, to reciprocate. Thus social reciprocity and social ties of mutual obligation are sustained through the spirit of the goods exchanged.

Mauss argues that such beliefs are out of place in an industrial capitalist world of rational exchange. For example, the concept of alienation is an 'economic prejudice', since it implies that commodities possess the stolen spirit of their producers (1990: 66). On the other hand, the flow of goods through consumption rituals still maps out and solidifies complex networks of social relationship. Mary Douglas (1979, 1984), particularly in her joint work with Baron Isherwood (1979), brought this perspective to bear on material culture in general and consumer culture in particular. Goods, she argues, can be regarded from the point of view either of their function or of their meaning. If the former is 'bracketed away for the moment' (62), we can see that goods are *primarily* 'needed for making visible and stable the categories of culture. It is standard ethnographic practice to assume that all material possessions carry social meanings and to concentrate a main part of cultural analysis upon their use as communications' (59). As communicators, goods are primarily 'markers' that indicate social relationships and classifications. Through the public meanings attached to goods and their public uses consumption organizes social order by making visible social divisions, categories, ranks and so on. Social meaning is generally shifting and unstable; consumption rituals as conventions of use tie these meanings down and 'set up visible public definitions'.

This is particularly clear in the case of overtly ritual consumption. To take a banal example, the Christmas turkey marks out a Christian community (or, in these days, a western commercial one), marks out time and periodicity (the annual Christmas season), marks out kinship and community ties (who is at the table) and, as centrepiece of the meal, can organize the progression of courses and roles taken (the man carves, thus marking patriarchal dominance) and affords a chance to demonstrate social knowledge and taste ('last year's was too dry') and so on. Through the use of goods we can construct and maintain an intelligible social universe, since by classifying, comparing, ordering the things we have and use we make sense of and organize our social relations, classifying persons and events. All consumption has a ritual character for Douglas: 'Goods . . . are ritual adjuncts; consumption is a ritual process whose primary function is to make sense of the inchoate flux of events.' Finally, because goods mark out social categories they can be used to discriminate ranks and values, identities and memberships. Indeed, 'the more numerous the discriminated ranks, the more varieties of food will be needed' (66). Consumption, then, is about stabilizing cognitive order in societies – turkeys will be on so many tables next December 25 not so much because they are good to eat but because, in Lévi-Strauss's phrase, they are 'good to think' (59).

Crucially, Douglas's whole approach, unlike semiotics, connects goods intrinsically to social contexts and relations, to practices. Firstly, the meanings of goods are neither socially arbitrary nor derived from an autonomous sign system. Rather, the classification systems that govern the meanings of things reflect the social order itself and are central to its reproduction as a moral order. Secondly, these meanings are used within everyday practices to 'make and maintain social relationships' (60). Not only do they organize practice (consumption rituals) through the categories of the social order, but through these practices the social order is reproduced. Douglas calls this an 'information approach'. Goods are not 'mere messages' but rather 'they constitute the very system [of information] itself. Take them out of human intercourse and you have dismantled the whole thing. In being offered, accepted or refused, they either reinforce or undermine existing boundaries. The goods are both the hardware and the software, so to speak . . . '.

Bourdieu's (1973) analysis of a Berber house offers a concise example of the 'mapping of the social' onto the domestic use of goods. Bourdieu analyses the spatial organization of the house and of the placement of objects and activities within it: for example, things are separated from other things by being placed inside versus outside, higher versus lower, in different rooms or in demarcated spaces. These separations correspond to the cognitive categories by which the social is organized, classified, differentiated – in a word, made sense of – such as man/woman, adult/child, kin/stranger. But this correspondence of categories and consumption is not just a matter of patterning according to an arbitrary sign system. It both originates in and itself reproduces this social order through practice. The spatial separation of men and women, for example, involves a real social organization of activities, information, events, values and so on. To use Douglas's terms, the physical organization of the Berber house makes 'the categories of culture' both 'visible' and 'stable'. The social order is displayed and affirmed through consumption, but it is also enacted, made operational, through these practices. Through our consumption we make social sense and social order not merely within the confines of a sign system but across a total social field of practices.

Douglas's view – like Durkheim's – is fundamentally 'integrative' (Webster 1987). Consumption as a flow of information integrates people into an intelligible social world. Knowledge of consumption codes and attendance at consumption rituals are essential to the 'project of creating intelligibility' and having it socially confirmed: 'the individual uses consumption to say something about himself, his family, his locality. . . . The kinds of statements he makes are about the kind of universe he is in.' Conversely, this generates an account of inequality. Poverty is not so much a lack of possessions but rather exclusion from participation in the flow of information; in consuming less, we are excluded from essential social events and knowledges. In fact both kinds of poverty go together, for exclusion from the flow of consumption information has direct material consequences. An example is the old boy network: getting access to good jobs, social opportunities and privileges depends on being linked into social networks of information flow. Access to such networks itself requires being able to use the codes of goods and their ritual uses appropriately, so that one is seen to be 'one of us'. Goods can be used for exclusion as well as inclusion; knowledge of categories (as in 'good taste') is necessary for inclusion. Moreover, one needs to stay in the information network in order to keep up to date with the information about goods on which remaining a member depends.

The meanings and rituals of consumption, then, mark out the categories and classifications which constitute the social order. However, this involves two problems. The first is a tendency to regard these meanings as merely reflecting a pre-existing social reality. Consumption practices can appear as passively structured by society (Miller 1987; Sahlins 1976: 117–20). Such a view can be overly deterministic and ignore the ways in which social order is not just reflected but constituted and certainly changed through practices. The second problem moves in the other direction. Douglas translates her perspective rather too easily to modern consumer culture, taking no account of the fact that as an information flow, public consumption meanings are not the prerogative of social networks but are increasingly managed by vested commercial interests with public technologies of design, marketing and advertising. The desire for 'cognitive order' like any other need is increasingly merely a means to the end of profit. Integration in this context is a matter of socio-economic power as well as of intelligibility (see Miller 1987: 146).

These problems are evident in some recent literature which extends to advertising the idea of 'consumption as an information system' (Jhally 1987; Kline and Leiss 1978; Leiss 1976, 1983; Leiss et al. 1986; Schudson 1981, 1984). With the decline of traditional social information systems such as religion, politics and the family, advertising fills the gap with its privileged 'discourse through and about objects'. Advertising offers maps of modernity, maps of the social order that are no longer available from traditional sources. The meanings advertising provides allow people to signal their attitudes, expectations and sense of identity through 'patterns or preferences for consumer goods', organized into lifestyles, taste cultures and market segments (Leiss et al. 1986: 3). Consumption and the messages of the market-place have 'gradually absorbed the functions of cultural traditions in providing guideposts for personal and social identity – telling one "who one is" or "what one might become" in life' (11). Leiss, Kline and Jhally's empirical work traces this usurpation, following the gradual shift of advertising over the century from a focus on utilitarian aspects of the product to the advertising of products through complex lifestyle imagery.

Unfortunately, these developments are not discussed (except in Jhally 1987) in terms of the commercial motives and opportunities for exploiting post-traditional anomie, but rather in terms of the usefulness of advertising as a modern system of cultural information. A central theme, for example, is that in complex modern systems both needs and goods become highly differentiated and confused (more so because they move further away from 'basic' needs and objects and into the realm of discretionary spending and leisure). However, 'when goods are little more than changing collections of characteristics, judgments about the suitability of particular goods for particular needs are, so to speak, "destabilized" ' (Leiss et al. 1986: 59). Advertising provides the social discourses that connect confused needs and diverse, constantly innovated things, and does so increasingly through lifestyle imagery which 'bonds together images of persons, products and well-being' (7). As in Douglas, this perspective on consumption is 'integrative' – it is an information system that bonds social members into a moral universe; extending this perspective to advertising, however, makes the latter look a little too benign, as if it were simply a helpful modern aid in sorting out modern confusions (Webster 1987).

Status and social difference

In Douglas's work, consumption goods and rituals make up a social information system through which schemes of social classification are deployed and controlled. Douglas is particularly concerned to demonstrate that consumption systems are, in effect, complete 'cosmologies'; they order an entire moral universe ('The choice between pounding and grinding [coffee] is . . . a choice between two different views of the human condition . . . ' (1979: 74)). On the one hand, they cannot be reduced to technical information (the functional utility of goods); but on the other hand, Douglas refuses to treat them as mere competitive signs, as status symbols. Yet it is through the latter idea that the connection between meaningful goods and social structure has most regularly been made. The meaning of goods, in this view, arises from their ability to act as markers of social status, symbols or badges indicating membership of, or aspiration to, high status groups. The style of one's consumption is then explained as the display of one's social status, one's desire for goods is a desire to emulate the consumption style of higher status groups, while the cultural as opposed to technical aspect of consumer goods is explicable in terms of status competition: goods, by virtue of their meanings, are tools of social climbing, social membership and social exclusion – their basic nature is to differentiate, but solely with respect to social hierarchy. In place of Douglas's broad Durkheimian concern with moral order and social classification as total 'cosmologies', there is a much narrower focus on status hierarchy and status display.

The *Ur*-model for status consumption is often found in anthropological evidence of multiple, separated spheres of exchange in non-modern societies. There can be a sharp division between, on the one hand, a sphere of mundane and necessary goods and, on the other, a sphere of prestige objects and activities (particular kinds of valued shells, jewellery, etc.). The latter sphere involves the negotiation of social power and prestige (having more shells, etc.). It also involves rituals of exchange and consumption that are 'really' rituals of status display and competition, for example competitive feasting (potlatch), circulation of symbols (kula). This feasting and exchange can take the form of massive waste or destruction of economic value (an original meaning of the word consumption) in order to secure *social* value for the individual, clan or kinship group.

A crucial aspect of this system is the separation of mundane consumption from prestige consumption (which is often interpreted as a division between basic needs and cultural ones). Goods from one sphere cannot be exchanged for goods from the other (food cannot be exchanged for prestige shells), a non-modern version of the idea that money cannot buy culture or social value. The function and the meaning of goods, one could say, seem literally and socially separated. The analytical leap from non-modern to modern systems of objects is often made by arguing that nowadays mundanity and prestige are no longer separated into different classes of objects and exchange but constitute different aspects of the same sphere of consumer objects: I can buy a Ford or a Jaguar within the same sphere of exchange. Of course this hardly fits the observably different statuses and consumption experiences of, say, a working class woman perpetually occupied in budget shopping for grocery staples as opposed to a middle-class man intermittently choosing a new car or new island on which to holiday (cf. Douglas and Isherwood 1979: 114–27).

Thorstein Veblen famously placed these kinds of distinctions at the centre of his work. The phrases he has passed on to everyday speech and academic discourse – 'conspicuous consumption', 'the leisure classes', 'invidious distinction' and so on – all arise from what he considered a structural principle of human history: that status is measured by one's distance or exemption from mundane, productive labour; consequently, the manner of consuming time and goods must demonstrate that distance. Remarkably, Veblen traces the evolution of status and consumption from the primacy of gender division. From the dawn of history the primary distinction in human societies is between women's 'drudgery' (the 'industrial' occupations of working on 'brute materials' (Veblen 1953 (1899): 27) to produce useful things) and men's 'exploit' (their assertion of prowess by expropriating the products of others' labour through warfare, slavery or other forms of domination). Whereas drudgery ('women's assiduous and uneventful shaping of materials') merely serves useful functions, exploit *signifies*: it testifies to skill, aggression, power, success. Thus 'the obtaining of goods by other methods than seizure comes to be accounted unworthy of man in his best estate' (30).

The 'trophy' is the first consumer good. What is stolen by conquest is desired not as an end in itself but as an indication of a man's honour, a sign that his role in life is to assert his prowess rather than carry out functional labour and that he is successful in this. Indeed, for Veblen the institution of ownership originates in the capture of women as trophies – this is the ultimate signification of a man's power to subordinate industry to his own ends without engaging in it himself. The aim of wealth is not increased consumption but rather the accumulation of marks of honour   wealth is an 'invidious distinction', a way of demonstrating one's status and inciting envy and emulation on the basis of one's visible exemption from productive labour.

Aside from trophies, the most obvious signifier of distance from productive labour is a life of comfortable leisure and consumption, the conspicuous waste of time and of goods. Leisure, Veblen argues, is not indolence: it can be very busy indeed so long as the activities that fill it are non-productive. Hence, we have an elite culture which signals status superiority by demanding knowledge of anything so long as it does not 'conduce directly to the furtherance of human life   the knowledge of the dead languages and the occult sciences; of correct spelling; of syntax and prosody; of the various forms of domestic music and other household art; of the latest proprieties of dress, furniture and equipage; of games, sports and fancy-bred animals, such as dogs and race-horses ... ' (Veblen 1953 (1899): 47), all of which forms of taste and culture provide 'serviceable evidence of an unproductive expenditure of time'. This list extends to the activities that fill the life of the bourgeois or upper-class woman and her domestic servants – her accomplishments, entertaining, good works, religion, fashion, etc.: all this is labelled 'vicarious consumption' whereby her time, her use of things and the appearance of her body are all engineered to signify, by their non-productive nature, her husband's status. The conspicuous wasting of both time and things comes together in yet another sense of culture, the cultivation of the aesthetic faculty for making endless discriminations of taste. Any of these activities and objects may be experienced by the consumer as useful or necessary, but none of them are. It is precisely their uselessness that is necessary to demonstrate status.

The lifestyle of the leisure class is constituted to distinguish them from productive classes of people. In modern societies it also regulates relations between classes, as well as culture as a whole. In modern, unlike traditional, status orders, the lines of demarcation between social classes have grown vague and transient, and wherever this happens the norm of reputability imposed by the upper class extends its coercive influence with but slight hindrance down through the social structure to the lowest strata. The result is that the members of each stratum accept as their ideal of decency the scheme of life in vogue in the next higher stratum, and bend their energies to live up to that ideal (70).

One's good name and repute depend on aping a lifestyle founded on non-productivity even when one's material conditions demand a constant daily grind of productive labour. Indeed, from the bourgeoisie downwards, the real inability of men to refrain from productive labour, while still trying to ape their betters, intensifies the vicarious use of women to demonstrate respectable (wasteful) leisure and consumption (and a concern with beauty and culture), while driving the men to an ever more intensely materialistic thirst for wealth.

This is a model of emulation. Emulation is one way of formulating the long-running idea that because goods can signify status they can also be used as tools for status competition. Goods are able to mark status because they are part of the lifestyle of a high status group. Consequently, lower status social climbers lay claim to higher status by emulating that lifestyle, by buying those goods, consuming after the fashion of the higher orders, 'aping' their manners, style, etiquette and so on. As we explored in chapter 3, both the dynamism and cultural depredations of modernity are often attributed to the fact that status symbols and manners can be bought with money rather than regulated through birth or breeding. Similarly, for example, the rise of both industry and consumer culture in Britain has been attributed to a social structure comprising numerous, permeable and intercommunicating ranks of 'middling sorts', who were both able and motivated to aspire to the wealth and lifestyle of those just above them.

However, a world in which emulation is possible is also one where the nature of both social status and status markers (consumer goods and manners of consuming) is profoundly changed. A wide range of goods are seen as 'positional' or 'relational' goods (really alternative terms for status symbols). Their value resides in their semiotic ability to mark social position. On the one hand, this gives rise to analyses of consumer dissatisfaction. Goods that have only relational value are points of constant and uneasy comparison; therefore, no consumption can be final (the 'need' to maintain status cannot be satisfied because status must be competitively maintained) and the whole dynamic of consumption takes the form of a self-defeating or zero-sum game (Hirsch 1976). A holiday in Marbella or a taste for nouvelle cuisine has a certain cachet until ten million other people are consuming it in packaged form. At this point it is devalued because it can no longer discriminate status and its wide availability cancels out the positional gains any individual consumer might have achieved by obtaining it. If we are consuming only signs of status then once enough of us have succeeded in copying the lifestyle of the next higher rank, we have all, by definition, failed. As consumer culture, it is argued, comprises a higher proportion of positional goods than of those satisfying basic needs, increasing standards of living simply intensify this dynamic and produce increasing dissatisfaction (Hirsch 1976; Leiss 1976, 1983).

At the same time, this dynamic gives rise to a popular, if somewhat circular (see Campbell 1989: 24) explanation of 'fashion': the constant change in tastes, goods, appearances, lifestyles that characterizes modernity, the constant remaking/remodelling of all the stuff of everyday life, both arises from and exploits the endless devaluation of positional goods. Being in fashion means conforming to the lifestyle of the leading edge consumers and, therefore, generally being (or emulating) those who by their status sit atop the fashion ladder, who make things fashionable by consuming them, who set the fashions. At the same time, producers intensify and exploit this dynamic, speeding it up through programmed cultural obsolescence and the constant renovation of markets by offering new spring and autumn fashions, by differentiating consumer electronics (videos, computers, hi-tech cameras) through infinitesimal but none the less 'must-have' features that – for the moment – have social rarity value. The cult of the designer label turned this positional competition into a very conscious manoeuvre. The *fact* that one's goods had labels, as much as the particular labels they had, indicated one's shamelessly yuppie-ist participation in status competition through consumption. A similar position is associated with Simmel, for whom fashion involves a dialectic of differentiation and conformity, individuality and imitation, all of which are seen as innate human characteristics that take social form in the use of goods simultaneously to conform to the class structures of taste and yet to mark out both oneself and one's group as unique and individual.

Concepts like emulation have been a preoccupation for western modernity from its start, as we saw in chapter 3. As an *explanation* of the dynamics of consumer culture, however, it is limited. Firstly, it reduces social motivation almost exclusively to a desire to 'ape one's betters', and generally understands this desire to be universal rather than to offer a sociological account of how and why (or indeed if) it has become generalized in modern society. Consumption can never be solely about marking and claiming status. Secondly, emulation theories assume that the consumption styles of any social rank have 'trickled down' from above. This assumes a rather mechanical view of hierarchies and the processes that maintain them and ignores the extent to which consumption styles can emerge from the internal resources and social experiences of a subordinated social group and from their opposition (indeed, class struggle) to higher ranks. Class competition can involve the very opposite of lifestyle emulation. Consider the bitter attacks of the bourgeois Rousseau or Laclos on the decadent lifestyles of the *noblesse d'épée*, or the complex inversions of conventional status symbols such as cars, jewellery, dress enacted by black youth cultures. Moreover, consumption styles may not only trickle down, but also trickle up and sideways: the suit adopted by upper-class men and then developed into the uniform of the respectable bourgeois citizen, of the white-collar worker and of working people in their respectable leisure time was first adapted from the riding costumes of the 'lower orders' by way of the military uniform (Fine and Leopold 1993).

Status symbols and emulation are but one example of the broader theme we discussed in relation to semiotics in the last chapter: the distinction between the function of a thing and its meaning. Indeed, in these concepts the function of goods is reduced to a single one: to signify and differentiate status. The only utility of a thing is in furthering status competition; any other practical functions are treated as mere rationalizations or 'alibis'. The only real social practice is social climbing. Thus, the basis of Veblen's caustic irony is precisely his obsessive demonstration that all the most cherished aspects of culture, from feminine beauty to classical learning, have no intrinsic merit whatsoever and are not even pursued for their own pleasures: they have value only as signifiers of rank. Veblen argues that they are able to signify rank only *because* they have no practical worth and are as remote as possible from productive labour, because utilitarian value has been entirely displaced by sign-value. Status ranking only takes the form of any activity at all (busy leisure) because total abstention from activity (which would be the purest indicator of status) would be unendurably 'stultifying' for even the most decadent aristocrat. Status consumption, therefore, relies on the separation of meaning from social practice. Conversely, the only significant social practice apparently is status competition.

In many respects, Barthes and Baudrillard in their distinctions between function and meaning (chapter 5) merely adopt Veblen's general idea that the only real function of goods is to signify status. They then generalize this to all classes and translate it into semiotic terms. Baudrillard takes this furthest, to the point of arguing that we no longer consume things but only signs. As in Veblen and Barthes, the putative function or utility of a consumer good is unmasked as merely a rationalization, an 'alibi': the good is really valuable because it marks a social position. Even its economic value or price is important only as a signifier. People will buy the most expensive version of a product not because it possesses more use-value than a cheaper version (though they might use this rationalization) but because it signifies status and exclusivity; and of course this status is likely to be marked by a designer or department store label. Hence through the logic of social differentiation not only use-value (function) but also exchange-value are subordinated to 'sign-value.'

Bourdieu: class and lifestyle

The exceptional significance of Bourdieu's work stems from his attempts to square some of the many circles involved in understanding the cultural nature of consumption without either collapsing consumer culture into abstract sign systems or reducing it to a reflection of pre-existent social order. He pursues this by way of a theory of practice in which taste – cultural patterns of choice and preference – is seen as 'a resource which is deployed by groups within the stratification system in order to establish or enhance their location within the social order' (Crompton 1993: 171). The key term for the social process going on here is 'distinction', a term that captures both the sense of classificatory schemes by which we distinguish between things and also the use of these things and their meanings to achieve distinction within hierarchical social relations.

Another way of saying that consumption is cultural is to say that in consuming we both exercise and display our taste or style. Taste is not, however, a matter of individual whim; rather it is socially structured. Indeed, it is stratified. We might classify structures of taste (as Bourdieu rather exhaustingly does) into 'highbrow', 'middlebrow' and 'lowbrow' tastes for different kinds of culture. This classification implies not only difference but also hierarchy, for example between those who like opera, those who like comic opera or musicals and those who like soap opera or variety. This is not primarily – at least for Bourdieu – a classification based on the objects themselves (let alone based on their intrinsic worth). Rather it is a classification of different structures of taste and indeed a set of expectations about the preferences of different classes of people. These sets of preferences are socially organized through 'habitus' or structures of predispositions. Bourdieu is concerned to explain both how these kinds of taste structure and lifestyle arise but also how they function socially. The two questions are bound up with each other in many ways, but a crucial one is evident in everyday life. In expressing or displaying our taste, we indicate to others a great deal about our social position. If I choose opera rather than musical comedy, you may infer a great deal about my educational and class background, current income and social aspirations and about the relation between my economic and cultural position. You may socially classify me in terms of the particular system of cultural classifications I display (my 'taste'). In Bourdieu's classic formulation, 'tastes classifics the classifier'.

Taste, much as in Barthes, is seen as a 'cultural arbitrary', a matter not of intrinsic value but of classifications grounded in social processes. But it is not *socially* arbitrary: tastes correlate closely with social divisions, above all class, which Bourdieu empirically investigates in great detail. The stratification of social divisions is matched by cultural stratification and hierarchy. Different tastes have different degrees of social legitimacy and value in the wider society. Cultural reproduction therefore involves various forms of competition and power ('symbolic violence') in which individuals and institutions have a stake, above all competition over value and legitimacy and competition over access to valuable 'cultural capital' (knowledge and competent ease in exercising taste and making distinctions). In the process culture comes to be seen as a battleground of class struggle and competition. However, it is not simply that culture is determined by class; rather culture becomes a means of class competition itself, with a crucial role in the formation, reproduction and transformation of class structures and divisions. A vivid example of this dynamic (discussed in detail in the next chapter) involves the 'new middle classes', who are characterized by a new position in production (employment in service and cultural industries), by a contradictory position in the class structure (one of mobility) and by exposure to both high and low cultural capital. This gives them an uncomfortable relation to existing taste hierarchies, yet at the same time prompts them to advocate, or at least to be comfortable with, a new and disruptive scheme of cultural distinctions and legitimations (postmodernism), which they can use to further their interests in the economic, social and cultural fields, and which correspondingly enters into the restructuring of the class structure itself.

In fact the relation between class and culture is a highly complicated issue in Bourdieu's work, one that is possibly best approached through his distinction between economic capital and cultural capital – accumulated knowledge and competence in using the codes of legitimate culture (for example one's ability to appreciate modernist art, or to behave properly in a gentlemen's club, or to decorate one's home in 'good taste').

Each of these 'capitals' involves a 'hierarchy of legitimacy'. For example, there is 'legitimate culture': high art and music for which taste is defined by established authorities (critics, scholars, collectors). There is also 'legitimizable culture' such as jazz, photography or cinema, for which taste could and in some respects does fall under the gaze of legitimating authorities so that, for example, film studies A-levels and university-level cultural studies become respectable. Similarly, postmodernism can be seen as a way of legitimating virtually any cultural pursuit or taste. The arts of consumer choice and shopping, the appreciation of kitsch, ironic connoisseurship of B-movies can be given serious, legitimating critical and academic attention. Finally, there is the sphere of the arbitrary (including much everyday consumer choice), where taste is understood as a matter of individual preferences. There are inevitable conflicts and competition over the power to define these grades of legitimacy and what tastes belong in each: for example, which classes, status groups, educational and cultural institutions and commercial institutions such as the media should have the power to decide which forms of culture and taste merit serious attention. There is also conflict over the power to decide legitimate good taste *within* any of these cultural areas. Who decides what is a good painting, a good film, a good meal? Moreover, the identity, power and interests of groups can depend on their power to legitimate taste.

In addition to power struggles over and within the hierarchy of legitimacies, there is also struggle over the 'hierarchy of hierarchies': that is to say, whether economic capital (the industrial, corporate and financial bourgeoisies with their generally middlebrow tastes) or cultural capital (the legitimate and legitimizing tastes of the bourgeois intelligentsia for modernist art, the highbrow, the reflexive and the cosmopolitan) should have the upper hand in defining structures of legitimate taste. The idea of a hierarchy of hierarchies also raises the issue of 'convertibility', on what terms of trade can economic capital be converted into cultural capital and vice versa. In the classic example, 'new money' (economic capital recently accumulated by rising businessmen) cannot be directly converted into cultural capital with much conviction or legitimacy; buying a country house does not make you aristocratic but merely *nouveau riche*, however much hunting you do and however big your contributions to the Tory party. On the other hand, sending your offspring through Eton and Oxbridge is the usual way of converting economic capital, the investment paying high dividends in their acquisition of cultural capital (though you risk their joining the 'dominated fraction of the dominant class', the intelligentsia). *Their* cultural capital (unlike the taste of those who are restricted by class and lack of economic capital to lower levels of formal and – crucially – informal education concerning legitimate taste) is easily convertible back into economic capital by virtue of their confident ability to claim high *status*, their place in the City assured by their school ties, their knowledge of the best year for claret, the names picked up at university and dropped at the business lunch.

Bourdieu's account differs from semiotic accounts in that he is concerned less with the internal structure of taste systems and more with the complex economic, social and cultural battles – involving practices, institutions and power relations – through which the classificatory systems gain or lose social legitimacy, and how they both relate to and reproduce class and status structures; however, he also differs from both Marxist and conventional accounts (including most market research) in that he is not so much concerned to correlate taste structures with a pre-given thing called 'class' (with the implication of a causal link: because you are middle class you will have these tastes) but is rather more interested in how culture actively enters into the formation of class itself.

In addition to an account of the relation between competition over taste structures and over social power, Bourdieu is also concerned to offer an account of the relation between social and cultural structures on the one hand and social agency on the other. Again unlike semiotic accounts, taste structures are not systems that position or constitute subjects, nor are they social norms or knowledges into which people are 'socialized' or which they learn. Bourdieu's central concept is habitus, a concept that attempts to relate agency and structure at the level of practice. The habitus is a structure of 'dispositions': schemas of classification, rules, expectations and so on which predispose the individual to certain choices and actions. In a sense, habitus is a Durkheimian classificatory grid by which the individual cognitively maps the social world and orients actions within it. However, Bourdieu gives it two important new twists. Firstly, the word habitus is derived from the ideas of habit and custom and of the state of things. Habitus is habitual and customary, a sense of the way things are. Habitus is 'unconscious' but in a practical rather than a psychoanalytic sense. For example, it is both learned and acted out through sensory and bodily experiences, the subtexts of encounters rather than explicit statements. Above all, habitus is embodied, learned and acted out at the level of the body. It is very much about, for example, the comfort or discomfort, the ease or self-consciousness we feel in the body when wearing formal middle-class clothing, or when we try to find and use the right spoon for the soup, when we have to show good posture and poise. It is through these bodily experiences in everyday consumption that we feel and communicate or betray our 'true' class and breeding. As Douglas puts it, culture and cultural judgement, taste 'should fit, not like a glove, but like a skin' (1979: 77).

Secondly, habitus is both subjective and objective – indeed it is the meeting point between the two because it incorporates individual and collective experiences of class and class structure. As one of Bourdieu's more opaque definitions has it, habitus crystallizes the 'subjective expectations of objective probabilities'. To give an example, in Paul Willis's *Learning to Labour* (1978), the working-class lads at secondary school will not conform to normative (middle-class) expectations: they therefore 'fail' academically. By their 'failure' the class system has succeeded. They reproduce themselves economically and culturally as working-class men bound for alienated jobs, limited income, social subordination and devalued culture. All this has been accomplished not through manipulation but through their own efforts. They are quite realistic about their life-chances, about the myths of social mobility, about who their friends and social supports really are (not teacher, but mates and the family networks from whom they do not want to be separated by middle-class tastes) and about the skills they really need (not high-cultural capital but a few technical skills and a lot of social ability to resist everyday domination by being sullen and uncooperative). This realistic structure of dispositions – this habitus – is learned through a family and community steeped in class experiences, and through the individuals' experiences, large and small, conscious and unconscious, of the million everyday insults and injuries of class.

Extended to consumer lifestyles, every object chosen and every consumer ritual can be related back to fine and realistic calculations of possible social moves and constraints, an inner sense of appropriate aspiration and how to act on it. Thus, for example, Bourdieu argues that working-class culture and consumption are determined by the 'choice of the necessary': 'nothing is more alien to working-class women than the typically bourgeois idea of making each object in the home the occasion for an aesthetic choice' (Bourdieu, 1984: 379). His point is not that they cannot afford the aesthetic because of immediate economic poverty, but rather that the 'necessary' is chosen out of a habitus, a structure of cognitions, formed by long and indeed collective and transmitted experiences of the economic limitations of their class position.

This is a disappointing conclusion, one that recapitulates some now-familiar prejudices and wishful thinking – that somehow the working class (or women or other others) are unclouded by ideology (or by 'mythology' in Barthes) because they are compelled by real necessity, by a functional relation to things, or because they know things through direct labour, through their hands. (For example, Veblen hinges his moral universe on the related notion of 'workmanship', in which the lower orders and women, who actually make useful things, are morally and cognitively purer than the 'cultured' classes.) Yet its implausibility is not unconnected with the enormity of the task Bourdieu has set himself, to produce an account of cultural taste that is both explanatory (acknowledges social structure and determination) yet also grounded in social agency.

Cultural studies

Similar issues concerning cultural legitimacy and social practice also appear in the project of cultural studies. Moreover, it has investigated these issues in close relation to consumer culture because of the kind of social relations it has looked at – above all youth and minority subcultures whose spectacular and expressive styles and tastes were constructed on the same terrain and generally out of the same material as consumer culture (appearance, clothes, cultural commodities like music, leisure activities). The original impulse of cultural studies was to understand these expressive activities as both legitimate (coherent social behaviour worthy of academic study) and (potentially) oppositional social practice engaged in by conscious social agents rather than cultural dopes.

We can see this in the two strands which originally formed cultural studies. Firstly, the work of Leavis, Williams, Thompson and Hoggart shifted the study of culture away from expressive forms legitimated by the establishment as high culture, and towards the study of culture as 'lived experience'. Culture as lived experience – particularly class experience – was treated neither as non-culture nor as culture debased by consumer capitalism, but as the medium through which class is lived and therefore – particularly in Thompson's work — a central medium through which class and class struggle are *formed* as well as contested, negotiated and transformed.

The second strand built on a largely sociological tradition, which studied subcultural and 'deviant' groups in terms of their social organization and meaningful coherence (as opposed to regarding deviants as mad or bad individuals). With its roots firmly in interpretative sociology (both Weberian and symbolic interactionist), the aim was to legitimate subcultural life by understanding it as sensible practice. Street corner kids in the 1930s, like Willis's (1975) 'motor-bike culture' and Hebdige's (1979) genealogy of mods, Teds and punks with their strange costumes and tribal rituals, make sense if viewed not with the uncomprehending and normalizing gaze of straight society, but from the inside, by understanding how these behaviours are meaningful and creative responses to their social positions (as defined by class mediated through generation, ethnicity and – rather later – gender). This sense is only accessible if one reads their objects and activities as culture, and understands culture as practice: their dress, language, leisure and so on are modes of both expression and action.

Crucially, these strands intertwined in the 1960s at a point when 'youth' was the focus of both the explosion of affluent hedonistic consumerism and of radical political and cultural opposition and rebellion. The teenager, for example, marked a new biographical breathing space between school and job-and-family adulthood, funded by some disposable income and rather more free time. This freedom could be channelled (by youth and consumer capitalism alike) into expressive objects and activities (music, clothes, scooters, juke boxes, hanging out at the coffee bar or disco), and these could be intensively commodified through, for example, the music and clothing industries. However, the rather slow response of these industries, and mainstream society's reactions of moral panic, relayed through the media and state institutions, also indicated the intrinsically challenging nature of youth. Culture and style conflict, expressed through consumption, often takes inter-generational form. But this went deeper in that the very means of satisfaction (consumer goods) became the vehicle for expressing a seemingly total dissatisfaction or provocation to the society that produced them.

Cultural studies regarded the relation of subculture to consumer culture as neither senseless and deviant nor conformist and manipulated but rather as part of a project of using the materials at hand (objects, symbols, time) to make sense of and practically deal with the very contradictory social situations that youth found itself in. Dick Hebdige's *Subculture: The Meaning of Style* (1979) probably gave the clearest picture of what was at stake in subcultural consumption. Each of the subcultures he studies comprise (male) youths caught in contradictions thrown up by changing class experiences mediated through generation and ethnicity. Available cultural resources – consumer goods, leisure activities, popular culture in the form of music and dress – are appropriated and reassembled through a process of '*bricolage*' (102–6) into meaningful patterns – styles – which can be understood in terms of the meanings, responses and strategies through which youth copes with its contradictory situation. (See Ewen (1988) for an alternative account of the relation between style and identity.)

For example, mod culture was characterized by Italian suits and scooters, punctilious, almost dandyish, attention to style and dress as an end in itself, pills, short hair, Union Jacks on parkas, soul music. The mods' 'cool' style 'enabled them to negotiate smoothly between school, work and leisure' (52) as working-class and lower-middle-class youth dealing with social and occupational mobility – the move to white-collar work and the decline of traditional working-class lifestyles and values. The mods, for example, turned the meaning of the office suit inside out by 'pushing neatness to the point of absurdity' (52) and adding 'an intangible detail (a polished upper, the brand of a cigarette, the way a tie was knotted) which seemed strangely out of place in the office or classroom' (52). Their dandyish sartorial style pushed all the attributes of the good white-collar worker (on whose 'appearance, dress and "general demeanour"' are placed 'fairly stringent demands') to an ironic but subtle limit: 'they were a little *too* smart, somewhat *too* alert, thanks to amphetamines' (52) – the polysemy of consumer goods was mobilized for a 'semiotic guerrilla war' (Eco, cited in Hebdige 1979: 103).

The mods used 'commodity selection' as 'weapons of exclusion', marking themselves off from Teds, beats and rockers. But their very focus on consumption was itself expressive:

Their 'furious consumption programme' – clothes, clubs, records, hair styles, petrol and drinamyl pills – has been described as 'a grotesque parody of the aspirations of [their] parents' – the people who lived in the new towns or on the new housing estates, the post-war working and lower-middle-class . . . The mods converted themselves into objects, they 'chose' (in order) to make themselves into mods, attempting to impose systematic control over the narrow domain which was 'theirs', and within which they saw their 'real' selves invested – the domain of leisure and appearance, of dress and posture (Hebdige 1988b: 110–11).

This 'narrow domain' of control through consumption also took the form of 'inventing an "elsewhere" ' – the weekend, the West End, the drugs, 'the noonday underground' of 'cellar clubs, discotheques, boutiques and record shops', all of which were beyond the 'limited experiential scope of the bosses and teachers' (53) who dominated their overground life, but also vastly different from the world of their parents. The mods were 'negotiating changes and contradictions which were simultaneously affecting the parent culture but they were doing so in the terms of their own relatively autonomous problematic' (79).

Much of the analysis is in terms of codes and inversions of codes which are analysed in semiotic and therefore generally linguistic terms. However, it is interesting – and closely related to important themes in, for example, Bakhtin and Bourdieu – that the oppositional force of subculture was so often seen in terms of its *non*-verbal character: it is rooted in music and image, dress and stance, dirty or neat bodies. Hence, consumer goods and activities seem appropriate materials for subcultural expression, however mass produced, codified, 'serial' (in Baudrillard's terminology), and they perform 'something like the same expressive function that language does in the more familiar (to the middle classes) culture' (Willis 1975: 234). For example, Willis's account of 'the expressive style of a [male] motor-bike culture' argues that most minority cultures do not use verbal codes and are therefore opaque to conventional sociology, state institutions and the media; but it is precisely *'because* these codes of expression are largely passed over, or misinterpreted, by the middle classes and their agencies of control that they can, and are allowed to, play such a vital part in the generation of minority cultures with critical stances towards the dominant culture' (233). Subcultural activities appear 'meaningless or random' to the verbal culture of the bourgeoisie; for that reason they are also liberating, oppositional and disruptive and seem able to find these potentials in everyday consumer goods and activities.

This kind of analysis – of people using the meanings of things, subverting them, squaring impossible circles of social contradiction through style – depends upon acknowledging, firstly, that things can have many different, changing and contradictory meanings (they are 'polysemic') and secondly that things can be the sites of struggle over meaning in and through which people contest, invert, reinvent, appropriate things in line with their own developing social practices. Cultural studies has explored these themes at various analytical levels. Firstly, it has used several theoretical frameworks to look at how social power is mediated through struggles over meaning. Most influential here has been the model of 'moral panics' (Cohen 1972) and its incorporation into a Gramscian perspective by Stuart Hall (Hall et al. 1978). Gramscian theory was used to argue against manipulationist and deterministic assumptions that meanings can be imposed on a population by a unified and implacable system. It was argued that power had a more provisional character, derived from the need to negotiate 'consent' to social arrangements on the part of diverse and often contradictory social constituencies. Central to this negotiation were the meanings involved in everyday life, both the common sense of lived experience and common symbols that could command the allegiance of diverse social groups. All of this assumed (on the basis first of theorists like Volosinov, later of post-structuralists) that the various signs through which 'us' and 'them' are identified (clothes, flags, skin colour, nations) could indeed be sites of competing meanings.

A second line of development was post-structuralist. In the 1970s, cultural studies was to a great extent dominated by Althusserian structuralism and by Screen theory, both of which took an extremely deterministic view of the powers of ideological and textual structures. These theories went beyond arguing that consumer culture manipulated people to assuming that cultural texts entirely constituted subjects by positioning them within their structures (for example Williamson 1978). One route out of this cul-de-sac involved an exploration of the contradictory nature of cultural texts whereby ideology is ever engaged in a battle to contain and close off the excessive or transgressive meanings they unleash. A Doris Day film may safely end with her tamed and married to Rock or Cary, but, in order to get to this point, she has been portrayed as brash or 'sassy', independent, wilful and just possibly sexual. This portrayal – which is necessary to filmic pleasure – introduces contradiction and 'trouble in the text' and opens up the possibility of the viewer's identification with a strong woman character which just might not be tamed by the narrative finale. The possibility of excessive and transgressive meaning created an opening for feminist theorists to appropriate and reinterpret such films (Clarke and Simmonds 1980); it also potentially posed a sociological question as to who had the upper hand or final say in the actual consumption of culture – the woman who identifies with the wayward Doris or the textual structure that marries her off? The same question can be asked of the meaning of a bin-liner or safety-pin. Is it the semiotic system of functional objects that is in control or the punk who subverts the system by wearing them as fashion items?

In Paul Willis's work – particularly in *Common Culture* (1990) – the polysemic nature of things and the social struggles over their meanings are brought together very clearly in terms of consumer culture. For Willis, consumption is necessarily creative and open-ended because it necessarily involves the negotiation of meaning by users rather than the simple consumption of goods whose meaning is already determined by producers. Consumers must engage in 'symbolic work' in order to appropriate even the most mass-marketed of goods. People 'have to make their own sense of what is commercially available, make their own aesthetic judgements, and sometimes reject the normative definitions and categories of "fashion" promoted [for example] by the clothing industry' (85). Conversely, consumer goods are the 'raw materials' (19) for creativity in everyday life, and contemporary consumer culture now offers an unprecedented 'range of usable symbolic resources for the development and emancipation of everyday culture. Certainly this emancipation has been partial and contradictory . . . [But] a whole continent of informal, everyday culture has been recognised, opened up and developed' (18). In *Common Culture*, as throughout his work, Willis confronts this situation ethnographically. The meanings of things cannot be read off the objects themselves or through general systems of meaning; they must be investigated where they actually emerge, in the unpredictable practices of people's symbolic labour.

However, both the idea of polysemy and the idea of struggle over signs bring their own problems to theorizing consumer culture. Both ideas seem to prioritize consumption over production or detach the two completely (McGuigan 1992), and to regard consumption as a rather unconstrained sphere of interpretative freedom. There is a strong tendency, considerably exacerbated by postmodernist themes, to argue, firstly, that because consumer things are polysemic consumers have an almost complete freedom to interpret and use them as they will and, secondly, that because the sign is a 'site of struggle' it is always therefore a site of *political* struggle, that consumer acts of interpretation and appropriation automatically have political significance or consequences. The first of these arguments involves a kind of anti-sociological 'indeterminism', the second a kind of misplaced radical hope, or even (given its Gramscian background) an 'optimism of the will'. John Fiske's work has been associated with both of these arguments. For example, in *Reading the Popular* (1989), Fiske applies to various popular cultural experiences de Certeau's (1984) rather more cautious account of consumerist subversion and strategies of resistance whereby, for example, the consumer as 'trickster' uses his or her knowledge of official rules to mock or invert them. Fiske (rather optimistically) interprets a bumper sticker – 'A woman's place is in the mall' – as a subversion of women's subordination to domestic slavery in the home. The shopping mall is a place 'where women can be public, empowered and free, and can occupy roles other than those demanded by the nuclear family' (18–20). Shopping itself has subversive aspects, such as carnivalesque qualities, the valuation of the woman's consuming skills and knowledge and the woman's spending of her husband's money as an act of resistance and power over him.

Similarly, in an analysis of Madonna fans, Fiske argues that 'If her fans are not "cultural dopes", but actively choose to watch, listen to, and imitate her rather than anyone else, there must be some gaps or spaces in her image that escape ideological control and allow her audiences to make meanings that connect with *their* social experience' (97). Yet the 'must be' in this quote seems to be a *non sequitur*: unless one adopts a neo-liberal position, the fact that fans choose does not necessarily imply the kind of freedom or autonomy Fiske is inferring. The problem in both examples is that the undeniable fact that people are not 'cultural dopes' is taken to warrant investigating their active 'symbolic labour' as if it were unconstrained by social relations and necessarily subversive of them. Consumption always seems to happen in the 'gaps or spaces' – a realm of free self-determination – rather than in the gritty practices of mundanity; and those gaps or spaces always seem to be spaces of rebellion. The result is a continuous production of 'redemptive readings', in which texts and objects are always viewed in terms of the spaces they offer for pleasures and fantasies through which people can 'make sense', and the consumer's redemptive readings will always neutralize whatever is 'bad' in the text (for example the inevitable taming of Doris Day).

The first argument – that texts are so utterly polysemic that their meanings are indeterminate and consumers are unconditionally free to make their own meanings – is contested on two grounds: that the meanings of things remain socially structured, and that the actual acts of reading and consuming are socially structured. Taking the first point, Morley (1992) for example returns to some extent to Stuart Hall's (1980) older model of encoding/decoding and 'preferred readings' – a text goes through processes of production, distribution and consumption, each of which is subject to highly diverse and conflicting social features, which have to be examined. At each stage different decodings of the text are possible, but all of them must be undertaken in some relation to the actual, material and structured sign with which the decoder is dealing. Producers obviously structure their texts and objects in order to produce particular social effects of meaning. Whether those meanings (the 'preferred reading') are actually accomplished is an empirical matter to be investigated but 'while the message is not an object with one real meaning, there are within it signifying mechanisms which promote certain meanings, even one privileged meaning, and suppress others: these are the directive closures encoded in the message' (Morley

1992: 21; see also Morley 1980b). This is precisely what is at stake in the social circulation of most consumer objects. For example, returning to Hebdige's account of mod subculture, the meaning of a scooter (or suit) involves – at one moment – a youth culture materially and culturally appropriating a ready-made consumer good and adapting it to its own cultural purposes and problems; but in the very process it constitutes a new market and new set of meanings, which the manufacturer can profitably commodify and sell on to wider markets. In the process, the meanings of the scooter are again appropriated and changed in relation to commercial interests, backed by redesign, marketing and advertising. This pattern can be investigated in a wide range of consumer or subcultural fields, such as the relations between independent music and the music 'majors' or between street style, high-street fashion and *haute couture*.

Similarly Miller's investigation (1987: Chapter 9; see also Miller 1994) of objectivism in consumption usefully questions whether all consumer objects are equally polysemic. In one example, the built environment of architecture and town planning is constructed through discourses and institutions which are relatively unresponsive to the ultimate users, and once built most public structures are fairly constraining and largely inflexible in relation to people's everyday practices. In a second example, children's sweets, a transitory and less committing consumer investment, are used by young consumers to subvert adult codes of acceptable foods (they are produced in the shapes and colours of vampires and dead bodies). Moreover, producers and consumers seem to collude, against parents, in producing ever more disgusting objects and meanings. What Miller is outlining here is not unconstrained meaning, let alone unconstrained subversion, but objects and social processes that allow different degrees of room for manoeuvre and negotiation between producers and consumers.

The structure of the consumer object, then, places social limits on polysemy and interpretative freedoms; so too do the social relations within which any act of reading or using takes place. This has been the particular focus of ethnographic formulations of media consumption (Morley 1980a, 1980b, 1986, 1992; Radway 1987; Silverstone 1990; Silverstone and Hirsch 1992), which have moved well away from looking at the 'readings' of a text to consider how the act of reading is socially constructed. For example, Morley's (1986) work investigates 'watching television' as a complex process of domestic consumption, which is therefore structured by, among many other things, gender relations within the home. This can involve quite immediate relations of power. For example, access to all these polysemic texts is limited when control over the flow of prime-time television is normally under the man's thumb on the remote control (and his thumb is fixed there partly because of the less than polysemic coding of technology as the 'male domain' (Gray 1987, 1992)). Moreover, the meaning of the act of watching television is known to be highly diverse and changes through the place people give it in relation to other activities (for example, it might be background noise in another room, or a focus of riveted attention). These diverse meanings of 'watching television', Morley argues, are deeply structured by gender relations of power. A man can watch television as a couch potato because the home is for him a place of leisure and non-work; a woman cannot because the home is for her a place of work and responsibility. 'Just watching television' involves guilt or unease about all the tasks undone, even if it were possible in the midst of family members' demands on her. A sociology of consumption would not stop at discovering that consumers are active in their consumption and diverse in the meanings that objects have for them. The issue is rather how to understand the structures of power and social relationship in which that activity is carried out.

In addition to the problem of sociologically framing the activity and freedom of the consumer, there is the second problem, about the political nature of struggles over meaning. Many authors at least implicitly acknowledge that whatever freedoms the consumer may have they do not constitute *power* in the sense that manufacturers and media conglomerates have power over things and meanings. They have neither the same command over resources nor the power to structure objects and messages (and choose which are to be produced), nor do their 'readings' have the same public significance and consequence, *except* in the one instance that cultural studies focused on for so long, spectacular subcultures. For the most part, meaningful appropriation of things by consumers is, firstly, simply an aspect of the intrinsically cultural nature of consumption (to use things we must make meanings). Secondly, where that 'activeness' appears more oppositional, it is – as de Certeau analyses it – a matter of people's survival strategies in which they 'make do with what they have', which is a lot less than producers have.

Being active in one's consumption – as opposed to being a manipulated mass cultural 'dope' – does not mean being free (textually or socially) let alone oppositional. Yet the association between being culturally active and culturally oppositional goes back to the origins of cultural studies. Cultural studies started, as we have seen, from an important political and academic impulse to legitimate the lived experience and expressive forms – the construction of ways of life through forms of consumption in the broadest sense – of marginal or dominated groups (the working class, youth, ethnic groups, etc.), whose culture could be seen as neither bad or irrational, nor subordinated and manipulated, but as active and oppositional, involving a creative making of inherently *political* meaning. However, forms of lived experience and consumption other than the spectacularly subcultural – 'mainstream consumption' – continued to be seen as conformist, manipulated and non–oppositional because they did not appear spectacular, expressive and therefore active. Conversely, 'mainstream consumption' appeared to cultural studies to be passive and conformist because it was not deemed to be politically or culturally oppositional, radical or disruptive. If a subcultural member dons an Italian suit *he* is a working-class hero engaging in creative and expressive *bricolage*; if anyone else does they are engaged in unthinking and conformist consumerism. Thus while the consumption activities of male subcultures involved agency, activity and opposition, mainstream consumption could seem conformist, manipulated, and basically as uninteresting to cultural studies as it was to manipulation theory.

The political revaluation of consumption most clearly splits along gender lines (Carter 1984; McRobbie 1978, 1980, 1984, 1991; Thornton 1995). Subcultures are uncomfortable places for young women who have neither the same freedom as men within the broader society nor the self-determining control over meaning within the subculture. If a young woman transgresses certain norms as part of her creative expressivity in material culture she is a 'slag' to both members and non-members. McRobbie therefore argues that we should look at the forms that girls' consumption and culture take in these circumstances: for example their bedroom culture, in which – excluded from the public and spectacular culture of the street – consumption and culture is focused on pop music and posters, cosmetics and fashion and the adulation of stars, which are consumed in private with girlfriends. Girls' consumption is rendered invisible by the focus on spectacular (male) consumption; it is also normalized and seen as uninteresting because it appears conformist, passive and non-political. McRobbie is concerned to make girls' experience visible and to legitimate it as an object of investigation. She is also concerned to explore the forms of activity and agency that bedroom culture involves (particular the spaces of 'pleasure' and 'fantasy' in which girls can make meanings). However, she, like all researchers into cultural studies, treads the fine line (which Fiske abandons) between acknowledging that this conformist consumption is active and assuming that it is oppositional. Between these two terms there remains the powerful original insight of the whole tradition, that consumption is part of a social process of making social sense (see McGuigan 1992: chapter 3).

Conclusion

These issues bring us back to the starting point of this chapter. How can we connect the cultural nature of consumption to a sustained analytical sense of 'the social'? How can we investigate the social meanings of things, needs and uses without reducing them either to omnipotent social structures (semiotic codes, grids of social classification generated by the social order itself, the structures of commercial capitalism) or regarding them as socially unconstrained, indeterminate, open, as a space of self-determined activity so free that it looks increasingly like the space of the sovereign liberal consumer? These issues become far more urgent as we move from cultural theory to concepts of post-Fordism and postmodernism in the next chapter, for each of these appears to give an account of the sociological dissolution of 'society' into 'sign' by way of consumer culture.

7
New Times?

Introduction

Consumer culture is always 'new', but there has been a different, more consequential kind of newness in the air over the past few decades, a sense of structural transformation within modernity itself, of ruptures in its economic, social and cultural modes of carrying on. This sense of an epochal shift has become the focus of most social theory, the main item on its agenda: postmodernism and postmodernity, 'New Times', the shift from Fordism to post-Fordism, from organized to disorganized capitalism, from commodities and exchange value to commodity-signs and sign-value.

On the one hand, it is argued that these shifts have important consequences for consumer culture. Above all, it is argued that the modern, Fordist mass production of standardized goods for mass consumption by homogeneous consumers has given way to the postmodern, post-Fordist specialized production of goods more specifically tailored for and targeted on precise consumer groups who are defined by lifestyles rather than by broad demographic variables like class, gender or age. There is a different dynamic of consumption.

On the other hand, the sense of newness is more radical than this. There is a sense that consumer culture has not simply been changed by these shifts but in various ways has been instrumental in bringing them about, and that it plays an altogether more central role in the new world that has succeeded the modern one. For example, in the post-Fordist system, it is argued, the driving seat of capitalism is no longer occupied by the engineers and production managers, by manufacturing or heavy industry, but rather by the marketing directors and design consultants, the retailers and the producers of 'concepts'. It is only with the emergence of postmodernity that consumer culture becomes central not just to the diagnosis of social pathologies (either cultural or economic) but also to social explanation at the highest systemic levels.

In this chapter we will see where this sense of newness comes from and where it might lead us, what social phenomena it brings into prominence and what issues it raises. The picture is very confusing, both because it is contemporary and because it is in fact confused. The biggest confusion arises around the term 'postmodernism'. On the one hand, postmodernism is an argument that in economic, social, political and cultural terms we now live predominantly in a world that is qualitatively different from the modern. It therefore makes various sociological claims about contemporary social life, which we can debate as we would any other sociological statements. In a word, we can do a sociology *of* postmodernity (an investigation into whether there have been decisive shifts and, if so, what society looks like now). This includes a sociology of postmodern*ism*, a study of shifts in the nature of culture – including everyday experience, aesthetic practices and social theory itself – which seem to be part of these new times. The first two sections of the chapter do that kind of work. We look first at post-Fordism and related ways of conceptualizing a restructuring of society around and through consumer culture. This in itself requires us to go back a bit further, to consider how people have thought through the role of consumption in social reproduction. We then consider a range of new developments that are held to exemplify postmodern consumer culture.

Beyond a sociology of postmodernity, however, there is postmodern sociology. This introduces a set of arguments to the effect that society in general, consumer culture in particular, can no longer be understood through old, modern concepts. For a figure like Baudrillard, the very things that modernism talked about – society, self, needs, utility – have disappeared from the postmodern world. His own account is – ironically – rather sociological, in that it generally accounts for these disappearances with claims about social changes which can be rationally investigated (and can prove to be unfounded). At the same time, the themes he raises also derive from post-structuralism and a kind of radical semiotics. These argue philosophically, rather than sociologically, that the old modern concepts were always fictions: it is not so much that they have disappeared as that we no longer believe in these myths. We will conclude by asking about the implications of this approach for the critique of consumer culture.

Consumption and capitalist reproduction

For many years, consumer culture was conventionally described in terms of the arrival of mass consumption as a counterpart to mass production:

generally speaking, the Fordist system. For about 30 years, it is now argued, we have seen the steadily accelerating break-up of this system and its replacement by fragmentation and diversification in both consumption and production. We will flesh out this picture in later sections. However, underlying the concepts of both Fordism and post-Fordism is a concern, which we will first need to look at in a wider context, to understand how production and consumption can be knitted together, or 'articulated', so that capitalist economy and society can be reproduced from one time-period to the next. Fordism and post-Fordism are ways of analysing two such modes of social reproduction.

Modernity has encouraged us to see consumption as a private and personal affair, yet paradoxically it also made of it a central tool of socio-economic management. The latter was a very long-term development, however, which required both economists and politicians to recognize that consumption is an integral part of economic and social reproduction and that while the consumption of *individuals* could be treated morally and politically as private, *aggregated* individual consumption – effective demand – was a major social force, which could be viewed *technically* in terms of its function in maintaining a stable or expanding system. It therefore becomes a legitimate object of state and corporate management, as well as of social and economic theory.

The key to this transition was the emergence of economic modes of thought and practice that tied individual consumption intrinsically to the health and growth of the body politic. In premodern Europe, famine and shortage (which continued in England until the mid-eighteenth century, in Ireland through the next century) could be viewed as periodic political crises of provisioning whose result was riot and mayhem – problems of public order rather than of social reproduction (Appleby 1993). Similarly, excessive consumption by lower orders, as we have seen, was labelled luxury and was seen as a problem more of 'cosmic order' (sin against natural hierarchy) than of economic stability (Sekora 1977).

As is frequently noted (OED; Williams 1976), until the eighteenth century the word consumption meant waste, using up, as in a consuming fire, or consumption as a wasting disease (Porter 1993a, 1993b). Similarly, in political and proto-economic terms, consumption was a loss, a departure of value from the social order, rather than part of the reproduction of that order, let alone a part of its expansion (though – in political terms – extravagant elite consumption could *represent* power). Mercantilist thought demonstrates this well. The wealth of the country is identified with the bullion contained in the coffers of the monarch: the health of the body politic is represented by the healthy household of the sovereign. Consumption will tend to deplete this wealth by drawing in imports – 'foreign fripperies that robbed this kingdom of its bullion' (Thirsk 1978: v). This is especially true in so far as monarchical power is bound up with international dynastic rivalry since wealth represents the political, military and economic capability to compete in war and adventure: excess consumption is not only waste but akin to treason. Moreover, in a context of low economic growth consumption appears to be a losing strategy in a zero-sum game: our contemporary positive valuations of consumption depend on the assumption of open-ended economic expansion.

From the late seventeenth century, there was a gradual redefinition of consumption as *demand*. Consumption as waste was a point of exit from the economy. Demand is something *within* economy, a nodal point within a circuit of material resources as it flows through a body politic. Unlike consumption, which saps the moral and political good, demand is both an opportunity and a necessity for the expanded reproduction of systematic social endeavour. Quesnay's *Tableau économique* was the most graphic demonstration of this shift. Representing the economy as a complex input–output table, Quesnay depicts an economy as a systematic set of relations between a multitude of endeavours, each seen from a specifically 'economic' point of view; consumption appears as an integral part of its operation.

The revaluation of consumption as part of social reproduction is not confined to economics. There is also a political revaluation, as theorized by, for example, Foucault, both in terms of bio-politics and liberal governmentality. This is the gradual reconceptualization of populations as a *resource* for national wealth and power. The people are to be 'policed' not only for social order but also in order to cultivate them as labour-power, military energy and self-governing political subjects. Their needs fit into the needs of national policy, their consumption into the reproduction of a social order. However, there is also a moral revaluation of consumption. This shift is exemplified by the furore over Mandeville's *Fable of the Bees* in the early eighteenth century, with its infamous announcement that 'private vices' rather than virtues generate public benefits. Mandeville argues, in verse, that even the most vicious and decadent of tastes and desires will stimulate the economic enterprise needed to satisfy them, thus increasing wealth and civic energy. Consumption is treated rigorously – if highly ironically and in its contemporary context cynically – from the point of view of wealth creation not moral judgement, in terms of its technical function within a process of expanded reproduction rather than its moral virtue or corruption: his standpoint is that of 'economic amoralism'. When Adam Smith, who owed much to Mandeville, argues less cynically and with less fanfare by 1776 that 'consumption is the sole end and purpose of production', he conjoins moral and technical concerns. He is certainly defending the consumer's right to goods produced efficiently and therefore cheaply under conditions of liberal economic deregulation, but he is also arguing that the potential for economic growth (and the division of labour) is determined by the size and extent of markets. A high wage economy allows those who create the wealth to share in its enjoyment, but it also produces the levels of demand necessary to an economy that is expanding to ever higher levels of activity (Smith 1986 (1776): 180–5).

Smith, like Mandeville, recognizes that in the form of demand consumption is integral to expanded reproduction. However, he does not yet recognize that the absence of demand is a potentially chronic source of crises in reproduction. The extent to which this recognition was absent in classical political economy is generally indicated by its decisive assumption of 'Say's law' that 'supply creates its own demand'. This postulate, though ambiguous in detail, states that a sum equivalent to the value of all commodities produced is paid out in the form of wages and profits to those involved in their production. There should, therefore, always and automatically be sufficient means in the economy to purchase the commodities produced: for every price asked there is – somewhere in the economy – a wage that has been paid. Say's law takes care of the macro-economic and longer-term balance between production and consumption; neo-classical economics took care of the short-run and micro imbalances through the price mechanism which automatically adjusts itself to bring supply and demand into equilibrium.

The idea that consumption can play a part in crises of economic and social reproduction was given centre stage in Ricardo's extensive defence of Say's law against attack from Malthus. Malthus argued that when incomes were saved rather than spent demand would not equal supply. In addition, saved money would contribute to an expansion of output. He argued this because (in common with most political economists) he assumed that saved money would be automatically invested in productive resources (capital) and thus lead to higher levels of production. A crisis of under-consumption would therefore be possible in which output could continue to expand on the basis of structurally ever-insufficient demand. Malthus's highly conservative solution to the dilemma was to laud the unproductive consumption of land-owning and rentier classes who lived on unearned income, that is to say income which funded increased demand for goods without generating any further supply.

This theme is central in Marx, as we shall see in a moment, but it became politically decisive through Keynes, in relation to the Great Depression. It was widely recognized before Keynes that low aggregate demand was a contributor to economic downturns. In line with Say's law, it was assumed however that equilibrium would be automatically restored when prices –

particularly of labour (the wage) and money (the interest rate) – reduced to a level that made investment attractive again, thus leading to the creation of new jobs and therefore an increase in demand for goods (because more wages are paid out). Why then the long years of depression? The patent failure of these laws and mechanisms to kick into operation during the Great Depression set the backdrop for Keynes's argument that equilibrium can be reached at levels well below full employment. A crucial variable here was the propensity to consume – the balance between saving and spending in individual household budgets. The propensity to consume tends to decrease as incomes rise (people have more disposable income and can save some of it for the future), thus lowering the rate of interest (since there is a larger supply of money its price goes down) but also decreasing demand and thus rendering unattractive those increases in productive investment that would generate more employment and hence increased demand. As a result saving and investment could reach equilibrium at lower than optimal levels of output – and *stay there*. While a propensity to consume is difficult to shift over a population (especially when it is considered, as Keynes did, to be determined by a psychological law), the same effects can be secured through macro-economic policy. Hence the role of government expenditure through public works and the expansion of the money supply, both of which attempt to increase aggregate demand while keeping the cost of investment (interest rates) low, thus seeking to secure the equilibrium between saving and investment at a level that will support full employment and maximum output. Basically, the government takes on the role of Malthus's 'unproductive consumers'.

It is important that consumption becomes a central and legitimate focus of economic theory and government policy simply as a *quantity*, a sum, that slots into the set of simultaneous equations by which the economy is modelled. Moreover, the aim of the whole exercise is quantitative and formal: higher levels of output and employment. Indeed, although *aggregate* consumption – the total quantity – is made an object of government intervention, Keynes made every effort not to politicize this intervention by dictating the content or substantive character of consumption. Hence, although Keynes is closely identified with the welfare state in Britain (much as Roosevelt and Hitler are closely associated with infrastructural government investment as a tool of demand management) he did not require that 'public works' be 'good works' or that aggregate effective demand take the form of any particular kind of consumption. Military rearmament would serve just as well as a national health service to overcome the multiplier effects of a declining propensity to consume, and of course a simple expansion of the money supply to fund higher wage settlements in the public sector became the established technique by the 1970s.

Where Keynes sees managerial problems (with solutions), Marx leads us into a labyrinth of intrinsic structural contradictions. As with Keynes, however, these contradictions regularly appear, at least in some of the Marxist tradition, as crises of under-consumption (for example in Hilferding, Luxembourg, Baran and Sweezy). Indeed, there have been long-running and rather sterile debates within Marxism between crises theories of over-production and under-consumption, yet all parties generally have to concede in the end that the basic point of Marxism, as for any other modern economic theory, is that production and consumption are intrinsically connected and in the very concrete sense that incomes from production and consumer buying power are two sides of the same coin.

As we have already seen in chapter 4, within the Marxist framework worker and consumer, capitalism and consumer culture, wage-labour and commodity consumption are born at the same moment: separation from the means of production entails both the sale of labour as a commodity and the buying of commodities to reproduce labour (the worker's needs are met by buying consumer goods through the market). In chapter 4, we looked at this in terms of alienation: how do needs, activities (work) and objects *appear* under these conditions?

However, Marx also generates an account of capitalist reproduction and crisis on the same basis. Commodities (including labour-power) are valued by their possessors not for their specific qualities (use-value), but for their abstract economic worth (exchange-value). However, in order to realize this economic worth, to sell these things, they must be use-values to *someone*, and to someone who has the money to buy them. There must be sufficient effective demand (enough of these someones) for individual firms to stay in business. Moreover, the imperative of capital accumulation drives capitalists to an enormous expansion of the technical means of production and thus to a titanic outpouring of commodities that have to be sold. This drive is structural. It is not driven by individual greed but rather by the conditions of capitalist competition – failure to develop productive capacity and efficiency on an expanded scale means that competing firms will capture markets through lower prices. The capitalist is left bankrupt, with a socially unnecessary stockpile of use-valueless widgets.

The need for the realization of exchange value, and therefore for ever higher levels of effective demand, thus arises from the separation of labour from the means of production and the consequent commodification of both labour and its products. But so too does the ever incipient failure of capitalism to meet this need. Firstly, the wage-relation on which capitalist production and expanded reproduction is based is one in which surplus value is extracted. The capitalist's entire aim is to maximize the gap (ultimately 'profit') between the value produced and the value paid for. However, this 'value paid for' is also the worker's wage, and hence the main constituent of effective demand in the market. Therefore, capitalism – as a result of its basic operating principle – simultaneously produces more goods and less effective demand to pay for them. (In the much longer run, the tendency for the rate of profit to fall through the increased organic composition of capital can also be expressed in the same form.) As any Marx primer will say, at root is a contradiction between forces and relations of production. Marx himself, as usual, puts it more colourfully:

> each capitalist does demand that his workers should save, but only *his own*, because they stand towards him as workers; but by no means the remaining world of workers, for these stand towards him as consumers. In spite of all his 'pious' speeches he therefore searches for means to spur them to consumption, to give his wares new charms, to inspire them with new needs by constant chatter, etc. (1973: 283).

Across the whole of the economy, then, and as a matter of capitalism's fundamental social logic, *every* capitalist is trying to decrease the wages and consumption of their own workers and entice everyone else's workers to consume to their limit and beyond.

Secondly, this structural contradiction is compounded by the market itself. Whereas for liberals the market solves all these problems through price adjustments (and for Keynes it will do so with a little strategic help), for Marx markets are always mechanisms of mystification. Precisely because markets mediate between production and consumption, the very basis of reproduction is in fact anarchic, irrational and endemically crisis-prone. Individual capitalists are driven to maximize output in advance of any knowledge of social need or even of effective demand. They do not know *ex ante* whether the labour they cause to be expended is socially necessary; the verdict is delivered *ex post* by empirical market behaviour: Did enough people actually buy? In an increasingly complex economy, the lines of sight become ever more hazy. Marx's most complete depiction of capitalist trade crisis argues that production in Department I (production of capital goods, of means of production themselves) can go on increasing for some considerable time before signals come back from Department II (consumer goods) that demand has dried up. By this point there is a mountain of both goods and productive capacity which has simply to be scrapped through bankruptcies.

It is important that this kind of logic drove Marxist responses to the post-war 'affluent society' in directions rather similar to Keynes or Galbraith. Most notably Baran and Sweezy (1977 (1966)) (but see also Sweezy (1942); Mandel (1976); Mattick (1971)) account for consumer culture in terms of 'absorption of the surplus': that is to say more value is produced than there is effective demand available to absorb it. Capitalism therefore requires extraordinary levels of waste in the old sense of 'non-productive consumption'. Military defence, Cold War arms races and contests for geopolitical dominance are good for wasting astronomical sums of money, in the process creating jobs but not commodities. Equally good – and indeed logically equivalent to war – is the 'sales effort': Baran and Sweezy argue that design and style changes, advertising, packaging and so on add extraordinary unproductive costs to production (i.e. costs occasioned by the commodity-form of goods as opposed to the use-value of things, as discussed in chapter 5) and therefore boost effective demand, while at the same time acting to suppress market competition by controlling the cultural content of that demand.

Consumption is therefore very much part of Marx's picture of capitalist reproduction and crisis. However, as for most other economists, it generally becomes part of the picture only when it is looked at as *effective demand*, an aggregated quantity of buying power. For the most part, when he is looking technically at systemic reproduction rather than substantively at commodity culture (alienation), Marx too treats needs (the actual use-values people want) as exogenous (for example, they are 'natural motives falling outside the economic process' (1973: 245); but compare Fine and Leopold (1993: 258–9)). To an extent this is because Marx agrees with liberal-utilitarians of every ilk that the capitalist economy is indeed formal and disembedded. His point is that this is *wrong* (it produces alienation and exploitation), not untrue, and also that it is not a natural situation but one that has been produced (and can be changed) by historical forces which it is his responsibility to discover and explain.

At the same time, there are a few crucial points at which Marx does relate substantive consumption to the formal capitalist economy, largely through the determination of wages. In each case, the qualitative character of consumption is directly connected to the level of wages, which represents the cost of reproducing labour. Firstly, and most crudely, by forcing wages down quantitatively the wage-relation and class exploitation also force them down qualitatively. As we saw in chapter 4, capitalism reduces workers to basic or even 'animal' needs.

A second account of consumption in Marx underpins this: precisely because of the formality of market economies, the price of labour is determined not by human need but by the supply and demand of labour-power on the market. When demand is high (periods of economic growth) or supply low (for example in nineteenth-century America) wages can be pushed up. However, when demand is low or labour is in over-supply (spilling over into a 'reserve army' of the unemployed), wages are pushed down to a minimum represented by the point at which the supply of labour dries up: that is to say, wages below the level at which workers can physically reproduce themselves (and their offspring) as labour-power - a point of starvation, chronic ill-health, exhaustion.

Thirdly, however, as a way of defining minimum wages and consumption levels the 'cost of reproducing labour' is historically variable and emerges from historical struggles over the standard of living, as Marx clearly recognizes. This cost cannot be defined either qualitatively or quantitatively by some natural or existential survival requirement: even under capitalism, labour is never just bodies, but people who are members of communities. There are – at any historical moment – different moral and political norms of what standard of living constitutes the bottom line of civilized life; there are traditional and customary – cultural – expectations and aspirations about lifestyle, not least among the workers themselves. Moreover, even from the capitalist's economic point of view labour is a variable whose reproduction requires different kinds of skill, discipline, manual and mental strengths, literacy and the transmission of these to the next generation. The most basic reproduction of labour thus involves culturally variable forms of consumption (such as education, parenting and a gender division of labour, housing, policing, religion and so on), which enter into defining as well as achieving that reproduction. Thus issues of culture, education, ideology, family life all enter into the labour costs of capitalism. They are part of setting the minimum consumption levels (and thus minimum wage) required for social reproduction. And although this minimum consumption norm enters into the negotiation of wage levels, it is not set by the market so much as by class struggle in its most general sense. Capitalists attempt to push wages down to the lowest levels compatible with reproducing the kind of labour force they require. The workers themselves use trade unions, industrial action, political parties, community resistance and religious movements   to define and struggle for what they believe is a *socially* minimum level of consumption for civilized life given available resources, cultural expectations and so on. Religious institutions, charities, philanthropies and welfare systems both public and private also join the game of trying to pin down something that is eminently mobile and historically variable: a basic standard of living, a level of consumption, which wages (plus these forms of welfare) must sustain at a given historical moment. (See Rowthorn (1980) for a good summary of Marx's theories of wages.)

Fordism

What is striking in Marx's perspective and what grounds theories of Fordism and post-Fordism is that while consumption norms are set by a complex of social, cultural, economic and political forces, *all of these* can be viewed from the perspective of the reproduction of labour and of the system. The consumption of the vast majority of the population must be set (quantitatively and qualitatively) in such a way that it strikes a balance between the systemic needs of, on the one hand, keeping labour costs low enough to maximize surplus value while still 'reproducing labour', and on the other hand, ensuring that wages are high enough to constitute an effective demand sufficient to realize the value which that labour produces. This perspective can result in a rather mechanistic functionalism: all social needs are explained in terms of the (functional or dysfunctional) part they play in keeping capitalism afloat. On the other hand, it can also give a powerful account of how production and consumption are, in practice, articulated in a system that ostensibly keeps them completely separate. (For a good critique of this perspective see Bagguley et al. 1990.)

The way labour is reproduced – the level of its consumption, some of its character (for example skills, labour discipline), the way in which it goes about its consumption (buying commodities) – is central to the reproduction of capital. Consumption norms, wage levels, effective demand and the size of markets are moments within an endless cycle of reproduction. A break at any point entails crisis. Capitalism needs to find 'modes of regulation' which prevent any such breaks. As a consequence, there is an imperative to link consumption as closely as possible into this cycle. But as consumption is about the way people live in general, not simply about their technical economic function, this linking involves not merely a regulation of capitalist economy, but of capitalist *society*.

'Fordism' and 'post-Fordism' are labels for two such modes of regulation. The latter term itself derives from the concept of neo-Fordism, developed by the French 'Regulationist School' of Marxist theory, centred around the work of Michel Aglietta and Alain Lipietz. They are far from the only theorists of Fordism, but they are certainly among the most influential (see Harvey 1982, 1988; Lee 1992). Their central point is that while the articulation of production and consumption is a functional necessity for capitalist reproduction it is not automatically secured. Rather, it is a historical achievement involving class struggle; there can be a failure to achieve it (resulting in crises), and ways of achieving it can reach their limits so that new ways have to be found (hence a move to post-Fordism). The general tendency over the course of modern capitalist development has, however, been fairly clear. Capital is 'a social structure that is produced by labour, but which subjects labour to the logic of its own reproduction . . . far from attenuating this social necessity, the evolution of capitalism in the twentieth century has generalized it to encompass the totality of social relations. The extension of wage-labour has made society homogenous as never before ... ' (Aglietta 1979: 24). This subjection flowed outwards to dominate all of capitalist society because capitalism 'transformed not only the labour process but also the process of reproduction of labour-power', thus producing a new 'characteristic mode of consumption of the wage-earning class, and ... integrating this mode of consumption into the conditions of production'.

Early modern capitalism (up to the late nineteenth century in America, as studied by Aglietta) separated workers from ownership of the means of production and reduced them to wage-labour but did not entirely transform their mode of consumption. Certainly communities were broken up as individuals and households moved to cities and industrial areas, and certainly they were increasingly brought into a cash economy in which they had to buy commodities. None the less, domestic consumption involved, to very late dates, domestic production, for example making clothes, growing vegetables, raising animals, making one's own entertainment (Braverman 1974). This lack of commodity consumption caused little discomfort to a capitalist economy which was focused predominantly on the production of capital goods (Department I) rather than consumer goods (Department II): wage-labourers would never constitute markets for the steel, coal, chemicals, etc. which then preoccupied capitalist accumulation.

Two major and interrelated shifts occur around the turn of the century. Firstly, the focus of capital accumulation moves 'forward' from producer to consumer goods, as it must. Only so much steel is necessary until there is a greater demand for, say, automobile production, which uses steel. Mass markets for consumer goods must now be found, or – to put it in terms of the concept of reproduction – the reproduction of labour-power (workers' consumption) must be based on buying commodities (the new consumer goods) rather than on domestic production. This requires both social transformation (destruction of traditional communities, already largely accomplished by the social disruption of industrial urbanization itself) and sufficient wages (accomplished by the Fordist notion of a high wage/high output growth economy based on collective bargaining on the assumption of a steadily rising standard of living).

The massive expansion in the production of consumer goods is related to the second shift, a transformation of the work process itself. Aglietta theorizes this as a shift from a regime of accumulation based on extracting from the worker 'absolute surplus-value' (increasing production by lengthening the working day, buying more hours worth of labour-power) to a regime based on 'relative surplus-value' (increasing the efficiency and therefore productivity of the same quantity of labour-power). This is accomplished through all the now-familiar tools of automation, intensive division of labour,

efficient management of inventory and throughput, strict cost-accounting
and so on. The epitome is the Fordist mass-production plant itself, the
Dearborne plant with its flow-past assembly line, a mechanized version of
Adam Smith's pin factory, in which the analytical breakdown of production
into individual, repetitive tasks is carried to its ultimate conclusion: the task
arrives at the worker's station so as not to require (or allow) any waste of
time in moving between jobs. Fordism, from this perspective, represents
systemic planning of every move within production by intensifying the
technical division of labour. Fordism is accompanied by Taylorism. Every
movement of the worker in carrying out a task is examined and analysed to
eliminate wasted effort and time, and then to formalize the resulting analysis
as a productivity norm which the worker must then meet. The worker is
completely subordinated to a production process planned in detail, and thus
loses any control over labour, is deskilled (Taylor once notoriously described
his workers as trained gorillas), loses any free time at work by losing control
over the pace of work (you can't chat, go to the loo, etc.) (Braverman 1974).
However, for Ford rationalization of the production progress always
extended beyond mechanical movements on the assembly line to the
inculcation of labour discipline through, for example, the 'company town'
which encouraged '100% Americanism' through education, moral policing
and Ford's infamous 'sociology department', but also through offering high
wages and therefore increased consumption possibilities as compensation
and incentive. Moreover, all such rationalization of life outside the work-
place was partly designed to counter the alienation produced by rationalization inside the workplace.

All these features, described by Aglietta in terms of relative surplus-value,
are also those described by authors such as Weber, Simmel and above all
Lukács in terms of rationalization and reification (see chapter 4), and the
same issue arises here, though in greater technical detail: how does this
rationalization of the worker's labour in production become generalized to
the reproduction of labour in consumption, and indeed to everyday life and
culture in general?

In fact, according to Aglietta, labour can be transformed and rationalized
without this logic being extended to the rest of everyday life. This is the
'extensive regime of accumulation' characteristic of western capitalism until
around the turn of the century: 'the traditional way of life may persist or be
destroyed, but it is not radically recomposed by the logic of utilitarian
functionalism' (1979: 71). That is to say, pre-capitalist social relations (close
relations between town and country, between work and the seasons and
customs, between public and domestic life) can be destroyed without
consumption becoming dominated by purchased commodities. An *intensive*
regime of accumulation, on the other hand, involves transformation a

transformation not merely of the labour process, but also of the reproduction of labour-power. High-volume mass production requires the mass consumption of commodities, and the separation of workers from the means of producing their own consumer goods cheaply and efficiently renders this at least a possibility. Yet although capitalism requires the consumption of commodities, Aglietta recognizes that consumption is predominantly private and cannot be the object of legitimate direct compulsion by the state or business. None the less, consumption is structured by the worker's life in production – it is 'subject to the general logic of the reconstitution of energies expended in social practices' (156). Mainly, rationalization of labour (Taylorism) and the separation of work and home allow no time for recuperation at work: all 'repair' is concentrated in leisure-time. Domestic consumption is therefore geared to keeping people mentally and physically fit for work (much like the Frankfurt School stress on consumption as recuperation, or Lefebvre's analysis of alienated leisure).

This consumption is focused on commodities and therefore conditioned by capitalist relations of production. Above all, modern (particularly American) consumption was governed by standardized housing and the automobile. Both are significant in that, firstly, 'It was important for the process of individual consumption to be organised and stable, while remaining compatible with the apparently individual and free relationships of commodity exchange' (159). The small family as primary unit of consumption, constructing a home and relating it to work through car transport, achieves this aim. Moreover, both house and car 'created complementarities which effected a gigantic explosion of commodities, supported by a systematic diversification of use values . . . whose evolution was governed by the replacement of direct activity at home by time-saving equipment'. That is, each of these commodities is at the centre of a whole universe of related commodity consumption. Secondly, both illustrate the domination of consumption by the logic of Fordist production in that they involve the consumption of standardized goods, subordinated to a 'functional aesthetic' which is amenable to automated mass production. That is to say, Fordist mass production requires not only a large quantitative scale of social consumption but also a qualitative form. Fordist consumption is built around economies of scale and therefore decreasing unit-costs, achieved by standardizing goods. Finally, Aglietta considers the cultural differentiation of consumer goods to be based on the representation of status positions, which he regards as an ideological process. These representations are organized into something rather similar to what other authors call lifestyle: 'acquired habits which stabilize the maintenance of labour-power into a routine' (157) and which can be learned via the family, advertising and so on.

Rather more original, and less functionalist, is Aglietta's analysis of how all this appears at the political level. This is probably best visualized in terms of national collective bargaining. Organized business has to keep wage-costs low; it has to ensure that labour is willing to submit to intensive planning and rationalization in the work place; and it has also to ensure that the massive output of goods can be sold. Organized labour – despite rumblings from its more radical elements – is convinced to give up all work-place power (though it demands, with some success, that government regulate certain conditions of work, such as health and safety) and to maintain labour discipline (honour their contracts, get to work on time, make their right to strike narrowly conditional, etc.). In exchange, labour demands steadily rising wages. This is fine by organized business because these wage levels are set so that they do not threaten profits, while at the same time they rise predictably enough to ensure reliable effective demand over the short and medium term. The rising standard of living – the social 'consumption norm' – is an organized and stable framework, and it is set, directly or indirectly, on the assumption that all consumption will involve the consumption of commodities. Finally, government is also a happy party to these negotiations, because in exchange for legally enforcing these arrangements it secures political and industrial peace, minimal structural threats to social order and, through full employment at reasonable wages, a reduced welfare bill. (It is important to recognize that the whole 'deal' emerges from negotiations involving unionized labour: the resulting 'social consumption norm' therefore does not apply to most women or ethnic minorities, who are excluded from direct participation in the process. This undermines much of the analysis (Bagguley, et al. 1990: 20).)

The idea that mass production requires or produces mass consumption is hardly original to Aglietta, let alone to debates on post-Fordism. Though the mechanisms by which the two are connected (usually advertising and manipulation) may be less theoretically sophisticated, the same central point is generally made, that mass consumption kills two capitalist birds with the single stone of a rising standard of living: firstly, it secures the markets necessary to absorb mass output; secondly, it secures industrial and political peace. Consumer culture constitutes a 'bribe' in that workers (at any rate skilled and organized workers) are offered freedom and relative plenty in the sphere of consumption in exchange for accepting intensive rationalization, alienation and utter lack of control over their work life, and for politically accepting a 'democratic' system that manages but does not fundamentally challenge capitalism. This theme extends from Lukács through the Frankfurt School analysis of mass culture as 'compensatory', and is made explicit in authors such as Braverman (1974), Ewen (1976) and Williams (1980).

Post-Fordism

In accounting for a shift away from Fordism and mass consumption, we are again dealing with a mode of regulation which interconnects numerous economic, political and cultural factors. A generic summary of the transition to post-Fordism would include the following considerations. Up to the early 1970s, consumer society is seen as part of a system that has overcome economic crises and trade cycles. From the early 1970s it becomes increasingly evident that this system is reaching its internal and external limits. The costs and time-scale of investment in Fordist production have become colossal, while the logic of high output and lower unit costs has been pushed to the point where vast quantities of goods have to be sold with decreasing margins. This has to be accomplished in the context of increasingly saturated consumer markets and of ever faster turn-over in fashions, tastes, trends (itself the result of decades of Fordist mass-marketing). Consider investing hundreds of millions over five years of research and development and plant-building in factories and distribution networks that are inflexibly dedicated to producing millions of units of yet another chocolate bar, which has to be sold in huge volumes alongside dozens of others to the consumers of half a decade into the future: the risk gets silly.

The response to this situation is reckoned to be 'flexibility' and 'flexible accumulation'. In place of dedicated plant churning out high volumes of standardized goods to achieve economies of scale, the aim is now to have flexible plant (and labour) that can cost-efficiently produce smaller batches of more customized goods. These can also be brought from design through production to the consumer at a speed appropriate to the turn-over rate of consumer tastes and styles. The capability to do this is largely associated with new technologies – particularly computerization and robotics – which replace the mammoth capital costs of scrapping or retooling dedicated plant when product lines are changed with the notional cost of reprogramming a robot arm to move slightly differently. Optimally, responding to changed consumer taste for widgets as opposed to sky-hooks should be as simple and cheap as using computer-aided design to specify a new product and to generate orders for materials, instructions for the plant and details for the retailers. Not only is the response fast and cheap, it also means that small and specifically customized runs of products are no more expensive to produce per unit than very long and standardized runs.

Flexibilization extends well beyond the production line, generally along the flow of information. For example, post-Fordism is associated with rapid and interconnected flows of information from points of sale through to material suppliers (as in the idea of 'Benetton capitalism'). 'Just-in-time' management relies on such flows to ensure that precise daily or even hourly breakdowns of sales of every item in a product range, in all its possible specifications, are fed back to the producer. This allows the producer to produce only as much as is needed, but also to order only so much of producers' goods as will be required in the very short term, thus reducing losses to profitability due to stockholding and high inventory by speeding up the flow of circulating capital. Flexibilization and information are also associated with decentralization and the devolution of powers and responsibility within the firm. The rigorously hierarchical chain of command of the Fordist system is rendered unnecessary by distributed information networks, while smaller, more autonomous work units comprising flexibly trained workers rather than Taylorized machine-tenders respond quickly and creatively and more in keeping with the new technologies themselves.

On the other hand, all this new flexibility is not purely production-led, for Fordism has also reached other internal limits, above all – at least for Aglietta – the limits of work-place alienation. Increasing industrial action (strikes, stoppages, sabotage, absenteeism and so on), accelerating rates of inflation and the new phenomenon of 'stagflation' seemed to indicate by the 1970s that the deal cut by Fordism was no longer so good for the parties involved. Above all, steadily rising standards of living were no longer sufficient compensation for the magnitude of alienation in either the work-place or the wider society. Either the standard of living was not rising fast enough (and could rise no faster without either reducing profits or increasing inflation unacceptably) or consumer culture itself was no longer sufficient compensation. Or – as in Bell's argument - it was consumer culture and the 'hedonistic ethic' encouraged by Fordism itself which eroded the work ethic and work discipline, and created a 'revolution of rising expectations' (Bell 1979: 233). Whichever was the case, leading-edge firms, it is argued, have increasingly moved from the Taylorist model of worker as deskilled machine-tender to the model of 'human resources' (Rose 1991). The firm is now to make use not only of the workers' labour-power in its traditional sense but also of their motivation, creativity, personality and indeed, as we move into the 1980s, of their enterprising character. At the same time, flexible (i.e. insecure) labour complements flexible technology.

As in the case of Fordism, we can relate these changes to an altered mode of consumption within an overall mode of regulation, in this instance a post-Fordist mode. Firstly – and this is usually the central theme – flexibilization is associated with a move from standardized products that are sold to homogeneous mass markets to customized products that are sold to segmented markets. This involves a shift away from models of social relations and structure which were implicit in earlier, Fordist marketing practices. The older model aimed at *differentiating* products from competing products (through their 'real or imagined' qualities) but *aggregating* individual consumers into mass and undifferentiated markets at a national or international scale. In so far as it had to take account of the underlying social differentiation of consumers, it did so through standard demographic categories: the division of the population into different occupations, genders, age groups and geographical regions (ethnicity scarcely figured – see, for example, Marchand 1986). The assumption was that different patterns of consumer taste and buying power mapped out fairly predictably along these classic dimensions of social structure.

Post-Fordist marketing, on the other hand, disaggregates markets and consumption into 'lifestyles', 'niche markets', 'target consumer groups', 'market segments'. These are not defined by broad social demographic structures (and do not correlate with them easily, if at all) but rather by cultural meanings which link a range of goods and activities into a coherent image. The broader claim is that lifestyle marketing not only identifies and targets existing lifestyles but rather *produces* them by organizing consumers according to meaningful patterns, constructed and distributed through design, advertising and the media (which are themselves increasingly segmented or 'narrowcast' rather than mass). As against Bourdieu's argument that taste and lifestyle do not merely reflect social structure but enter into its constitution through forms of social practice, the further argument of post-Fordism is that culturally constituted lifestyle categories have now replaced, or increasingly *dis*place, social structural categories like class and gender, which are associated with modern as opposed to postmodern stratification. The endpoint of this argument – for example Baudrillard – is that the object formerly known as society has now dissolved into an endless and unanchored production of lifestyles by the codes and templates of marketing and similar logics. The less extreme argument – for example the 'New Times' line (Hall and Jacques 1989; Mort 1989) – is that (post)modern citizens associate self-definition, identity, pleasure, freedom and so on with their everyday life in consumption as opposed to production (which is unsurprising given workplace alienation, the centrality of choice and the centuries-long modern association of individual meaning and worth with the private domain). On this basis, forms of association and identity based on work or citizenship rather than consumption – for example trade-unions and political parties – lose the interest and allegiance of most people and become increasingly ineffective as social forces.

All these developments are associated with the ending of the Fordist roles of the state. Beleaguered if not bankrupted by the cost of its demand management and welfare obligations, side-lined by the internationalization of capital, its traditional constituencies disaggregated into mobile lifestyles and 'new social movements', unable to find, let alone manage, the 'commanding heights of the economy', the state enters a period of retrenchment and neo-liberal deregulation. There is a move away from demand management to a devolution of all social decision making to the sphere of market-mediated consumption.

We will take up a number of these elements in the following pages, but a few general points need making. Firstly, arguments about post-Fordism (like those about post-industrial and post-capitalist society) have from the start been mixed up with futurology: we are reading trends and sometimes tea-leaves. For example, the extent of actual roboticization is still uncertain, while the decentralization and disaggregation of firms may simply be a long-term, and cyclical, feature of capitalism in general. Secondly, as stressed by contemporary debates on globalization and localization, notions like flexibilization, disaggregation and market segmentation do not imply that capitalism is getting smaller or cosier. Even the capacity to target market may depend on industrial and marketing technologies capable of operating on a global scale. Similarly, the quintessential postmodern play-space represented by the shopping mall depends on levels of investment and rationalization never achieved even by Fordism. Thirdly, there are questions about the significance of these new times for both economy and culture. While some commentators are concerned to argue that post-Fordism represents new adaptations within a system that is still very much capitalist, others argue that they spell the dissolution of 'economy' as such. Similarly, a more flexible response to consumers or the treatment of workers as human resources rather than trained gorillas can be interpreted as offering either new spaces for human autonomy (or resistance) or simply a far deeper and more insidious integration of social subjects within the old, familiar systemic requirements of capitalism.

Lastly, to whatever extent new forms of marketing now predominate, the historical and conceptual distinction between product differentiation and market segmentation, the move from the mass to the fragmented and from social structure to lifestyle culture may be rather overdrawn (Slater 1985, 1993: 202–3). For example, Ford's mass production/mass consumption strategy of 'any colour you want so long as it's black' was rapidly superseded – in his own market – by 'Sloanism' at General Motors, as early as the mid-1920s (Rothschild 1973). Sloan organized a highly differentiated range of cars around lifestyle categories, especially biographical segments (for example a car for single people, for young marrieds, families and so on). General Motors was not an eccentric pioneer but the largest corporation in the world for most of the so-called Fordist period. Evidence that market segmentation existed alongside product differentiation within Fordism is often obscured by attempts to generalize across industries (Leiss et al. 1986) that do not look at the development of marketing within particular industries (compare Fine and Leopold 1993). Finally, there is a conceptual problem in separating product differentiation from market segmentation, let alone in assigning them to different historical epochs: as any marketer will say, the two are inextricable because a product difference must be a difference *for* a particular consumer segment for whom that difference has relevance.

Consumer culture and the postmodern

In theorizing consumer culture today, the notoriously confused notion of the postmodern summarizes the idea of an epochal shift or new organization and dynamic of consumption. The idea of a postmodern culture is clearly bound up with post-Fordism: the domination of information, media and signs, the disaggregation of social structure into lifestyles, the general priority of consumption over production in everyday life and the constitution of identities and interests. However, possibly the central theme linking the two is the dematerialization of objects and commodities, indeed of the economy and ultimately of society as a whole. This theme is sometimes glossed with the Baudrillardian slogan that we no longer consume things but only signs. However, in the context of post-Fordism, dematerialization can point to at least four different social developments.

Firstly, non-material goods play an ever greater role in the economy and in consumption. Broadly, there is the notable shift in the centre of economic gravity (in terms of value, volume and employment) from manufacturing to service industries. In fact, 'service' is a very ambiguous term (Bagguley et al. 1990; Gershuny and Miles 1983), and many services can include a considerable material component (McDonald's sells billions of very physical hamburgers, tourism involves major infrastructural development). None the less, much consumption comprises such things as information, advice and expertise, leisure events and activities, entertainment. Much of this testifies to the fact that more of the social world, including social relations and experiences, can be made in the form of a saleable commodity for consumption.

Secondly, even material commodities appear to have a greater non-material component. This includes the extension of 'commodity aesthetics', so that much of a product seems to comprise design, packaging and advertising imagery, and these elements seem to be dominant in the object's constitution (in production, distribution and consumption). A more general sense of this dematerialization is indicated by the fact that, whereas people used to talk about the consumption of goods and services, we now tend to talk about product 'experiences': Mars does not sell chocolate bars but rather a 'taste experience'.

Thirdly, part of this increasingly non-material composition is attributed to the *mediation* of goods. That is to say, we encounter objects (and services, experiences and activities that have become objectified as commodities) increasingly in the form of representations: in advertising, in portrayals of lifestyle in films, TV, magazines, in mediated encounters with celebrities and stars and so on. It is part of the paradox of alienation, one could say, that things become more objective and less material at the same time. This is certainly one implication of both the 'society of the spectacle' and Baudrillard's 'hyper-reality'. The phantasmagoria of signs becomes more substantial as the reality it once represented evaporates.

Fourthly, the dematerialization of consumer goods is often closely related to the equally non-material nature of producer goods, above all the commodity 'labour-power'. A long and exceptionally disparate line of thinkers (for example Bell, Toffler, Tourraine, Mills, Riesman, Lyotard) argue that regardless of the materiality of the final product, the process of production is increasingly governed by non-material functions involving knowledge, science, expertise, systems, planning and cybernetic skills. The raw material of much industry is increasingly non-material, as a result of technological developments, the rationalization of corporate management and the increasing abstraction of international financial and investment networks.

This results in, firstly, new and expanding markets in non-material commodities: databases, computer systems and software design, information, specialist knowledges sold by consultants, subcontracted management, planning and marketing functions, personnel and client relations management and so on. Secondly, less labour, it is argued, is spent on transforming matter and rather more on such things as dealing with customers, getting along with colleagues and effecting their co-operation, representing the firm, sales and marketing. One long-running contention, which we glimpsed in chapter 3, is that as 'human labour' is increasingly seen as 'human resources', the company no longer buys a quantity of abstract labour, but buys 'personality', commitment, personableness and social skills, sincerity, emotional warmth and so on (Hochschild 1983). What Sinclair Lewis castigated in the 1920s and Riesman and Mills chronicled for the 1950s seems to become the principle of the postmodern 1980s and 1990s: as labour, you have to sell your personality; this requires *work* – carried out through consumption – to dress well, look right, be attractive, stay up-to-date on culture, news and fashion. *Personality* is exemplary of the dematerialized commodity and its culture: what you are, what you sell and what you consume seem to have formed a frightening unity.

The dematerialization of things has a profound impact on the way they circulate and enter into everyday life as consumer goods. Firstly, there is an enormous speed-up in the circulation of capital and consumption in all their phases. Turn-over times, re-investment and capital deployment, rates of innovation and obsolescence of both producer and consumer goods, style changes – all reach hysterical velocities (Jameson 1984; Lash and Urry 1987, 1993; Mandel 1976). Secondly, dematerialization raises new issues of power. For example, if, as Lash and Urry (1993) point out, flows of information and signs become so central to control, production, work and consumption then access to and control over information networks arbitrate social power. Lash and Urry discuss information 'ghettos': social spaces off the networks are plunged into a vicious spiral of economic, social and cultural poverty. In a sense, this returns us to Bourdieu's notion of 'cultural capital' (or Douglas and Isherwood's analysis of information exchange) but gives it considerably added force since culture has become *literally* a form of capital.

Finally, all these elements of the dematerialization of the object are aspects of what Featherstone describes as a general 'aestheticization of everyday life' (Featherstone 1991b: 67–8), the sense of a world saturated by the flow of signs and images, a world encountered through images and in the form of images, in which – as Baudrillard argues – things appear to be set free from their material or even social determinations to be elaborated purely as commodity-signs or sign-values. (For an interesting attempt to 'screen' these developments for the marketing community itself, see Brown (1994)).

The unstable sign

Dematerialization of the object and the triumph of signs is associated with many forms of instability, maleability and fluidity of culture. Above all, dematerialization seems to imply a break-down or 'implosion' of the difference between representation and reality, sign and material good, culture and economy. It therefore evidences possibly the central theme of the postmodern: the break-down, instability or transgression of boundaries and distinctions. Lash (1990), for example, analyses this as a process of 'de-differentiation'. Modernity involved the constitution of different social realms, each of which is capable of autonomous development and even progress, and each of which is constituted through fundamental analytical distinctions as well as through social and conceptual hierarchies. In postmodern culture, these realms and distinctions blur or implode, and the vertical hierarchies are consequently flattened into a horizontal plane of equivalence. The list of modernist distinctions that are now considered blurred and flattened is fairly endless: high culture / mass culture, truth/fiction, mind/body, science/art, culture/society, art / everyday life, dominant culture / subculture. The list generally also includes standard social structural distinctions such as class, gender and 'race' or ethnicity.

In most accounts of postmodernity, consumer culture both exemplifies the blurring and flattening of modernist distinctions and indicates the medium through which it happens; it may even constitute an explanation. In watching the flow of television, for example, we may be watching soap opera one minute, opera the next; flick from melodrama to politics, to a drama–documentary that merges the two; attend more pleasurably to an advert than to a programme; observe a real war in progress or a political event staged for the camera. Things which inhabited different worlds and value systems, and were consumed by different audiences, now occupy a single cultural space. Moreover, that single cultural space may seem to be occupied by everyone, everywhere, at the same time, as in McLuhan's image of the 'global village'. The flattened plane of signs breaks down temporal, geographic and demographic boundaries (for example Meyrowitz 1986). Earlier accounts of capitalism might attribute this to spreading commodification: all things, whether culturally high or low, public or private, can be made equivalent as things to be bought and sold. In the notion of postmodern culture, commodities have been dematerialized and now exist purely as signs circulating within a 'political economy of signs'. However seemingly infinite the number of different signs in circulation, they are all completely the same in being 'just signs'. Within this circulation of signs, there can be nothing but choice – things have no intrinsic meaning or anchorage in the world; they simply constitute a selection of signs from which to pick and mix. 'Eclecticism is the degree zero of contemporary general culture: one listens to reggae, watches a western, eats McDonald's food for lunch and local cuisine for dinner, wears Paris perfume in Tokyo and "retro" clothes in Hong Kong; knowledge is a matter for TV games' (Lyotard, quoted in Callinicos 1989: 162). Where there are only signs, there is only difference, but differences that cannot be differentially valued or hierarchized; only different signs that are all equivalent to each other.

The crucial 'de-differentiation' for accounts of postmodern culture is the implosion of sign and reality, or, in semiotic terms, of sign and referent, connotation and denotation. The plane of signs and culture can no longer be plausibly anchored in, as Baudrillard puts it, 'finalities' in the external world. Consumption is no longer anchored in the finality of need, nor knowledge in truth, technocracy in progress, history in a metanarrative characterized by causation and teleology. These external anchors for meaning are now revealed, and indeed experienced, as being internal to the arbitrary game of culture and signification. As a result, contemporary experience is 'depthless': there is nothing credible beneath or beyond the flat landscape of endless signification. For example, time and history no longer constitute a logic or context of change (and explanation) comprising real social processes and relations. History is reduced to signifiers – styles, references, images, objects – which can circulate independently of their original contexts. Hence, postmodern architecture assembles styles from different periods and places them into 'pastiches' which aim at immediate effect without any obligation to historical coherence; fashion endlessly recycles, revives and recombines period clothing; national cultures and 'heritage' are torn from their contexts to be moulded into consumable tourist commodities ('Merrie Olde England', peasant costume, theme park history) (Jameson 1984; see also Lukács's (1971: 90) analysis of reification as the reduction of time to space). In each case, the consumable sign does not refer to a real historical sequence but rather to a grab-bag of equivalent and contemporaneous styles or images which mean (and compete) in relation to each other. Hence, for example, Jameson's (1984) account of the 'schizophrenic' subject of postmodernity, who inhabits a purely present tense and is therefore unable to form a coherent ego (which requires the capacity to formulate projects with temporal duration) and instead swims chaotically down a never-ending river of signification.

This schizophrenic subject becomes one of two exemplars of the postmodern consumer (and the consumer becomes exemplary of the postmodern subject). On the one hand, the consumer, inhabiting a perpetual present, confronts all of social life as a field of simultaneous and depthless images from which to choose, but to choose without reference to any externalities or anchors ('finalities' like need or value or truth). Consumer culture is a fancy-dress party in which we dress up our everyday lives in ever-changing costumes, drawn from an inexhaustible wardrobe and driven by impulses which are themselves prompted by the life of the party rather than the life outside it. On the other hand, the postmodern consumer is reckoned to be ironic and knowing, reflexive and aware of the game being played. In a sense, the mass consumer of modernity was suckered – was truly conformist, really wanted things, was really *in* the game. The postmodern consumer in contrast is hyper-aware of the game itself (indeed, that is the only way to play it). This consumer must have considerable cultural capital in order both to make sense of the wealth of mobile and detached signs and to be able to treat them as *just* signs; must obtain pleasure not from the things themselves but from the experience of assembling and deconstructing images; must be free of obligations to finalities in order to keep in view the play of signs, and keep up with it. For example, unlike the romantic traveller in search of authenticity, or the mass package holiday maker who captures a 'real' experience in snapshots, the 'post-tourist' *knows* that she or he is a tourist and 'that tourism is a series of games with multiple texts and no single, authentic tourist experience' (Urry 1988: 154; see also Bagguley et al. 1990; MacCannell 1989; Urry 1990).

Because signs are said to be no longer anchored in finalities, postmodernity can be understood as 'post-responsibility', in both a positive and negative sense. Either one is liberated from old and domineering myths and free to play with newly liberated symbolic resources, or one is exonerated from all moral and collective obligations, as well as from the reckoning of truth, and ruled only by libidinal impulses in a purely relativist world. We will take up some of these divisions below, but it is necessary to register from the start the political ambiguity of postmodernism: it is perpetually veering between the two traditional characterizations of consumer culture, unable to decide whether it represents the ultimate in anomie or in freedom.

Baudrillard and the death of 'the social'

Underlying postmodern accounts of consumer culture is the 'loss of the real': through the dematerialization of the object in contemporary capitalist production and consumption, and through the corresponding consumer and cultural experiences of a world constituted in and through signs, not only objects but all finalities are reduced to signs positioned in protean codes. The 'real' that is lost is not only needs and objects but also social structural realities of class, gender, ethnicity and indeed the social itself: all of these are reduced to *images* of the social and lived out through the imagistic medium of lifestyle.

We can thank Baudrillard, as ever, for pushing this logic to its ultimate conclusions. He does so by pursuing the radical semiotics we looked at in chapter 5. As we saw there, Baudrillard defines the social logic of consumption in terms of the 'logic of social difference'. This logic is 'semiotic': the meanings of goods derive entirely from their relational position in social codes (codes of function, prestige, aesthetics etc.). Moreover, for Baudrillard the idea of 'the Code' is not a methodological tool of analysis but a social fact, indeed a social process or even social agent that arises with the development of advanced capitalism. Thus commodity exchange – the rule of exchange value initiated by early capitalism – produced the idea of use-value: signs and things must refer to finalities, to referents, realities in the world such as real needs and real objects with properties that satisfy them. In this industrial capitalist world, life is dominated by the referent (real needs and objects); and 'the social bond' is effected via exchange value (people are connected by the equivalence of value as they pursue their separate interests). Yet the very emergence of this system indicates that objects have been released from their traditional contexts and no longer relate to the real world but only to each other: 'they are homogenous as cultural signs and can be instituted in a coherent system' (Kellner 1989: 10). We no longer consume products (referents) but rather signs, and indeed the system of signs: what we buy in and through the consumer good is the social place it maps out in relation to all the other commodity-signs in the system. Conversely, we now secure social place and identity solely through the commodity-sign rather than through our position in social structural referents such as class. The value of goods no longer arises from their use or even from their abstract economic exchange: rather, it is their sign-value that defines them. The commodity, once liberated as 'sign' can 'float free from the referent or product, and domination and the "social bond" are no longer achieved through the referent but the sign. Moreover, our identities are constructed through the exchange of sign-values, and the means of legitimation of the signifier (or the image) is the signified' (Kellner 1989: 29), which is *within* the semiotic code, rather than the referent, which is external and final.

Firstly, then, the sign becomes increasingly autonomous of social determinations. It has no referent, but only self-referentiality, its relational position within codes. Secondly, codes come to dominate social production and consumption. They structure reality, rather than merely reflect or represent it, by organizing production and ordering consumption (which has become the consumption of signs). Thirdly, now that signs no longer reflect but rather produce 'the real', the boundary between sign and referent, representation and reality, code and materiality is blurred and uncertain, largely irrelevant: it is imploded. The boundary, the differentiation, is dismantled and the two spheres merge. Finally, as a consequence of this implosion, all of social life takes on the characteristics of the code (as defined by semiotics). Everything is equivalent to everything else as a sign (just as everything used to be equivalent as exchange values), everything is arbitrary (any sign can replace any other), everything is indeterminate, and nothing is any more real or more true than anything else (there are no finalities, no ultimate anchors for the code that stand outside the code).

In many respects it is the second step that is crucial, the idea that codes structure and constitute reality. Baudrillard is partly making the conventional point that mediated experience (signs, media, images) increasingly replaces real face-to-face interactions, and so the social bond is effected through the logic of signs. However, he is also making the more radical (but not unprecedented) point that the logic of signs dominates the constitution of reality through all forms of production and organization. For example, in arguments reminiscent of Bell or Riesman, Baudrillard assumes a post-industrial society dominated by information and knowledge commodities and in which labour has been transformed from work on materials to social management using social skills; the 'mode of production' is transformed into a 'code of production'. The planning function, simulation models and cybernetic systems – rather than the brute movement of materials – now dominate production and the techno-industrial apparatus. Baudrillard's term for this situation is 'simulation': representation neither mimics the world nor simply reproduces it endlessly (as in Fordist mass production) but generates it through its own models. The things it generates are not real but 'hyperreal', defined as copies for which no original exists. The airport lounge, the McDonald's hamburger, the theme park, muzak – all endlessly duplicated across the globe – are not reproductions of some original referent; they are rather more or less perfect instantiations of a genetic code that generates them. Hence, once again, the stuff of everyday life is utterly without depth and bears no connection to nor the imprint of social relations evolved over time. Living in the postmodern world means knowing or flowing with the codes that generated it.

But the social has indeed disappeared according to Baudrillard. The interrelations and activities of civil society – Hume's world of commerce – have been replaced by the cybernetic abstractions of opinion polls, market research, elections, the media. These again are simulations and quantitative models rather than social relations, and they kill off social relations even in the attempt to construct or simulate the illusion of a society (as in the phone-in radio programme or studio audience). As in the spectacular society, the 'masses' can only confront them passively. Moreover, as in Lefebvre and Debord, the result of the death of the social is a people that is neither manipulated nor rebellious (rebel in the name of *what?*), neither conformist nor possessed of even the concept of the revolutionary (except as a signifier for advertising's announcement of something entirely new, which is always the same). Rather they are terminally bored, indifferent, neutralized. Indeed, for Baudrillard, but not for Debord, their only proper response to consumer culture is an ever more intense passivity, an absorption of yet more signs and meanings in the attempt to expose the utter meaninglessness of all these signs. This is the 'black hole' of the 'silent majorities' which by absorbing and killing all the meaning that consumer culture can throw at them will expose the death (whose announcement is far from premature) of the social. If the critique of alienation and reification argues – in terms comparable to Baudrillard's – that modernity has reduced everyone to consumers of a world, Baudrillard argues that in postmodernity the only 'oppositional' activity is to consume yet more intensely.

Who is postmodern?

In a society divided by wealth and power we would expect forms of culture and experience to be divided too. For example, although I can recognize that I have 'postmodern experiences', they do not constitute the whole of my everyday life. Moreover, it is difficult to imagine many people who can afford the eclecticism in which one 'wears perfume in Tokyo and "retro" clothes in Hong Kong'. Even if we grant the entire post-Fordist and postmodern arguments combined, there would remain sociological questions as to *who* is a postmodern consumer, when and under what conditions? Yet arguments for the existence of a postmodern culture tend to be 'totalistic' (though rarely as total as Baudrillard's) and therefore produce a rather non-sociological account of capitalist consciousness as such or *in toto*. Whereas Frankfurt School or Situationist theory could be equally totalizing, they none the less sought to relate the alienated appearance of capitalism to the reality of the system that necessarily produces it. For Baudrillard there is no reality left, only the code, appearance without depth. The problem of relating postmodern experience to social structure or to the structural positions of social groups does not arise because – rather circularly – postmodern experience also serves to explain their disappearance. Postmodern experience is total because it has swallowed up 'the social' which would otherwise differentiate it.

But the sociological questions do still arise. If postmodern experience depends on access to consumer goods or, more generally, on the ability to construct one's life along the model of the consumerist lifestyle, then money and power quite directly restrict access to postmodern culture. Bauman (1987, 1988), for example, distinguishes the 'seduced' from the 'repressed', the two-thirds of society able to enter the consumer playground (the same two-thirds who make up Galbraith's 'culture of contentment') from the other third dependent on the state and therefore subject to their planning and management. This, as Warde (1994a) points out, does scant justice to the egalitarian and democratic potential (if not reality) of public provision. Nor does it recognize the highly rationalized planning and management in private provision. It does, however, make the point that differentials of wealth and power can divide society (as well as the planet), not only between different scales and levels of consumption but also into entirely different *modes* of consumption and therefore quite different structures of everyday life and everyday need.

Moreover, the borders between the different modes of consumption are heavily guarded and policed, both privately and by the state. A clear example of this is the regulation of space, and particularly cities, in contemporary society. Postmodern transformations of the city are generally associated with a shift from the industrial city to the city as a place of consumption, entertainment and services. Much research has therefore focused, for example, on the building of shopping malls and precincts, the 'museumification' of industrial and pre-industrial districts (such as dock areas, older markets, buildings), the '24-hour city' and the shift of city labour to consumer and financial services. All these spatial transformations imply new forms of urban sociality and experiences. Yet they are all equally clearly designed for specific social sectors (or markets). Cities are transformed to attract, through the consumption, leisure and entertainment facilities they offer, tourists and other international movements of people (for example business conferences, major sporting events), middle-class consumers who took to the suburbs during late modernity and 'gentrifying' folk working in professional and financial services.

Zukin (1991) gives a powerful account of the very material struggles that stand behind such postmodern inner cities. The reclamation or creation of inner cities fit for tourists and professionals involves making extraordinary numbers of the poor, the homeless or simply the indigenous vanish into thin air. Similarly, Davis's (1990) account of 'Fortress LA' documents the policing of malls, homes and neighbourhoods as zones of exclusion of those who do not fit or cannot afford postmodern culture. There are multiple and interconnected lines of exclusion from any form of consumer culture. Hispanics are frog-marched (or far worse) out of Californian shopping malls not only because they are poor but because they are people of colour, and the connection between the two features is fairly obvious.

Concepts of postmodern culture and consumption, in line with their stress on the replacement of the social by the signifying, argue that consumption is organized by lifestyle as opposed to traditional 'ascribed' identities or modern structural divisions. This is linked closely to notions such as neo-tribalism and self-identity, as discussed in chapter 3. Yet many people are structurally excluded from this postmodern experience of mobile identity by clearly ascribed identities such as female, black, Jew, old, non-U, or by compulsory norms of identity, such as the universal assumption of heterosexuality. That is to say, it is diffi-cult to deal with racism and sexism if it is assumed that 'essentialism' has gone the way of all other 'finalities' or that the social has dissolved into signification. It simply has not. In a similar vein, concepts like neotribalism and lifestyle assume that we pick up and drop memberships and identities rapidly, easily and without commitment, and that these memberships and identities relate to unstable, image-based groupings with unpoliced borders and no relevant continuity over time. In fact, people continue to be part of communities with considerable longevity, which do demand commitment as well as the learning and observance of established norms. For example there are still some families, churches and careers left, as well as old boy networks, trade unions and political organizations.

New middle classes

One attempt to analyse a shift to postmodern culture and consumption in terms of a continuing and differentiated social structure relates it to the emergence of new middle classes in the transition to post-Fordism (Featherstone 1991b; Lash 1990; Lash and Urry 1987, 1993; Lee 1992). Interestingly, this is in line with a consistent theme in accounts of consumer culture and modernity, that changes in the mode of consumption are almost invariably associated with the emergence of new sectors of the 'middling sorts'. In the eighteenth century it is the new commercial and trading classes. In the transition to Fordism (as analysed by the Regulationist School), new white-collar workers and middle management – a class fraction created by the increasing bureaucratic complexity of the Fordist firm – constitute the original market for Fordist mass-produced goods (Aglietta 1979: 85). The argument to be discussed here is that the transition to post-Fordism throws up yet another new middle class, which is predisposed to, or has an 'elective affinity' with, postmodern culture and consumption.

This analysis draws on Bourdieu's work in both style and substance. The 'old bourgeoisie' of early and modern capitalism exemplified the split between economic and cultural capital, being itself split between the bourgeoisie proper and the intelligentsia (generally comprising its own offspring). Each side of the split not only had different taste structures, but 'the prestige, legitimacy, relative scarcity and therefore social value of [the intelligentsia's] cultural capital is dependent on a denial of the market in cultural goods' (Featherstone 1991b: 89), thus maintaining the illusion of an autonomous sphere of high culture. This strategy also enhances the prestige of the intelligentsia as a class fraction by giving them a monopoly on defining legitimate taste and good culture.

The situation is altered by the emergence of new middle classes as part of the structural changes that come with post-Fordism. A new bourgeoisie emerges whose members are high in both economic and cultural capital. This class fraction

is the initiator of the ethical retooling required by the new economy . . . whose
functioning depends as much on the production of needs and consumers as on the
production of goods. The new logic of the economy rejects the ascetic ethic of
production and accumulation, based on abstinence, sobriety, saving and calculation, in favour of a hedonistic morality of consumption, based on credit, spending
and enjoyment (Bourdieu 1984: 310).

The new bourgeoisie are the go-getting executives of finance, design and
marketing, of non-material sectors of production.

Their natural allies, but subordinates, are the 'new petite bourgeoisie',
which 'collaborates enthusiastically in imposing the new ethical norms
(especially as regards consumption) and the corresponding needs' (Bourdieu
1984: 366). It does this in a variety of ways, corresponding to the new
occupational requirements and categories emerging within what comes to be
called post-Fordism. Firstly, as we have seen, not only the new service
occupations but also most roles even within manufacturing appear to
demand less in the way of simple labour or even technical skills and more
and more human and social skills. 'That is the skills of welcoming, selling,
soothing, and so on . . .' (Crompton 1993: 176), the care of both customers
and colleagues (through human resources management), and a reliance on
personnel and experts to manage themselves and each other with a view not
simply to maximize output on the Taylorist model but to 'build a
commitment to the organization at all levels of employment' (176). Secondly,
a vast range of public service workers emerge with the growth of education,
social services, health services, even in police departments and the military,
to handle people's needs, workers whose professional concern is with 'the
management of the body and the emotions' (176). Thirdly, there is the
emergence of 'need merchants' and 'new cultural intermediaries', the
workers in occupations involving presentation and representation, symbolic
goods and services, from those directly employed in the vastly expanding
media to advertisers, marketers and PR and press officers. The new petite
bourgeoisie identify with and carry out the exemplary activities of
postmodernity: they are the communicators and sign-producers who have
displaced the commodity-producers of organized capitalism (Lash and Urry
1987).

However, the new petite bourgeoisie are (upwardly or downwardly)
mobile, and therefore lack the class confidence of their public school mentors
in the new bourgeoisie. They go to the old polytechnics and new universities
rather than to Oxbridge or even the redbricks. They are uneasy in their
habitus, in their very body (Featherstone 1991b: 90) and are therefore
intensely self-conscious, self-monitoring and narcissistic, constantly attempting
to acquire cultural capital, and they are suckers for self-help, body
maintenance techniques and so on. They take taste and lifestyle very

seriously indeed. This makes them, according to Featherstone, natural consumers, but also for similar reasons automatic postmodernists: lacking elite cultural capital yet intimately involved by background and occupation in both learning cultural skills and producing cultural objects, 'they seek to legitimate the intellectualization of new areas of expertise such as popular music, fashion, design, holidays ... which increasingly are subjected to serious analysis' (91). They do not promote a particular style but rather a serious interest in the general idea of style. And unlike the split between old bourgeoisie and old intelligentsia, the new petite bourgeoisie not only do not require, but positively cannot allow a split between commerce and culture, between economic and cultural capital, for through postmodernism they are seeking to legitimate precisely the cultural activities that constitute their economic occupations and those of their class.

Postmodernism and post-structuralism

We noted earlier that postmodernism is ambivalent as to whether contemporary consumer culture is the ultimate in anomie or in freedom. The issue of politically 'mapping the postmodern' (Huyssen 1986) is in this respect similar to some of the issues we broached in relation to cultural studies, but more intense. The dissolution, mobility or implosion of social boundaries and hierarchies and the inability to anchor social categories in 'the real', in finalities of need, social structure or nature, can appear as a liberation of the active social subject who is now able to *play* with social symbolic resources rather than be determined by social structure, who can now treat representations of the social as mere images and raw materials for the construction of new realities. Or this liberation can be seen as anomic to the point of schizophrenia. There can no longer be foundations, values, truth, authenticity, real needs or real objects; by the same token there can be no critique, and the unhinged individual (no longer an ego, but a fragmented subjectivity) is merely constituted through the flow of codes constructed by the system and its agents.

This ambivalence is complicated to an extraordinary degree by another factor: postmodernism, one could say, is made up of one part post-Fordism and one part post-structuralism. The two parts seem to point in quite opposite directions. The post-Fordist aspect of postmodernism offers a sociological account of interrelated changes in economy and culture, largely characterized by the predominance of signs in both production and consumption. Even when Baudrillard argues that the social has dissolved, he generally arrives at this conclusion through a socio-historical account which presumes that it once existed or indeed could do so again. In this respect he is no different from critics of alienation and reification who also offer accounts of the death of the social (for example one-dimensional society or the society of the spectacle). Indeed, he can be fairly close to 'culture and society' arguments (chapter 3), which hold that the real social (organic society) has been replaced by the ersatz false social of commercial and consumer culture. These traditions retain some notion of reality or truth (for example 'symbolic exchange'), which serves to produce a critique of the society that has repressed it. The 'real' can be as absent from the contemporary social world as it is for Baudrillard, but the aim is to account for how it has disappeared and how it can be recovered.

Much of Baudrillard conforms to this. He traces historical realities to the point of their disappearance. However, he also follows another train of thought which can illustrate the post-structuralist side of postmodern thought: he often examines concepts such as needs, use-values, social relations not as historical realities to be studied but as myths that are to be deconstructed. Need never existed, only the ideology of need; society never existed, only its myth. Baudrillard then uses deconstructive techniques to demystify the central terms of modern thought (need, the individual, labour, society) and to reveal – much as in semiotic demystification - that they represent cultural constructs rather than objective realities. Thus, the coherent ego or self, the natural body, reason, needs, identities such as gender and 'race', all emerge as fictitious unities, bolted together by and on behalf of forms of social power, which unities must be dissolved into their component processes, discourses and practices.

Ironically, postmodern consumer culture can be treated as if it were a kind of deconstructionism within everyday life, dissolving the fictions of ego, society, need and so on, and can be presented as if it were an agent of truth and demystification bursting mythical bubbles, dissolving false unities and eroding popular belief in the foundations and certainties which underwrote oppression. Consumer culture involves, for example, the schizophrenic, pastiching consumer of Jameson's (1984) account, the demise of the social in Baudrillard's; the dethronement of elitist or absolute cultural values by the relativistic but now socio-economically empowered preferences of 'decentred' subjects. Thought itself is reduced to a series of consumer choices, which are made in terms not of truth or reason but of rhetorical style and textual pleasures.

However, if it is argued that consumer culture has become a vehicle or a result of *de*mystification and free, pleasurable libidinal play, then postmodernism can find itself in strange company. At the limit point postmodernism argues that social subjects are being liberated from the (false) certainties which modernity offered, much as modernity offered liberation from the certainties of traditional society. This parallel can place postmodernism very close to liberalism and neo-liberalism, and it is worth pursuing this parallel to get a better sense of what kinds of liberation are on offer today.

Postmodernism and neo-liberalism can rather often find themselves on the same side of the barricade, with critical theorists and social conservatives on the other. The last two, as we have seen, are committed to finding substantive social values that can be grounded in something beyond or above the individual (reason, tradition and historicity, nature). Their concepts of needs and goods are derived from this imperative. The first two, on the other hand, attack all such foundations as unwarranted, on various grounds (for example the separation of facts from values, the mythological nature of finalities), and both view belief in such finalities as socially dangerous, as inimical to freedom: both, for example, can attack public welfare provision, high culture, public service broadcasting and a range of other modernist totems not only as wrong, but as acts of power in which a truth about people's needs and desires is institutionally imposed upon them and restricts the free flow of their desires and actions. Society constrains. Indeed, whereas for traditions of culture and of critique society has been destroyed, for liberalism and post-structuralism it never really quite exists: the one reduces it to individuals, the other to cultural mythology.

Both liberalism and postmodernism, then, refuse the possibility or desirability of socially authoritative definitions of substantive needs and values, or of a distinction between real and false needs. The two are, therefore, often joined in a similar populism and anti-elitism that regards people's pleasures, desires, tastes and wants as self-legitimating. Both regard modernity as irredeemably pluralistic (liberalism) or relativistic (postmodernism) and argue that politics and ethics must accord with this. They thus argue, variously, for 'respect for difference', democratic and civil rights, individual freedom, consumer sovereignty. Finally, liberals and most postmoderns (at least the optimistic ones) regard consumers and other social agents as creative, active, self-defining.

On the other hand, the differences between liberalism and postmodernism are decisive and powerfully highlight the radical nature of a postmodernist view of consumer culture. Firstly, liberalism argues that individuals are free in so far as they are rational. Critical theory attacks *formal* rationality as a source of distortion, alienation and reification of substantive values. Postmodernism tends to argue that people are free, creative or autonomous in so far as they are irrational. This is partly because post-structuralism distrusts any form of rationality as bound up with the totalitarian project of the Enlightenment, and this includes the formal rationality of economic action. Indeed, in Foucault the argument comes close to Weberian and Frankfurt School critiques of instrumental rationality. The rational enterprising self – producer and consumer – of liberalism can be seen as the imposition of another totalitarian model of modernity, a form of normalization and tool of governance. Thus, whereas liberalism historically sought to combat social domination through the individual's inner resource of rational autonomous thought, postmodernism's main resource for struggle against social authority (which now includes the authority of reason) is irrationality: impulse, desire, libido, the body, the unconscious, hedonism, carnivalesque inversions and excesses of meaning that transgress codes. The irrational, rather than rational, consumer becomes the hero of postmodernism.

This divergence arises partly from different accounts of the subject. Liberalism tends to see the consumer as a coherent and calculating self (the Ego) acting in relation to non-rational desires which it can know and rationally pursue, a reality principle in the service of the pleasure principle. For most liberalism, this rational self is the reality or truth of social actors, a truth expressed, as we have seen, in the figure of economic man rather than the consumer *per se*. Postmodernism, on the other hand, largely as a result of its post-structuralist origins, argues that the self is a fiction of coherence, that the reality is a decentred subject, one that deconstructs into the incoherence of multiple discourses, unconscious drives, the amorphousness of desire, the primacy of the body, the endless flow of signs and difference. It is neither rational nor unified. In so far as this sea of impulses seems to be contained within organized frameworks (such as liberalism's rational economic actor or self-interested social agent) this is either a fiction or a form of oppression (for example, see Deleuze and Guattari 1977).

Secondly, the key term for liberalism is the market or civil society, for postmodernism it is culture. The former worships social mechanisms which impersonally coordinate the self-interested actions of autonomous egos; the latter, dissolving the ego into the more basic units of desire or sign, regards the flow of meaning as the mechanism of social coordination or organization. This accounts for the centrality of consumer culture in both. Society, such as it is, is constituted by the way in which desire is produced and channelled. Traditions of culture and critique, on the other hand, emphasize being and making over using and consuming and therefore argue that social co-ordination should be achieved by way of organic relations between humans and nature.

Thirdly, though liberalism and postmodernism both inhabit a post-traditional world of irreconcilable values and identities, they characterize it quite differently. Liberalism asserts *pluralism*: diversity can be socially managed within mechanisms like the market and political democracy, which allow diverse interests to co-exist and be coordinated. Pluralism therefore asserts formal values (reason, equality, freedom) that regulate, contain or frame the diversity of desires and interests. Postmodernism by contrast asserts *relativism*. There are *no* values that stand above the fray, not even values that could regulate it. There can be no Geneva Convention for postmodernism, only strategies for survival or conquest. Critical theorists, on the third hand, continue their impossible game of reasoning their way into unshakeable, foundational but substantive values.

Conclusion

Over the past decade or so, the interlinked themes of post-Fordism, postmodernism and post-structuralism have so dominated the agenda of consumer culture (and have so powerfully thrust consumer culture onto the wider agenda of social analysis) that many students and scholars take it as read that we do indeed live in new times, and that these new times represent a decisive discontinuity with modernity. It is beyond the framework of this book to assess whether we do or do not, though it is important to emphasize that the issue is still very much open: post-Fordism and postmodernity are *debates*, not *facts*. At the same time, the structure and themes of this book should indicate fairly clearly that most of the issues and conceptual tools of postmodernity, if not its conclusions, come out of the very long-term concern with consumer culture that is coextensive with modernity. Above all, the post-Fordist side of postmodernism continues a concern with the socio-economic role of consumption in the reproduction of social order that goes back to Smith and beyond, while its post-structuralist concern with the ontological, epistemological and moral-political status of needs and values reprises themes that have been constitutive of the entire modern interest in consumption.

Afterword

In this book, I have not tried to solve any of the theoretical or practical issues which consumer culture has raised in the modern mind, nor have I refuted through sustained critique any of the 'solutions' offered by the literatures we have reviewed. The more limited aim has been to put the questions into some manageable order and context so that when you encounter this large and expanding field you can go to the heart of it with a clearer sense of what is at stake. I hope it is clear by now just how much is at stake. Above all, I hope it is clear that, because consumer culture is about how we collectively handle the relation between social order and the intimate spheres in which people come to define who they are, what they want and how to live, 'what is at stake' is profoundly and fundamentally *political*. It is about our power of disposal over our lives, and over the resources necessary to define and to live the lives we wish to lead.

As Foucault has argued, power is not monolithic, and it is in some respects productive rather than repressive. None the less, there are domineering social forces, and these have to be recognized and contested by someone, acting from somewhere, in the name of something. Otherwise who would there be who could feel that something is wrong? In modern thought, this critical, oppositional someone, somewhere and something have very fundamentally been identified, and have identified themselves, through the concept of needs and the part it plays in defining identities, interests, values, collectivities and cultures. By stating a need, I commit myself to particular social values and aims, identities and memberships. And in my everyday life, it is through the experience of being unable to formulate such statements on my own terms, or to pursue those needs satisfactorily in the social world, that I most directly, intimately and oppressively meet something I call power. It is as a woman whose very desire to articulate her own needs is rendered a matter of guilt by patriarchal relations; it is as a child offered commodities instead of nurture; it is as a Third World citizen condemned to poverty, war, genocide, cultural stagnation because of the economic and geo-political *needs* of the over-developed world; it is as an invalid or elderly person unable to pay for the commodities of health care, housing, heating because his or her own commodity – a functional body and mind – has lost its market value; it is as an intellectual whose own critical activity has been alienated through commodification or academic productivity norms; it is as a member of an ethnic group whose needs are as invisible in the public spheres of politics and the media as they are dashed by structural racism in the worlds of work, housing and education – it is through the experience of these people, through the needs they name and all the potential needs they are prevented from naming, that we know about power. And it is through these experiences that we are launched into critical theory and practice.

How does consumer culture stand up to the critique posed by their needs? As we have seen, the answers given to this question not only have been polarized but are part and parcel of all the central political debates of modern times concerning freedom, solidarity, equality, identity, values, pluralism and so on. Consumer culture has offered critical thought a powerful vantage from which to reckon the costs of modernity, and now postmodernity. On the other hand, consumer culture is certainly found to be problematic in its failures to meet needs due to the structural inequalities that underlie it and the poverty that therefore accompanies it. But even where it 'meets needs' – the argument goes – it meets only those needs that emerge at the end of an impossibly long gauntlet of mediation by inequalities in material and symbolic power, by cultural intermediaries, by the 'impersonal steering mechanisms' of the market, by the instrumental rationality of corporate planning – a gauntlet so long that those needs that do emerge from it are battered to a pulp that is virtually unrecognizable by those to whom they putatively belong.

On the other hand it is strongly claimed as either fact or hope that – contrary to the overweight irony of an Adorno or the glib nihilism of a Baudrillard – most of us, even in the depths of poverty or the heights of conformist affluence, are very far from being mindless consumerist zombies. We can and do reinterpret, transform, rework, recuperate the material and experiential commodities that are offered to us; indeed, we *have to* be capable of all this simply in order to make sense of what is on offer and to assimilate it into everyday life in either critical *or* conformist mode. We also deploy a wide variety of devices ironically to distance ourselves from identification with the system of goods, to make it a matter of play, into something superficial and endlessly transformable rather than deep, fixed and fixing; we engage in tactical resistance and guerrilla warfare as de Certeau or Fiske would have it. And of course we often have fun doing any or all of this.

None the less, there are times when playing in the consumer playground threatens to tip into something else, when play becomes serious, when the cost gets too high, when we do not want a postmodernism (or liberalism) that, as Plant (1992: 7) puts it, offers 'a manual for survival . . . in a capitalist world which seems immune to transformation', which reassures us 'that it is quite natural to feel lost, confused, and uncertain of the solidity of the ground beneath one's feet'. It is at such times that one reaches back to those traditions of critical social thought that have struggled both to rationally grasp and practically transform modernity since the time when it first gave rise to market society and consumer culture.

Bibliography

Adburgham, A. (1981) *Shops and Shopping*. London: Barrie & Jenkins.

Adorno, T. and Horkheimer, M. (1979) *Dialectic of Enlightenment*. London: Verso.

Aglietta, M. (1979) *A Theory of Capitalist Regulation: The US Experience*. London: Verso.

Agnew, J. (1986) *Worlds Apart: The Market and the Theater in Anglo-American Thought, 1550–1750*. New York: Cambridge University Press.

Altvater, E. (1993) *The Future of the Market: An Essay on the Regulation of Money and Nature after the Collapse of 'Actually Existing Socialism'*. London: Verso.

Anderson, P. (1983) *In the Tracks of Historical Materialism*. London: Verso.

Appadurai, A. (1986) *The Social Life of Things: Commodities in Cultural Perspective*. Cambridge: Cambridge University Press.

Appleby, J. (1993) 'Consumption in early modern social thought', in J. Brewer and R. Porter (eds), *Consumption and the World of Goods*, 162–73. New York: Routledge.

Appleby, J. O. (1978) *Economic Thought and Ideology in Seventeenth-Century England*. Princeton, NJ: Princeton University Press.

Bagguley, P. (1991) 'Post-Fordism and enterprise culture', in R. Keat and N. Abercrombie (eds), *Enterprise Culture*. London: Routledge.

Bagguley, P., Mark-Lawson, J., Shapiro, D., Urry, J., Walby, S. et al. (1990) *Restructuring: Place, Class and Gender*. London: Sage.

Baran, P. A. and Sweezy, P. M. (1968) *Monopoly Capital*. Harmondsworth: Penguin.

Baran, P. A. and Sweezy, P. M. (1977 (1966)) *Monopoly Capital: An Essay on the American Economic and Social Order*. Harmondsworth: Penguin.

Barthes, R. (1977) *Elements of Semiology*. New York: Hill and Wang.

Barthes, R. (1986) *Mythologies*. London: Paladin.

Baudrillard, J. (1968) *Le Système des objets: la consommation des signes*. Paris: Denoel/Gonthier.

Baudrillard, J. (1975) *The Mirror of Production*. St Louis, MO: Telos.

Baudrillard, J. (1981) *For a Critique of the Political Economy of the Sign*, St Louis, MO: Telos.

Baudrillard, J. (1983) *Simulations*. New York: Semiotext(e).

Bauman, Z. (1983) 'Industrialism, consumerism and power', *Theory, Culture and Society*, 1 (3).

Bauman, Z. (1987) *Legislators and Interpreters: On Modernity, Post-modernity and Intellectuals Cambridge*: Polity Press.

Bauman, Z. (1988) *Freedom*. Milton Keynes: Open University Press.

Bauman, Z. (1990) *Thinking Sociologically*. Oxford: Blackwell.
Bauman, Z. (1991) *Modernity and Ambivalence*. Cambridge: Polity Press.
Bauman, Z. (1993) *Postmodern Ethics*. Oxford: Blackwell.
Beck, U. (1992) *Risk Society: Towards a New Modernity*. London: Sage.
Bell, D. (1979) *The Cultural Contradictions of Capitalism*. London: Heinemann.
Benjamin, W. (1989) *Charles Baudelaire: A Lyric Poet in the Era of High Capitalism*. London: Verso.
Benson, S. P. (1986) *Counter Culture: Saleswomen, Managers, and Customers in American Department Stores, 1890–1940*. Urbana, IL: University of Illinois Press.
Berman, M. (1970) *The Politics of Authenticity*. New York: Atheneum.
Berman, M. (1983) *All That is Solid Melts into Air: The Experience of Modernity*. London: Verso.
Berry, C. J. (1994) *The Idea of Luxury: A Conceptual and Historical Investigation*. Cambridge: Cambridge University Press.
Boorstin, D. (1962) *The Image*. Harmondsworth: Penguin.
Boorstin, D. J. (1973) *The Americans: The Democratic Experience*. New York: Vintage Books.
Bordo, S. (1987) *The Flight to Objectivity: Essays on Cartesianism and Culture*. Albany, NY: State University of New York Press.
Bourdieu, P. (1973) 'The Berber house or the world reversed', in M. Douglas (ed.), *Rules and Meanings*. Harmondsworth: Penguin.
Bourdieu, P. (1984) *Distinction: A Social Critique of the Judgement of Taste*. Cambridge, MA: Harvard University Press.
Bourdieu, P. (1989) *Outline of a Theory of Practice*. Cambridge: Cambridge University Press.
Bowlby, R. (1987) 'Modes of modern shopping: Mallarmé at the Bon Marché', in N. Armstrong and L. Tennenhouse (eds), *The Ideology of Conduct: Essays in Literature and the History of Sexuality*, 185–205. New York: Methuen.
Braudel, F. (1981) *The Structures of Everyday Life*. London: Fontana.
Braverman, H. (1974) *Labour and Monopoly Capital: The Degredation of Work in the Twentieth Century*. New York: Monthly Review Press.
Breitenbach, H., Burden, T. and Coates, D. (1990) *Features of a Viable Socialism*. Brighton: Wheatsheaf.
Brewer, J. and Porter, R. (eds) (1993) *Consumption and the World of Goods*. New York: Routledge.
Brittan, S. (1988) *A Restatement of Economic Liberalism*. London: Macmillan.
Bronner, S. J. (ed.) (1989) *Consuming Visions: Accumulation and Display of Goods in America, 1880–1920*. New York: Norton.
Brown, S. (1994) *Postmodern Marketing*. London: Routledge.
Buck-Morss, S. (1989) *The Dialectics of Seeing: Walter Benjamin and the Arcades Project*. London: MIT Press.
Burchill, G. (1991) 'Peculiar interests: civil society and governing the system of natural liberty', in G. Buchill, C. Gordon, and P. Miller (eds), *The Foucault Effect: Studies in Governmentality*. London: Harvester/Wheatsheaf.
Callinicos, A. (1989) *Against Postmodernism: A Marxist Critique*. Cambridge: Polity Press.
Campbell, C. (1989) *The Romantic Ethic and the Spirit of Modern Consumerism*. Oxford: Blackwell.
Carter, E. (1984) 'Alice in the consumer wonderland: West German case studies in gender and consumer culture', in A. McRobbie and M. Nova (eds), *Gender and Generation*. London: Macmillan.

Castle, T. (1986) *Masquerade and Civilization: The Carnivalesque in Eighteenth-Century Culture and Fiction*. London: Methuen.
Certeau, M. de (1984) *The Practice of Everyday Life*. Berkeley, CA: University of California Press.
Chambers, I. (1986) *Popular Culture: The Metropolitan Experience*. London: Routledge.
Chaney, D. (1983) 'The department stores as a cultural form', *Theory, Culture and Society*, 1 (3).
Chaney, D. (1991) 'Subtopia in Gateshead: the MetroCentre as a cultural form', *Theory, Culture and Society*, 7.
Chaney, D. (1993) *Fictions of Collective Life: Public Drama in Late Modern Culture*. London: Routledge.
Clarke, J. and Simmonds, D. (1980) *Move over Misconceptions: Doris Day Reappraised*. London: British Film Institute.
Clarke, S. (1982) *Marx, Marginalism and Modern Sociology: From Adam Smith to Max Weber*. London: Macmillan.
Coats, A. W. (1958) 'Changing attitudes to labour in the mid-eighteenth century', *Economic History Review*, 2nd series, IX: 35–51.
Cohen, S. (1972) *Folk Devils and Moral Panics: The Creation of the Mods and Rockers*. London: Paladin.
Coward, R. (1989) *The Whole Truth: The Myth of Alternative Health*. London: Faber & Faber.
Crompton, R. (1993) *Class and Stratification: An Introduction to Current Debates*. Cambridge: Polity Press.
Cross, G. (1993) *Time and Money: The Making of Consumer Culture*. London: Routledge.
Cunningham, H. (1980) *Leisure in the Industrial Revolution, c.1780–c.1880*. London: Croom Helm.
Dabydeen, D. (1987) *Hogarth, Walpole and Commercial Britain*. London: Hansib.
Davis, M. (1990) *City of Quartz: Excavating the Future in Los Angeles*. London: Verso.
Deleuze, G. and Guattari, F. (1977) *Anti-Oedipus: Capitalism and Schizophrenia*. London: Athlone Press.
DiMaggio, P. (1990) 'Cultural aspects of economic action', in R. Friedland and A. F. Robertson (eds), *Beyond the Marketplace: Rethinking Models of Economy and Society*. Chicago, IL: Aldine.
Dore, R. (1983) 'Goodwill and the spirit of market capitalism', *British Journal of Sociology* 34: 459–82.
Douglas, M. (1979) *Implicit Meanings: Essays in Anthropology*. London: Routledge.
Douglas, M. (1984) *Purity and Danger: An Analysis of the Concept of Pollution and Taboo*. London: Routledge & Kegan Paul.
Douglas, M. and Isherwood, B. (1979) *The World of Goods: Towards an Anthropology of Consumption*. Harmondsworth: Penguin.
Doyal, L. and Gough, I. (1991) *A Theory of Human Needs*. London: Macmillan.
Du Gay, P. (1996) *Consumption and Identity at Work*. London: Sage.
Durkheim, E. (1987) *Suicide: A Study in Sociology*. London: Routledge & Kegan Paul.
Eagleton, T. (1983) *Literary Theory: An Introduction*. Oxford: Blackwell.
Eco, U. (1979) *A Theory of Semiotics*. Bloomington, IL: Indiana University Press.
England, P. (1993) 'The separative self: androcentric bias in neoclassical assumptions', in M. A. Ferber and J. A. Nelson (eds), *Beyond Economic Man: Feminist Theory and Economics*. Chicago, IL: University of Chicago Press.
Etzioni, A. (1988) *The Moral Dimension: Toward a New Economics*. New York: Free Press.
Eversley, D. E. C. (1967) 'The home market and economic growth in England 1750–

1780', in E. L. Jones and C. E. Mingay (eds), *Land, Labour and Population in the Industrial Revolution*. London: Edward Arnold.

Ewen, S. (1976) *Captains of Consciousness: Advertising and the Social Roots of Consumer Culture*. New York: McGraw-Hill.

Ewen, S. (1988) *All Consuming Images: The Politics of Style in Contemporary Culture*. New York: Basic Books.

Featherstone, M. (1991a) 'The body in consumer society', in M. Featherstone, M. Hepworth and B. Turner (eds), *The Body: Social Process and Cultural Theory*. London: Sage.

Featherstone, M. (1991b) *Consumer Culture and Postmodernism*. London: Sage.

Featherstone, M., Hepworth, M. and Turner, B. (1991) *The Body: Social Process and Cultural Theory*. London: Sage.

Feher, F., Heller, A. and Markus, G. (1984) *Dictatorship over Needs: An Analysis of Soviet Societies*. Oxford: Blackwell.

Ferber, M. A. and Nelson, J. A. (eds) (1993) *Beyond Economic Man: Feminist Theory and Economics*. Chicago, IL: University of Chicago Press.

Fine, B. and Leopold, E. (1990) 'Consumerism and the Industrial Revolution', *Social History*, xv: 151–79.

Fine, B. and Leopold, E. (1993) *The World of Consumption*. London: Routledge.

Finkelstein, J. (1991) *The Fashioned Self*. Cambridge: Polity Press.

Fiske, J. (1989) *Reading the Popular*. Boston, MA: Unwin Hyman.

Foucault, M. (1988) 'The political technology of individuals', in L. Martin, H. Gutman and P. Hutton (eds), *Technologies of the Self: A Seminar with Michel Foucault*. Amherst, MA: University of Massachusetts Press.

Fox, R. W. and Lears T. J. (1983) *The Culture of Consumption: Critical Essays in American History, 1880–1980*. New York: Pantheon.

Frankel, B. (1987) *The Post-Industrial Utopians*. Cambridge: Polity Press.

Fraser, W. H. (1981) *The Coming of the Mass Market, 1850–1914*. London: Macmillan.

Friedman, M. (1957) *A Theory of the Consumption Function*. Princeton, NJ: Princeton University Press.

Frisby, D. (1988) *Fragments of Modernity*. Cambridge: Polity Press.

Gaines, J. and Herzog, C. (eds) (1990) *Fabrications: Costume and the Female Body*. London: Routledge.

Galbraith, J. K. (1969) *The Affluent Society*. London: Hamish Hamilton.

Gambetta, D. (1989) *Trust: Making and Breaking of Cooperative Relations*. Oxford: Blackwell.

Gardner, C. and Sheppard, J. (1989) *Consuming Passion: The Rise of Retail Culture*. London: Unwin Hyman.

Gellner (1992) *Reason and Culture*. Oxford: Blackwell.

Geras, N. (1983) *Marx and Human Nature: Refutation of a Legend*. London: New Left Books.

Gershuny, J. and Miles, I. (1983) *The New Service Economy: The Transformation of Employment in Industrial Societies*. London: Francis Pinter.

Giddens, A. (1991) *Modernity and Self-Identity: Self and Society in the Late Modern Age*. Cambridge: Polity Press.

Gilboy, E. W. (1967) 'Demand as a factor in the Industrial Revolution', in R. M. Hartwell (ed.), *Causes of the Industrial Revolution in England*. London: Methuen.

Gilroy, P. (1993) *The Black Atlantic: Modernity and Double Consciousness*. London: Verso.

Godelier, M. (1972) *Rationality and Irrationality in Economics*. New York: Monthly Review Press.

Godelier, M. (1986) *The Mental and the Material: Thought, Economy and Society*. London: Verso.

Goldthorpe, J. and Lockwood, D. (1968–9) *The Affluent Worker*. Cambridge: Cambridge University Press.

Gorz, A. (1982) *Farewell to the Working Class: An Essay on Post-Industrial Socialism*. London: Pluto Press.

Gorz, A. (1989) *Critique of Economic Reason*. London: Verso.

Gottdiener, M. (1995) *Postmodern Semiotics: Material Culture and the Forms of Postmodern Life*. Oxford: Blackwell.

Granovetter, M. (1985) 'Economic action and social structure: the problem of embeddedness', *American Journal of Sociology*, **91** (3): 481–510.

Gray, A. (1987) 'Behind closed doors: video recorders in the home', in H. Baehr and G. Dyer (eds), *Boxed In: Women and Television*. London: Pandora.

Gray, A. (1992) *Video Playtime: The Gendering of a Leisure Technology*. London: Routledge.

Habermas, J. (1991) *The Structural Transformation of the Public Sphere: An Inquiry into a Category of Bourgeois Society*. Cambridge, MA: MIT Press.

Hacking, I. (1986) 'Self-improvement', in D. C. Hoy (ed.), *Foucault: A Critical Reader*. Oxford: Blackwell.

Hall, S. (1980) 'Encoding/decoding', in S. Hall, D. Hobson, A. Lowe and P. Willis (eds), *Culture, Media, Language*. London: Hutchinson.

Hall, S., Critcher, C., Jefferson, T., Clarke, J., and Roberts, B. (1978) *Policing the Crisis: Mugging, the State, and Law and Order*. London: Macmillan.

Hall, S. and Jacques, M. (eds) (1989) *New Times: The Changing Face of Politics in the 1990s*. London: Lawrence & Wishart.

Harland, R. (1987) *Superstructuralism: The Philosophy of Structuralism and Post-Structuralism*. London: Methuen.

Harvey, D. (1982) *The Limits to Capital*. Oxford: Blackwell.

Harvey, D. (1988) *The Condition of Postmodernity: An Enquiry into the Origins of Culture*. Oxford: Blackwell.

Haug, W. F. (1986) *Critique of Commodity Aesthetics: Appearance, Sexuality & Advertising*. Cambridge: Polity Press.

Hayek, F. A. (1976) *The Road to Serfdom*. London: Routledge & Kegan Paul.

Hebdige, D. (1979) *Subculture: The Meaning of Style*. London: Methuen.

Hebdige, D. (1988a) *Hiding in the Light: On Images and Things*. London: Comedia.

Hebdige, D. (1988b) 'Object as image: the Italian scooter cycle', in *Hiding in the Light: On Images and Things*. London: Comedia.

Hebdige, D. (1988c) 'Towards a cartography of taste 1935–1962', in *Hiding in the Light: On Images and Things*. London: Comedia.

Heelas, P. and Morris, P. (eds) (1992) *The Values of Enterprise Culture: The Moral Debate*. London: Routledge.

Hirsch, F. (1976) *Social Limits to Growth*. Cambridge, MA: Harvard University Press.

Hirschman, A. (1977) *The Passions and the Interests*. Princeton, NJ: Princeton University Press.

Hobbes, T. (1972 (1651)) *Leviathan*. London: Fontana.

Hochschild, A. (1983) *The Managed Heart: Commercialization of Human Feeling*. Berkeley, CA: University of California Press.

Hodgson, G. (1984) *The Democratic Economy: A New Look at Planning, Markets and Power*. Harmondsworth: Penguin.

Hodgson, G. (1988) *Economics and Institutions: A Manifesto for a Modern Institutional*

Economics. Cambridge: Polity Press.

Hodgson, G. M. and Screpanti, E. (1991) *Rethinking Economics: Markets, Technology and Economic Evolution*. Aldershot: Edward Elgar.

Hoggart, R. (1977 (1957)) *The Uses of Literacy*. Harmondsworth: Penguin.

Horowitz, D. (1985) *The Morality of Spending: Attitudes Toward the Consumer Society in America, 1875–1940*. Baltimore, MA: Johns Hopkins University Press.

Hoskins, W. (1963) 'Rebuilding of rural England, 1570-1640', in W. Hoskins (ed.), *Provincial England: Essays in Social and Economic History*, 131-48. London: Macmillan.

Huyssen, A. (1986) *After the Great Divide: Modernism, Mass Culture and Postmodernism*. London: Macmillan.

Ignatieff, M. (1984) *The Needs of Strangers*. London: Hogarth Press.

Ironmonger, D. S. (1972) *New Commodities and Consumer Behaviour*. Cambridge: Cambridge University Press.

Jameson, F. (1984) 'Postmodernism, or the cultural logic of late capitalism', *New Left Review*, **146**.

Jhally, S. (1987) *The Codes of Advertising: Fetishism and the Political Economy of Meaning in the Consumer Society*. London: Frances Pinter.

Kahneman, D., Knetsch, J. and Thaler, R. (1987) 'Fairness and the assumptions of economics', in R. Hogarth and M. Reder (eds), *Rational Choice*. Chicago, IL: University of Chicago Press.

Kant, I. (1983) 'An answer to the question: what is Enlightenment?', in I. Kant (ed.), *Perpetual Peace and Other Essays*. Indianapolis, IN: Hackett.

Keat, R. and Abercrombie, N. (eds) (1991) *Enterprise Culture*. London: Routledge.

Kellner, D. (1989) *Jean Baudrillard: From Marxism to Postmodernism and Beyond*. Cambridge: Polity Press.

Kline, S. and Leiss, W. (1978) 'Advertising, needs and commodity fetishism', *Canadian Journal of Political and Social Theory*, **2** (1).

Lancaster, K. (1966) 'A new approach to consumer theory', *Journal of Political Economy*, **74**: 132–57.

Lancaster, K. (1971) *Consumer Demand: A New Approach*. New York: Columbia University Press.

Lane, R. E. (1991) *The Market Experience*. Cambridge: Cambridge University Press.

Langholz Leymore, V. (1975) *Hidden Myth: Structure and Symbolism in Advertising*. London: Heinemann.

Lansley, S. (1994) *After the Gold Rush: The Trouble with Affluence, 'Consumer Capitalism' and the Way Forward*. London: Century Business Books.

Lasch, C. (1979) *The Culture of Narcissism*. London: Abacus.

Lash, S. (1990) *Sociology of Postmodernism*. London: Routledge.

Lash, S. and Urry, J. (1987) *The End of Organized Capitalism*. Cambridge: Polity Press.

Lash, S. and Urry, J. (1993) *Economies of Signs and Space*. London: Sage.

Lears, T. J. (1983) 'From salvation to self-realization: advertising and the therapeutic roots of the consumer culture, 1880–1930', in R. W. Fox and T. J. Lears (eds), *The Culture of Consumption: Critical Essays in American History, 1880–1980*. New York: Pantheon.

Leavis, F. R. (1930) *Mass Civilisation and Minority Culture*. Cambridge: Minority Press.

Leavis, F. R. and Thompson, D. (1933) *Culture and Environment: The Training of Critical Awareness*. London: Chatto & Windus.

Lee, M. J. (1992) *Consumer Culture Reborn: The Cultural Politics of Consumption*. London: Routledge.

Leiss, W. (1976) *The Limits to Satisfaction: On Needs and Commodities*. Toronto: University of Toronto Press.

Leiss, W. (1983) 'The icons of the marketplace', *Theory, Culture and Society*, 1 (3): 10–21.

Leiss, W., Kline, S. and Jhally, S. (1986) *Social Communication in Advertising: Persons, Products & Images of Well-Being*. London: Methuen.

Lewis, S. (1922) *Babbitt*. New York: Harcourt Brace Jovanovich.

Lovejoy, A. O. (1936) *The Great Chain of Being*. Cambridge, MA: Harvard University Press.

Lukács, G. (1971) 'Reification and the consciousness of the proletariat', in G. Lukács (ed.), *History and Class Consciousness: Studies in Marxist Dialectics*. London: Merlin Press.

Lunt, P. K. and Livingstone, S. (1992) *Mass Consumption and Personal Identity: Everyday Economic Experience*. Buckingham: Open University Press.

MacCannell (1989) *The Tourist: A New Theory of the Leisure Class*. New York: Schocken Books.

McCracken, G. (1990) *Culture and Consumption*. Bloomington, IN: Indiana University Press.

McGuigan, J. (1992) *Cultural Populism*. London: Routledge.

McKendrick, N. (1959–60) 'Josiah Wedgwood: an eighteenth-century entrepreneur in salesmanship and marketing techniques', *Economic History Review*, 2nd series, 12 (3): 408–33.

McKendrick, N. (1964) 'Josiah Wedgwood and Thomas Bentley: an inventor-entrepreneur partnership in the Industrial Revolution', *Transactions of the Royal Historical Society*, XIV: 1–33.

McKendrick, N. (1974) 'Home demand and economic growth: a new view of the role of women and children in the Industrial Revolution', in N. McKendrick (ed.), *Historical Perspectives: Studies in English Thought and Society in Honour of J. H. Plumb*. London: Europa.

McKendrick, N., Brewer, J. and Plumb, J. H. (1983) *The Birth of a Consumer Society: The Commercialization of Eighteenth-century England*. London: Hutchinson.

McRobbie, A. (1978) 'Working class girls and the culture of femininity', in Women's Studies Group (ed.), *Women Take Issue*. London: Hutchinson.

McRobbie, A. (1980) 'Settling accounts with subculture', in T. Bennett (ed.), *Culture, Ideology and Social Process*. London: Batsford/Open University Press.

McRobbie, A. (1991) *Feminism and Youth Culture: From 'Jackie' to 'Just Seventeen'*. Basingstoke: Macmillan Educational.

McRobbie, A. and Nova, M. (1984) *Gender and Generation*. London: Macmillan.

Mandel, E. (1976) *Late Capitalism*. London: NLB.

Marchand, R. (1986) *Advertising the American Dream: Making Way for Modernity – 1920–1940*. Berkeley, CA: University of California Press.

Marcuse, H. (1964) *One Dimensional Man*. London: Abacus.

Marcuse, H. (1972) *Negations: Essays in Critical Theory*. Harmondsworth: Penguin.

Marcuse, H. (1973 (1955)) *Eros and Civilisation*. London: Abacus.

Marcuse, H. (1973 (1969)) *An Essay on Liberation*. Harmondsworth: Penguin.

Marx, K. (1959) *Capital*, Vol. III. London: Lawrence & Wishart.

Marx, K. (1973) *Grundrisse*. Harmondsworth: Penguin / New Left Review.

Marx, K. (1975) *Early Writings*. Harmondsworth: Penguin / New Left Review.

Marx, K. (1976) *Capital*, Vol. I. London: Penguin / New Left Review.

Mattick, P. (1971) *Marx and Keynes: The Limits of the Mixed Economy*. London: Merlin.

Mauss, M. (1990) *The Gift: The Form and Reason for Exchange in Archaic Societies*. New York: W. W. Norton.

Meyrowitz, J. (1986) *No Sense of Place: The Impact of Electronic Media on Social Behaviour*. New York: Oxford University Press.

Miller, D. (1987) *Material Culture and Mass Consumption*. Oxford: Blackwell.

Miller, D. (1994) *Modernity – An Ethnographic Approach: Dualism and Mass Consumption in Trinidad*. Oxford: Berg.

Miller, D. (ed.) (1995) *Acknowledging Consumption: A Review of New Studies*. London: Routledge.

Miller, M. (1981) *The Bon Marché: Bourgeois Culture and the Department Store*. London: Allen & Unwin.

Mills, C. W. (1951) *White Collar*. London: Oxford University Press.

Millum, T. (1975) *Images of Women: Advertising in Women's Magazines*. London: Chatto & Windus.

Mintz, S. (1985) *Sweetness and Power: The Place of Sugar in Modern History*. New York: Viking.

Morley, D. (1980a) *The 'Nationwide' Audience*. London: Comedia.

Morley, D. (1980b) 'Texts, readers, subjects', in S. Hall, D. Hobson, A. Lowe, and P. Willis (eds), *Culture, Media, Language*. London: Hutchinson.

Morley, D. (1986) *Family Television: Cultural Power and Domestic Leisure*. London: Comedia.

Morley, D. (1992) *Television, Audiences and Cultural Studies*. London: Routledge.

Mort, F. (1989) 'The politics of consumption', in S. Hall and M. Jacques (ed.), *New Times: The Changing Face of Politics in the 1990s*. London: Lawrence & Wishart.

Mui, H.-C. and Mui, L. H. (1989) *Shops and Shopkeeping in Eighteenth-Century England*. London: Routledge.

Mukerji, C. (1983) *From Graven Images: Patterns of Modern Materialism*. New York: Columbia University Press.

Nelson, J. A. (1993) 'The study of choice or the study of provisioning? Gender and the definition of economics', in M. A. Ferber and J. A. Nelson (eds), *Beyond Economic Man: Feminist Theory and Economics*. Chicago, IL: University of Chicago Press.

Nove, A. (1983) *The Economics of Feasible Socialism*. London: George Unwin and Allen.

O'Neill, J. (1985) *Five Bodies: The Human Shape of Modern Society*. Ithaca, NY and London: Cornell University Press.

Packard, V. (1977) *The Hidden Persuaders*. Harmondsworth: Penguin.

Perkin, H. (1968) *The Origins of Modern English Society*. London: Routledge.

Plant, R. (1989) 'Socialism, markets and end-states', in J. Le Grand and S. Estrin (eds), *Market Socialism*. Oxford: Clarendon Press.

Plant, S. (1992) *The Most Radical Gesture: The Situationist International in a Postmodern Age*. London: Routledge.

Plumb, J. H. (1983) 'Commercialization and society', in N. McKendrick, J. Brewer and J. H. Plumb (eds), *The Birth of a Consumer Society: The Commercialization of Eighteenth-century England*. London: Hutchinson.

Pocock, J. G. A. (1975) *The Machiavellian Moment*. Princeton, NJ: Princeton University Press.

Pocock, J. G. A. (1985) *Virtue, Commerce and History*. Cambridge: Cambridge University Press.

Polanyi, K. (1957a) 'The economy as instituted process', in K. Polanyi, C. Arensberg and H. Pearson (eds), *Trade and Markets in Archaic Societies*, 243–69. Chicago, IL: Free Press.

Polanyi, K. (1957b) *The Great Transformation: The Political and Economic Origins of Our Time*. Boston, MA: Beacon Press.

Polhemus, T. (1994) *Streetstyle*. London: Thames and Hudson.

Pope, D. (1983) *The Making of Modern Advertising*. New York: Basic Books.

Porter, R. (1982) *English Society in the Eighteenth Century*. Harmondsworth: Penguin.

Porter, R. (1993a) 'Baudrillard: history, hysteria and consumption', in C. Rojek and B. S. Turner (eds), *Forget Baudrillard*. London: Routledge.

Porter, R. (1993b) 'Consumption: disease of the consumer society?', in J. Brewer and R. Porter (eds), *Consumption and the World of Goods*, 58–81. New York: Routledge.

Radway, J. (1987) *Reading the Romance: Women, Patriarchy and Popular Literature*. London: Verso.

Reekie, G. (1993) *Temptations: Sex, Selling and the Department Store*. London: Allen & Unwin.

Richards, T. (1991) *The Commodity Culture of Victorian England: Advertising and Spectacle, 1851–1914*. London: Verso.

Riesman, D. (1961) *The Lonely Crowd: A Study of the Changing American Character*. New Haven: Yale University Press.

Ritzer, G. (1993) *The McDonaldization of Society: An Investigation into the Changing Character of Contemporary Social Life*. London: Pine Forge Press.

Robinson, J. (1983) *Economic Philosophy*. Harmondsworth: Penguin.

Rojek, C. (1985) *Capitalism and Leisure Theory*. London: Methuen.

Rose, G. (1978) *The Melancholy Science: An Introduction to the Thought of Theodor W. Adorno*. London: Macmillan.

Rose, N. (1991) *Governing the Soul: The Shaping of the Private Self*. London: Routledge.

Rose, N. (1992a) 'Governing the enterprising self', in P. Heelas and P. Morris (eds), *The Values of the Enterprise Culture: The Moral Debate*. London: Routledge.

Rose, N. (1992b) 'Towards a critical sociology of freedom', inaugural lecture. London: Goldsmiths' College.

Rosenberg, N. (1968) 'Adam Smith, consumer tastes, and economic growth', *Journal of Political Economy*, 7.

Rothschild, E. (1973) *Paradise Lost: The Decline of the Auto-Industrial Age*. London: Allen Lane.

Rousseau, J. J. (1984 (1755)) *A Discourse on Inequality*. London: Penguin.

Rowthorn, B. (1980) 'Marx's theory of wages', in B. Rowthorn (ed.), *Capitalism, Conflict and Inflation*. London: Lawrence & Wishart.

Rule, J. (1992) *Albion's People: English Society, 1714–1815*. London: Longman.

Ryan, A. (ed.) (1987) *Utilitarianism and Other Essays: J. S. Mill and Jeremy Bentham*. London: Penguin.

Sahlins, M. (1974) *Stone Age Economics*. London: Tavistock.

Sahlins, M. (1976) *Culture and Practical Reason*. Chicago, IL: University of Chicago Press.

Schama, S. (1989) *Citizens: A Chronicle of the French Revolution*. London: Penguin.

Schudson, M. (1981) 'Criticizing the critics of advertising: towards a sociological view of marketing', *Media, Culture & Society*, 3.

Schudson, M. (1984) *Advertising, the Uneasy Persuasion: Its Dubious Impact on American Society*. New York: Basic Books.

Scitovsky, T. (1976) *The Joyless Economy*. New York: Oxford University Press.

Scitovsky, T. (1986) *Human Desire and Economic Satisfaction*. Brighton: Wheatsheaf.

Sekora, J. (1977) *Luxury: The Concept in Western Thought, Eden to Smollet*. Baltimore, MA: Johns Hopkins University Press.

Sen, A. (1985) *Commodities and Capabilities*. Amsterdam: Elsevier.

Sen, A. (1987a) *The Standard of Living: The Tanner Lectures*. Cambridge: Cambridge University Press.

Sen, A. K. (1987b) *On Ethics and Economics*. New York: Blackwell.

Sennett, R. (1977) *The Fall of Public Man*. Cambridge: Cambridge University Press.

Shammas, C. (1990) *The Preindustrial Consumer in England and America*. Oxford: Oxford University Press.

Shammas, C. (1993) 'Changes in English and Anglo-American consumption from 1550–1800', in J. Brewer and R. Porter (eds), *Consumption and the World of Goods*, 177–205. New York: Routledge.

Shields, R. (1990) *Places on the Margin: Alternative Geographies of Modernity*. London: Routledge.

Shields, R. (ed.) (1992) *Lifestyle Shopping: The Subject of Consumption*. London: Routledge.

Shilling, C. (1993) *The Body and Social Theory*. London: Sage.

Silverstone, R. (1990) 'Television and everyday life: towards an anthropology of the television audience', in M. Ferguson (ed.), *Public Communication: The New Imperatives*. London: Sage.

Silverstone, R. and Hirsch, E. (eds) (1992) *Consuming Technologies: Media and Information in Domestic Spaces*. London: Routledge.

Simmel, G. (1950) 'The metropolis and mental life', in K. Wolff (ed.), *The Sociology of Georg Simmel*. London: Collier-Macmillan.

Simmel, G. (1990) *The Philosophy of Money*. London: Routledge.

Simmel, G. (1991a (1896)) 'The Berlin Trade Exhibition', *Theory, Culture and Society*, 8: 119–23.

Simmel, G. (1991b (1896)) 'Money in modern culture', *Theory, Culture and Society*, 8: 17–31.

Slater, D. R. (1985) 'Advertising as a commercial practice: business strategy and social theory', PhD thesis. Cambridge University.

Slater, D. R. (1987) 'On the wings of the sign: commodity culture and social practice', *Media, Culture and Society*, 9.

Slater, D. R. (1989) 'Corridors of power: research into advertising', in D. Silverman and J. Gubrium (eds), *The Politics of Field Research*. London: Sage.

Slater, D. R. (1993) 'Going shopping: markets, crowds and consumption', in C. Jenks (ed.), *Cultural Reproduction*. London: Routledge.

Slater, D. R. (1995) 'Photography and modern vision: the spectacle of "natural magic" ', in C. Jenks (ed.), *Visual Culture*. London: Routledge.

Slater, D. R. (1996) 'Consumer culture and the politics of need', in M. Nava. A. Blake, I. MacRury and B. Richards (eds.), *Buy This Book: Contemporary Issues in Advertising and Consumption*. London: Routledge.

Smith, A. (1986 (1776)) *The Wealth of Nations*. London: Penguin.

Smollett, T. (1985) *The Expedition of Humphrey Clinker*. London: Penguin.

Sontag, S. (1983) *Illness as Metaphor*. Harmondsworth: Penguin.

Soper, K. (1981) *On Human Needs: Open and Closed Theories in a Marxist Perspective*. Sussex: Harvester Press.

Soper, K. (1986) *Humanism and Anti-Humanism*. London: Hutchinson.

Soper, K. (1990) *Troubled Pleasures: Writings on Politics, Gender and Hedonism*. London: Verso.

Spufford, M. (1981) *Small Books and Pleasant Histories*. London: Methuen.

Spufford, M. (1984) *The Great Reclothing of Rural England: Petty Chapmen and Their*

Wares in the Seventeenth Century. London: Hambledon Press.

Swedberg, R. (1987) 'Economic sociology', *Current Sociology*, 35: 1–21.

Sweezy, P. M. (1942) *The Theory of Capitalist Development: Principles of Marxian Political Economy*. New York: Modern Reader.

Sydie, R. A. (1987) *Natural Women, Cultured Men*. Milton Keynes: Oxford University Press.

Talmon, J. L. (1986 (1952)) *The Origins of Totalitarian Democracy: Political Theory and Practice During the French Revolution and Beyond*. London: Peregrine.

Taylor, C. (1989) *Sources of the Self: The Making of the Modern Identity*. Cambridge: Cambridge University Press.

Thirsk, J. (1978) *Economic Policy and Projects: The Development of a Consumer Society in Early Modern England*. Oxford: Clarendon Press.

Thompson, D. (1964) *Discrimination and Popular Culture*. Harmondsworth: Penguin.

Thompson, E. P. (1971) 'The moral economy of the English crowd in the eighteenth century', *Past and Present*, 50: 78–98.

Thompson, E. P. (1975) *Whigs and Hunters: The Origin of the Black Act*. London: Allen Lane.

Thompson, E. P. (1978) *The Making of the English Working Class*. London: Penguin.

Thompson, G., Frances, J., Levacic, R. and Mitchell, J. (1991) *Markets, Hierarchies and Networks: The Coordination of Social Life*. London: Sage.

Thompson, K. (ed.) (1985) *Readings from Emile Durkheim*. London: Ellis Horwood / Tavistock.

Thornton, S. (1995) *Club Cultures: Music, Media and Subcultural Capital*. Cambridge: Polity Press.

Timpanaro, S. (1980) *On Materialism*. London: Verso.

Todd, J. (1986) *Sensibility: An Introduction*. London: Methuen.

Toqueville, A. de (1955 (1856)) *The Old Regime and the French Revolution*. New York: Doubleday Anchor Books.

Trilling, L. (1972) *Sincerity and Authenticity*. Cambridge, MA: Harvard University Press.

Turner, B. (1985) *The Body and Society: Explorations in Social Theory*. Oxford: Blackwell.

Turner, B. (1987) 'The rationalization of the body: reflections on modernity and discipline', in S. Whimster and S. Lash (eds), *Max Weber, Rationality and Modernity*, 222–41. London: Allen & Unwin.

Turner, B. S. (1986) 'Simmel, rationalization and the sociology of money', *Sociological Review*, 34 (1): 93–114.

Urry, J. (1988) 'Cultural change and contemporary holiday-making', *Theory, Culture and Society*, 5 (1).

Urry, J. (1990) *The Tourist Gaze: Leisure and Travel in Contemporary Societies*. London: Sage.

Veblen, T. (1953 (1899)) *The Theory of the Leisure Class: An Economic Study of Institutions*. New York: Mentor.

Vichert, G. (1971) 'The theory of conspicuous consumption in the eighteenth century', in P. Hughes and D. Williams (eds), *The Varied Pattern: Studies in the Eighteenth Century*. Toronto: McMaster University.

Walkowitz, J. R. (1992) *City of Dreadful Delight: Narratives of Sexual Danger in Late-Victorian Britain*. London: Virago.

Warde, A. (1994a) 'Consumers, identity and belonging: reflections on some theses of Zygmunt Bauman', in R. Keat, N. Whiteley and N. Abercrombie (eds), *The Authority of the Consumer*, 58–74. London: Routledge.

Warde, A. (1994b) 'Consumption, identity-formation and uncertainty', *Sociology*, 28 (4):

877–98.

Waters, M. (1995) *Globalization*. London: Routledge.

Weatherill, L. (1988) *Consumer Behaviour and Material Culture in Britain 1660-1760*. London: Routledge.

Weatherill, L. (1993) 'The meaning of consumer behaviour in late seventeenth- and early eightenth-century England', in J. Brewer and R. Porter (eds), *Consumption and the World of Goods*, 206–27. New York: Routledge.

Webster, F. (1987) 'Advertising the American dream', *Media, Culture and Society*, 9.

Wernick, A. (1991) *Promotional Culture: Advertising, Ideology and Symbolic Expression*. London: Sage.

Whyte, W. H. (1957) *The Organization Man*. New York: Doubleday Anchor Books.

Wiles, R. C. (1968) 'The theory of wages in later English mercantilism', *Economic History Review*, 2nd series, XXI: 113–26.

Willan, T. S. (1970) *An Eighteenth-Century Shopkeeper: Abraham Dent of Kirkby Stephen*. Manchester: Manchester University Press.

Willan, T. S. (1976) *The Inland Trade*. Manchester: Manchester University Press.

Williams, R. (1976) *Keywords: A Vocabulary of Culture and Society*. Glasgow: Fontana.

Williams, R. (1980) 'Advertising: the magic system', in R. Williams (ed.), *Problems in Materialism and Culture*. London: Verso.

Williams, R. (1982) *Dream Worlds: Mass Consumption in Late C19th France*. Berkeley, CA: University of California Press.

Williams, R. (1985) *Culture and Society: 1780–1950*. Harmondsworth: Penguin.

Williamson, J. (1978) *Decoding Advertisements: Ideology and Meaning in Advertising*. London: Marion Boyars.

Williamson, J. (1979) 'The history that photographs mislaid', in Photography Workshop (ed.), *Photography/Politics: One*. London: Photography Workshop.

Willis, P. (1975) 'The expressive style of a motor-bike culture', in J. Benthall and T. Polhemus (eds), *The Body as a Medium of Expression*. London: Allen Lane.

Willis, P. (1978) *Learning to Labour*. London: Saxon House.

Willis, P. (1990) *Common Culture: Symbolic Work at Play in the Everyday Cultures of the Young*. Milton Keynes: Open University Press.

Wilson, E. (1991) *The Sphinx in the City*. London: Virago.

Wolff, J. (1985) 'The invisible *flâneuse*: women and the literature of modernity', *Theory, Culture and Society*, 2 (3): 37–47.

Wrigley, E. A. (1967) 'A simple model of London's importance in changing English society and economy, 1650–1750', *Past and Present*, 37: 44–60.

Xenos, N. (1989) *Scarcity and Modernity*. London: Routledge.

Zukin, L. A. (1991) *Landscapes of Power: From Detroit to Disney World*, Berkeley, CA: University of California Press.

Zukin, S. and DiMaggio, P. (eds) (1990) *Structures of Capital: The Social Organization of the Economy*. New York: Cambridge University Press.

INDEX